OpenShift in Action

OpenShift in Action

JAMIE DUNCAN
JOHN OSBORNE

MANNING

SHELTER ISLAND

For online information and ordering of this and other Manning books, please visit www.manning.com. The publisher offers discounts on this book when ordered in quantity. For more information, please contact

    Special Sales Department
    Manning Publications Co.
    20 Baldwin Road
    PO Box 761
    Shelter Island, NY 11964
    Email: orders@manning.com

Manning Publications Co.
20 Baldwin Road
PO Box 761
Shelter Island, NY 11964

Development editor:	Toni Arritola
Review editor:	Ivan Martinović
Technical development editor:	Dani Cortés
Project manager:	Kevin Sullivan
Copyeditor:	Tiffany Taylor
Proofreader:	Melody Dolab
Technical proofreader:	Eric Rich
Typesetter:	Gordan Salinovic
Illustrations:	Chuck Larson
Cover designer:	Marija Tudor

ISBN 9781617294839
Printed in the United States of America
1 2 3 4 5 6 7 8 9 10 – EBM – 23 22 21 20 19 18

For Molly and Elizabeth. Thank you for your understanding, your immeasurable assistance, and making me take time off to play with the chickens.

—J.D.

To my wife and two daughters, thank you for always giving me spontaneous reasons to laugh.

—J.O.

brief contents

contents

foreword

Containers are becoming the primary way applications are built and deployed. They're one of those rare technologies that comes along and not only cuts operating costs, but also increases productivity. Containers also provide the flexibility to keep organizations from getting locked into any one technology. Our vision at Red Hat is to become a default choice for organizations looking for a partner to help them build any applications and deploy them in any environment.

Enter Red Hat OpenShift: Red Hat's answer to bringing together the best and most popular projects and developer services to emerge around containers—such as Kubernetes and Ansible—in a single, scalable, rock-solid container platform combined with all the services developers need.

In the pages that follow, you'll find something unique: the first holistic view of OpenShift in print. *OpenShift in Action,* written by two of Red Hat's top contributors, is the first book that takes a soup-to-nuts approach in combining both the developer and operator perspectives and covering everything from deployment to the top of the application stack.

As you read, you'll discover how containers reduce costs, increase productivity, and address the Holy Grail of software: the power to write code once and then reuse it multiple times. In the past, the heavy cost of architecting and building a reusable infrastructure has been a difficult barrier to cross. With containers working in cooperation with microservices, we finally have a lightweight technology that has kicked off an IT revolution.

Large-scale applications are moving to hybrid and multicloud environments, and more organizations are choosing containers to easily build applications, deploy them, and move them across clouds. By abstracting applications from underlying resources, OpenShift makes developers and operators more efficient and productive in delivering feature functionality.

We have long had a front-row seat in seeing how large enterprises and organizations with massive tech footprints struggle to implement the latest technology. Red Hat was early to embrace containers and container orchestration and contribute deeply to related open source communities. Just as we've done with Red Hat Enterprise Linux for decades, we created OpenShift as a way to bring the power of the community to the enterprise while making it consumable in a safe, secure, and reliable way.

Read on to get your own glimpse of how open source is leading the way in this emerging new paradigm of computing.

JIM WHITEHURST, PRESIDENT AND CEO, RED HAT

preface

When we first began developing *OpenShift in Action*, it was going to be a book focusing on the ops side of DevOps in OpenShift. Existing books focus on OpenShift's developer experience, and we wanted to be their counterpoint. As we continued to work on the content and look at what we wanted to teach, it became apparent that we didn't want to be a counterpoint. We didn't want to represent one side of anything. Instead, we decided to create a complete example of OpenShift with a strong experience for both operators and developers. *OpenShift in Action* takes a holistic view of OpenShift, giving equal weight to both perspectives represented in DevOps.

We think this is important, because the ultimate goal of DevOps is to enable and enhance communication between developer and operations teams that historically have been placed in adversarial (at best) relationships. To accomplish this, the two authors each specialize in one of these roles. For us, writing this book has been an amazing learning experience in how DevOps can work for just about anything, including writing a book.

We can't cover every OpenShift topic in a single book. But we hope *OpenShift in Action* gives you the fundamental knowledge from both developer and operation perspectives to allow you to deploy and successfully use OpenShift in your own environments. We also hope you can use OpenShift to accomplish meaningful work using containers. Most important, we hope the content in this book expands your knowledge through hands-on experience with OpenShift and becomes a reference for you for years to come.

OpenShift has a great web-based user interface, powerful command-line utilities, and a robust API. Almost any of the examples we go through in *OpenShift in Action* can be accomplished using any of those interfaces. We try to give you examples using all of these methods, but you'll notice as you read and work through the examples that we tend to focus on command-line workflows to accomplish tasks. There are two primary reasons we did this:

- With the electronic versions of the book, you can copy and paste most of the examples directly into the command line to run them.
- In our experience at Red Hat, working with hundreds of customers and helping them effectively use OpenShift, the command line is the most common interface for power users.

OpenShift in Action was written using the experience we've gained helping countless Red Hat customers over the years. We cover a wide range of topics, and we've done our best to organize them in a way that will be relevant and useful as you begin this exciting journey. We hope this book is as helpful to you as the process of writing it has been to us.

acknowledgments

We'd like to thank the OpenShift and Kubernetes communities. These technologies are changing how IT solutions are delivered. This book wouldn't have been possible without immeasurable help from those communities, as well as the other open source communities whose software makes OpenShift the industry-leading Kubernetes-based platform. To call out individuals would be nearly impossible. We'd also like to thank Red Hat for its sponsorship and leadership in open source endeavors globally.

We want to thank the people at Manning who made this book possible: publisher Marjan Bace and everyone on the editorial and production teams who worked behind the scenes.

We also want to thank Dani Cortés and Eric Rich for giving the book a thorough technical review and proofread. Several other reviewers also looked over the manuscript at various stages of development: Alexandros Koufoudakis, Andrea Cosentino, Andrea Tarocchi, Areg Melik-Adamyan, Bruno Vernay, Carlos Esteban Feria Vila, Derek Hampton, Ioannis Sermetziadis, Jorge Quilcate, Juan Lopez, Julien Pohie, Mario-Leander Reimer, Michael Bright, Paolo Antinori, Paul Balogh, Rick Wagner, Tony Sweets, Vinicius Miana, and Zorodzayi Mukuya. We appreciate all their time and feedback.

about this book

Our goal in this book is to give you working knowledge of how to build, deploy, and maintain applications running on OpenShift. We use practical examples to build core knowledge of the platform. Throughout, we explore the inner workings of containers within the Linux kernel all the way up through running a CI/CD pipeline. While Open-Shift has a fast release cadence, this book is designed to be relevant for future releases by focusing on foundational concepts instead of latest-and-greatest features. We hope it gives you the fundamental tools to succeed and is a reference for you going forward.

Who should read this book

OpenShift in Action is for any IT professional who's investigating OpenShift specifically, or containers in general from a developer or operations perspective. Countless blog posts and documentation sites are available online, but this is the first book that takes a view of OpenShift from top to bottom. Included in that is how to use container runtimes like docker as well as information about Kubernetes. This book brings all that information together in a single source.

How this book is organized: a roadmap

This book has 4 parts and 11 chapters. Part 1 explains OpenShift at a high level and explores deploying a cluster, creating your first applications, and how applications work in containers:

- Chapter 1 provides a high-level overview of how OpenShift works and how it fits modern business needs.

- Chapter 2 walks you through deploying an OpenShift cluster. It also covers the components in OpenShift and creating your first containerized applications.
- Chapter 3 is a deep dive into how applications in containers are isolated on an OpenShift node, using examples of the applications you've just deployed.

Part 2 focuses on working with cloud-native applications in OpenShift:

- Chapter 4 examines the OpenShift components that make up a deployed application. It also demonstrates how to set liveness and readiness probes for applications to ensure that they're functioning correctly.
- Chapter 5 demonstrates how to set up metrics-based application autoscaling.
- Chapter 6 uses Jenkins to deploy an entire CI/CD pipeline in OpenShift.

Part 3 is about using OpenShift to deploy stateful applications:

- Chapter 7 goes through the process of deploying persistent storage and making it available for applications in OpenShift.
- Chapter 8 deploys an application using persistent storage and covers managing application session persistence and other challenges for distributed stateful applications.

Part 4 focuses on the operational aspects of OpenShift and handling security challenges:

- Chapter 9 configures user roles to control access, resource limits, and quotas, and investigates how Linux cgroups enforce these constraints.
- Chapter 10 is a deep dive into how the software-defined networking layer is set up and managed.
- Chapter 11 deals with core aspects of security, including SELinux and working with security contexts.

Part 1 will be especially helpful to you if containers are a new concept; chapter 3 is the deepest technical chapter in the section. Parts 3 and 4 cover both operations and developer topics. Part 4 is primarily focused around operations but will still appeal to developers who have a need or desire to understand the OpenShift platform more deeply.

About the code

Beginning with chapter 2, each chapter has extensive code samples and source code; these are available for download at the book's website, www.manning.com/books/openshift-in-action, and at https://github.com/OpenShiftInAction. Because OpenShift evolves so quickly, we'll continue to update the samples on GitHub even after the book is printed. Please join us there or at the book's forum (https://forums.manning.com/forums/openshift-in-action) to let us know if you run into issues or have questions around the examples in the book. If you're looking for additional resources, you can find the official OpenShift documentation repository at https://docs.openshift.com.

This book presents source code both in numbered listings and in line with normal text. In both cases, it's formatted in a `fixed-width font like this` to separate it from ordinary text.

In many cases, the original source code has been reformatted; we've added line breaks and reworked indentation to accommodate the available page space in the book. When even this wasn't enough, listings include line-continuation markers (➥). Additionally, comments in the source code have often been removed from the listings when the code is described in the text. Code annotations accompany many of the listings, highlighting important concepts.

Book forum

Purchase of *OpenShift in Action* includes free access to a private web forum run by Manning Publications where you can make comments about the book, ask technical questions, and receive help from the authors and from other users. To access the forum, go to https://forums.manning.com/forums/openshift-in-action. You can also learn more about Manning's forums and the rules of conduct on the forums at https://forums.manning.com/forums/about.

Manning's commitment to our readers is to provide a venue where a meaningful dialogue between individual readers and between readers and the authors can take place. It isn't a commitment to any specific amount of participation on the part of the authors, whose contribution to the forum remains voluntary (and unpaid). We suggest you try asking the authors some challenging questions lest their interest stray! The forum and the archives of previous discussions will be accessible from the publisher's website as long as the book is in print.

about the authors

JAMIE DUNCAN is a recovering history major with 11 years of experience working professionally with Linux. Six of those years have been at Red Hat, focusing increasingly on the operations-oriented features of OpenShift. Jamie spends his days explaining how containers are an integral part of the Linux operating system, and he's had this discussion with customers, OpenShift advocates, and technology fans on multiple continents. That fundamental knowledge of how containers work helps people treat containers like the revolutionary technology they are, using them strategically to solve their challenges. When not knee-deep in OpenShift, Jamie's a wanna-be farmer and Formula 1 racing fan.

JOHN OSBORNE is a principal OpenShift architect dedicated to Red Hat public sector customers. He's been at Red Hat for five years, with a strong focus on Kubernetes and DevOps. Before his arrival at Red Hat, he worked at a startup and then spent seven years with the U.S. Navy developing high-performance applications and deploying them to several mission-critical areas across the globe. He enjoys making cutting-edge technologies useful and practical for people trying to solve business problems. He lives in northern Virginia with his wife and two daughters.

about the cover illustration

The figure on the cover of *OpenShift in Action* is captioned "Morning Habit of a Lady of the City of Pera in Natolia in 1568." Pera was the name of a district on the European side of Istanbul, separated from the historic old city by the Golden Horn, an inlet of the Bosporus. The illustration is taken from Thomas Jefferys' *A Collection of the Dresses of Different Nations, Ancient and Modern,* published in London between 1757 and 1772. The title page states that these are hand-colored copperplate engravings, heightened with gum arabic. Thomas Jefferys (1719–1771) was called "Geographer to King George III." He was an English cartographer who was the leading map supplier of his day. He engraved and printed maps for government and other official bodies and produced a wide range of commercial maps and atlases, especially of North America. His work as a mapmaker sparked an interest in local dress customs of the lands he surveyed and mapped; they are brilliantly displayed in this four-volume collection.

Fascination with faraway lands and travel for pleasure were relatively new phenomena in the eighteenth century, and collections such as this one were popular, introducing both the tourist and the armchair traveler to the inhabitants of other countries. The diversity of the drawings in Jefferys' volumes speaks vividly of the uniqueness and individuality of the world's nations centuries ago. Dress codes have changed, and the diversity by region and country, so rich at one time, has faded away. It is now often hard to tell the inhabitant of one continent from another. Perhaps, trying to view it optimistically, we have traded a cultural and visual diversity for a more varied personal life—or a more varied and interesting intellectual and technical life.

At a time when it is hard to tell one computer book from another, Manning celebrates the inventiveness and initiative of the computer business with book covers based on the rich diversity of national costumes from centuries ago, brought back to life by Jefferys' pictures.

Part 1

Fundamentals

As with most things, the best place to start with OpenShift is with the fundamentals. If you're an experienced OpenShift user, this part of the book may seem familiar. If this is your first look at OpenShift, these chapters may be very valuable.

Chapter 1 is a high-level overview of what OpenShift does and the issues it's designed to solve. We'll talk about the business problems and lay out the use cases where OpenShift and containers provide advantages over previous technology solutions.

Chapter 2 gets down to the bits and bytes. After deploying an OpenShift cluster, you'll deploy your first container-based applications on top of it. Using these examples, we'll discuss the OpenShift components that work together to make applications function correctly.

Chapter 3 takes you down to the bottom of the Linux kernel. We'll talk about how the containers used by OpenShift isolate the applications inside them. This is a fundamental concept of how containers work, and we feel that it's important for people who develop applications in containers as well as people who operate OpenShift clusters to have this essential knowledge.

Getting to know OpenShift

This chapter covers

- How container platforms are changing IT
- Comparing containers to virtual machines
- Understanding when containers don't fit
- Designing OpenShift

Containers are changing how everyone in the IT industry does their job. Containers initially entered the scene on developers' laptops, helping them develop applications more quickly than they could with virtual machines or by configuring a laptop's operating system. As containers became more common in development environments, their use began to expand. Once limited to laptops and small development labs, containers worked their way into the enterprise. Within a couple of years, containers progressed to the point that they're powering massive production workloads like GitHub (www.github.com).

NOTE The success of Pokémon GO running on a container platform makes for interesting reading. Pokémon GO runs on Google Cloud Platform. Its massive workloads are documented in the blog post "Bringing Pokémon GO to life on Google Cloud" by Luke Stone (September 29, 2016, http://mng.bz/dK8B). The next time you're stalking a Pikachu across your local park, remember that it's all happening in a container.

As powerful as container are—and we'll be discussing that throughout this book—they aren't a solution on their own. Containers are a new way to deliver applications. But the platform that serves those applications needs to have a lot more going for it than just containers. To effectively use containers, they need to be part of a *container platform* like OpenShift. Container platforms provide orchestration and other services that containers need in order for users to take full advantage of containers.

1.1   *What is a container platform?*

A *container platform* is an application platform that uses containers to build, deploy, serve, and orchestrate the applications running inside it. OpenShift uses two primary tools to serve applications in containers: a *container runtime* to create containers in Linux and an *orchestration engine* to manage a cluster of servers running containers. Let's discuss the container runtime first.

1.1.1   *Containers in OpenShift*

A container runtime works on a Linux server to create and manage containers. For that to make sense, we need to look at how containers function when they're running on a Linux system.

In subsequent chapters, we'll dig deeply into how containers isolate applications in OpenShift. To start, you can think of containers as discrete, portable, scalable units for applications.

Containers hold everything required for the applications inside them to function. Each time a container is deployed, it holds all the libraries and code needed for its application to function properly (see figure 1.1).

Applications running inside a container can only access the resources in the container. The applications in the container are isolated from anything running in other containers or on the host. Five types of resources are isolated with containers:

- Mounted filesystems
- Shared memory resources
- Hostname and domain name
- Network resources (IP address, MAC address, memory buffers)
- Process counters

We'll investigate these in more depth throughout this book.

In OpenShift, the service that handles the creation and management of containers is *docker* (https://github.com/docker). Docker is a large, active, open source project started by Docker, Inc. The resources that docker uses to isolate processes in containers

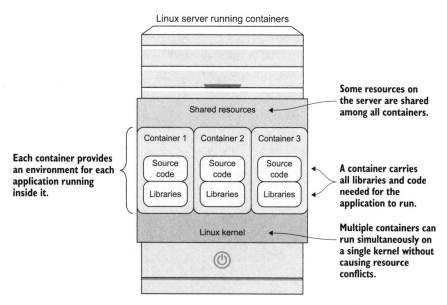

Figure 1.1 Overview of container properties

all exist as part of the Linux kernel. These resources include things like SELinux, Linux namespaces, and control groups (cgroups), which will all be covered later in the book. In addition to making these resources much easier to use, docker has also added several features that have enhanced its popularity and growth:

- *Portability*—Earlier attempts at container formats weren't portable between hosts running different operating systems. This container format is now standardized as part of the Open Container Initiative.[1]
- *Image reuse*—Any container image can be reused as the base for other container images.
- *Application-centric API*—The API and command-line tooling allow developers to quickly create, update, and delete containers.
- *Ecosystem*—Docker, Inc. maintains a free public hosting environment for container images; it now contains several hundred thousand images.

1.1.2 Orchestrating containers

Although the docker engine manages containers by facilitating Linux kernel resources, it's limited to a single host operating system. Although a single server running containers is interesting, it isn't a platform that you can use to create robust applications. To deploy highly available and scalable applications, you have to be able to deploy application containers across multiple servers. To orchestrate containers across multiple servers effectively, you need to use a *container orchestration engine*: an application that manages a

---

[1] More information is available here: https://github.com/opencontainers/image-spec.

container runtime across a cluster of hosts to provide a scalable application platform. OpenShift uses *Kubernetes* (https://kubernetes.io) as its container orchestration engine.

Kubernetes is an open source project that was started by Google. In 2015, it was donated to the Cloud Native Computing Foundation (www.cncf.io).

NOTE   Kubernetes is a bit of a challenge to type or spell. It's often abbreviated as *kube* or *k8s*, which stands for "k + 8 letters + s."

Kubernetes employs a master/node architecture. Kubernetes master servers maintain the information about the server cluster, and nodes run the actual application workloads (see figure 1.2).

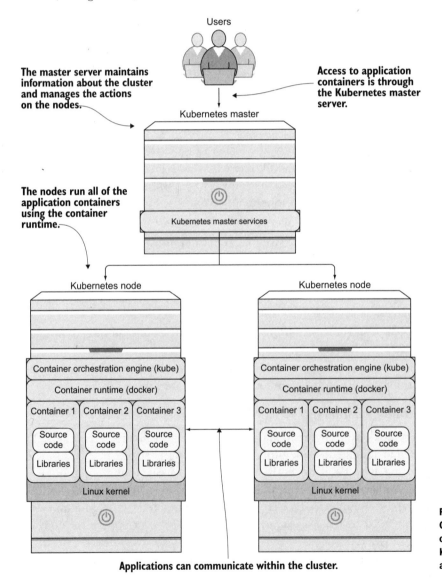

Figure 1.2
Overview
of the
Kubernetes
architecture

Kubernetes is a great open source project. The community around it is quickly growing and incredibly active. It's consistently one of the most active projects on GitHub. But to realize the full power of a container platform, Kubernetes needs a few additional components. OpenShift uses docker and Kubernetes as a starting point for its design. But to be a truly effective container platform, it adds a few more tools to provide a better experience for users.

1.2 Examining the architecture

OpenShift uses the Kubernetes master/node architecture as a starting point. From there, it expands to provide additional services that a good application platform needs to include out of the box.

1.2.1 Integrating container images

In a container platform like OpenShift, container images are created when applications are deployed or updated. To be effective, the container images have to be available quickly on all the application nodes in a cluster. To do this, OpenShift includes an integrated *image registry* as part of its default configuration (figure 1.3).

An image registry is a central location that can serve container images to multiple locations. In OpenShift, the integrated registry runs in a container.

In addition to providing tightly integrated image access, OpenShift works to make access to the applications more efficient.

1.2.2 Accessing applications

In Kubernetes, containers are created on nodes using components called *pods*. There are some distinctions that we'll discuss in more depth in chapter 2, but they're often similar. When an application consists of more than one pod, access to the application is managed through a component called a *service*. A service is a proxy that connects multiple pods and maps them to an IP address on one or more nodes in the cluster.

IP addresses can be hard to manage and share, especially when they're behind a firewall. OpenShift helps to solve this problem by providing an integrated *routing layer*. The routing layer is a software load balancer. When an application is deployed in OpenShift, a DNS entry is created for it automatically. That DNS record is added to the load balancer, and the load balancer interfaces with the Kubernetes service to efficiently handle connections between the deployed application and its users (see figure 1.3).

With applications running in pods across multiple nodes, and management requests coming from the master node, there's a lot of communication between servers in an OpenShift cluster. You need to make sure that traffic is properly encrypted and can be separated when needed.

Users access the API, web interface, and command line tools through the master server.

Users access applications through the routing layer.

Users

Master server manages all actions inside the cluster.

Routing layer provides easy DNS access and a consistent endpoint for all applications in OpenShift.

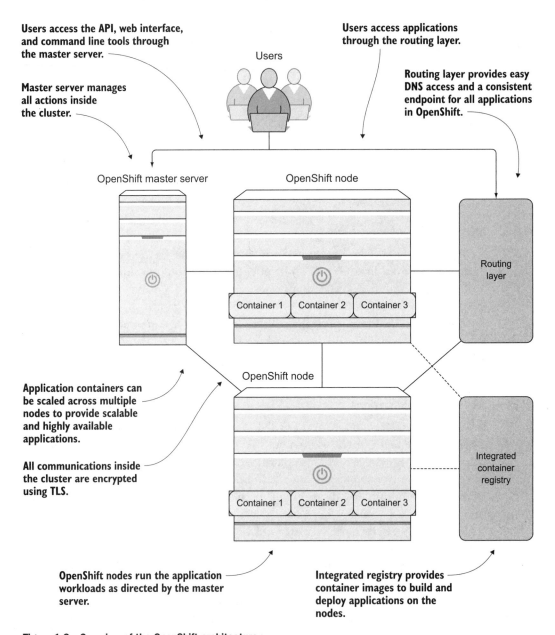

OpenShift master server

OpenShift node

Container 1 Container 2 Container 3

Routing layer

Application containers can be scaled across multiple nodes to provide scalable and highly available applications.

All communications inside the cluster are encrypted using TLS.

OpenShift node

Container 1 Container 2 Container 3

Integrated container registry

OpenShift nodes run the application workloads as directed by the master server.

Integrated registry provides container images to build and deploy applications on the nodes.

Figure 1.3   Overview of the OpenShift architecture

1.2.3 Handling network traffic in your cluster

OpenShift uses a software-defined networking (SDN) solution to encrypt and shape network traffic in a cluster. OpenShift SDN, an SDN solution that uses Open vSwitch (OVS, http://openvswitch.org) and other open source technologies, is configured by default when OpenShift is deployed. Other SDN solutions are also supported. We'll examine OpenShift SDN in depth in chapter 10.

Now that you have a good idea of how OpenShift is designed, let's look at the lifecycle of an application in an OpenShift cluster.

1.3 Examining an application

OpenShift has workflows that are designed to help you manage your applications through all phases of its lifecycle:

- Build
- Deployment
- Upgrade
- Retirement

The following sections examine each of these phases.

1.3.1 Building applications

The primary way to build applications is to use a *builder image*. This process is the default workflow in OpenShift, and it's what you'll use in chapter 2 to deploy your first applications in OpenShift.

A builder image is a special container image that includes applications and libraries needed for an application in a given language. In chapter 2, you'll deploy a PHP web application. The builder image you'll use for your first deployment includes the Apache web server and the PHP language libraries.

The build process takes the source code for an application and combines it with the builder image to create a custom application image for the application. The custom application image is stored in the integrated registry (see figure 1.4), where it's ready to be deployed and served to the application's users.

1.3.2 Deploying and serving applications

In the default workflow in OpenShift, application deployment is automatically triggered after the container image is built and available. The deployment process takes the newly created application image and deploys it on one or more nodes. In addition to the application pods, a service is created, along with a DNS route in the routing layer.

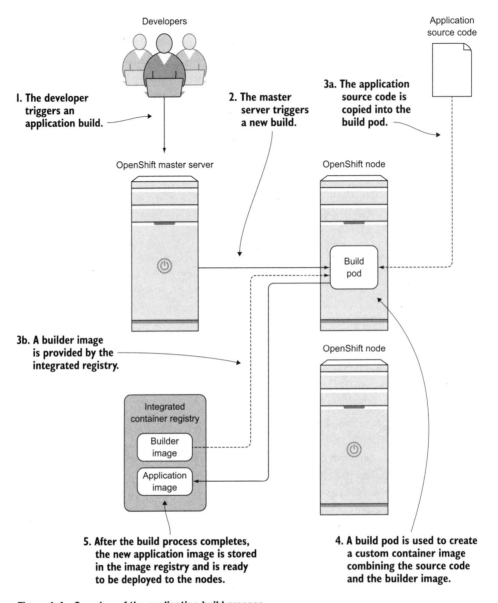

Figure 1.4   Overview of the application build process

Users are able to access the newly created application through the routing layer after all the components have been deployed (see figure 1.5).

Application upgrades use the same workflow. When an upgrade is triggered, a new container image is created, and the new application version is deployed. Multiple upgrade processes are available; we'll discuss them in more depth in chapter 6.

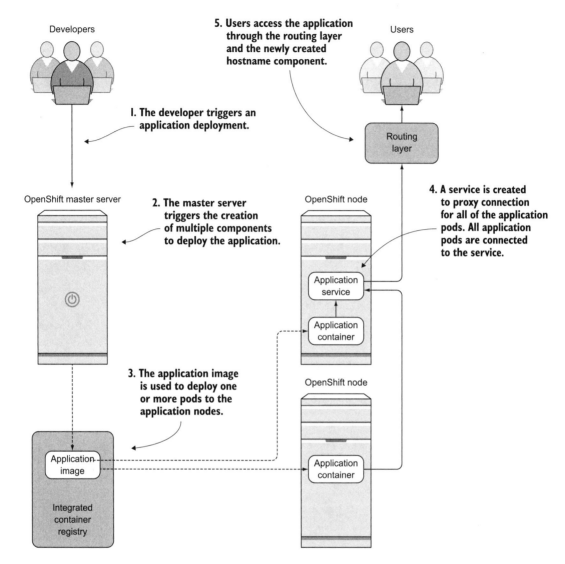

Figure 1.5 Overview of application deployment

That's how OpenShift works at a high level. We'll dig much deeper into all of these components and mechanisms over the course of this book. Now that you're armed with a working knowledge of OpenShift, let's talk about some of the things container platforms are good (and sometimes not so good) at doing.

TIP For a more comprehensive list of how OpenShift integrates with and expands the functionality of Kubernetes, visit www.openshift.com/container-platform/kubernetes.html.

1.4   *Use cases for container platforms*

The technology in OpenShift is pretty cool. But unless you can tie a new technology to some sort of benefit to your mission, it's hard to justify investigating it. In this section, we'll look at some of the benefits OpenShift can provide. Let's start by exploring its technological benefits.

1.4.1   *Technology use cases*

If you stop and think about it for a minute, you can hang the major innovations in IT on a timeline of people seeking more efficient process isolation. Starting with mainframes, we were able to isolate applications more effectively with the client-server model and the x86 revolution. That was followed by the virtualization revolution. Multiple virtual machines can run on a single physical server. This gives administrators better density in their datacenters while still isolating processes from each other.

With virtual machines, each process was isolated in its own virtual machine. Because each virtual machine has a full operating system and a full kernel (see figure 1.6), it must have all the filesystems required for a full operating system. That also means it must be patched, managed, and treated like traditional infrastructure.

Containers are the next step in this evolution. An application container holds everything the application needs to run:

- Source code or compiled code for the application
- Libraries or applications needed for the application to run properly
- Configurations and information about connecting to shared data sources

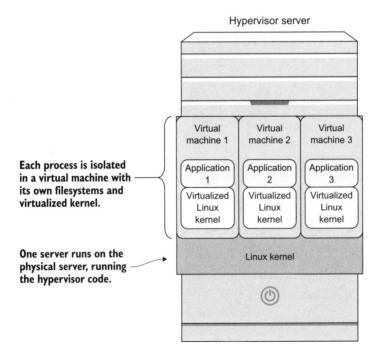

Figure 1.6   Virtual machines can be used for process isolation.

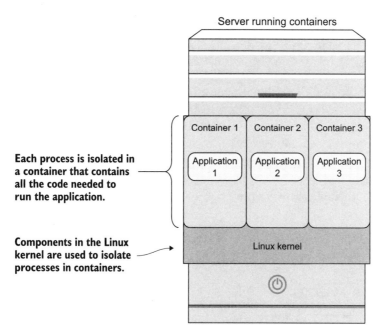

Each process is isolated in a container that contains all the code needed to run the application.

Components in the Linux kernel are used to isolate processes in containers.

Figure 1.7   Containers use a single kernel to serve applications, saving space and resources and providing flexible application platforms.

What containers *don't* contain is equally important. Unlike virtual machines, containers all run on a single, shared Linux kernel. To isolate the applications, containers use components inside the kernel (see figure 1.7) that we'll discuss in chapters 3 and 9.

Because containers don't have to include a full kernel to serve their application, along with all the dependencies of an operating system, they tend to be much smaller than virtual machines both in their storage needs and their resource consumption. For example, whereas a typical virtual machine starts out with a 10 GB or larger disk, the CentOS 7 container image is 140 MB.

Being smaller comes with a couple of advantages. First, portability is enhanced. Moving 140 MB from one server to another is much faster than moving 10 GB or more.

Second, because starting a container doesn't include booting up an entire kernel, the startup process is much faster. Starting a container is typically measured in milliseconds, as opposed to seconds or minutes for virtual machines.

The technologies behind containers provide multiple technical benefits. They provide business advantages as well.

1.4.2   Use cases for businesses

Modern business solutions must include time or resource savings as part of their design. Solutions today have to be able to use human and computer resources more efficiently than in the past. Containers' ability to enable both types of savings is one of the major reasons they've exploded on the scene the way they have.

MORE EFFECTIVE RESOURCE UTILIZATION WITH CONTAINERS

If you compare a server that's using virtual machines to isolate processes to one that's using containers to do the same thing, you'll notice a few key differences (see figure 1.8):

- Containers consume server resources more effectively. Because there's a single shared kernel for all containers on a host, instead of multiple virtualized kernels as in virtual machines, more of the server's resources are used to serve applications instead of for platform overhead.
- Application density increases with containers. Because the basic unit used to deploy applications (container images) is much smaller than the unit for virtual machines (virtual machine images), more applications can fit per server. This means more applications require fewer servers to run.

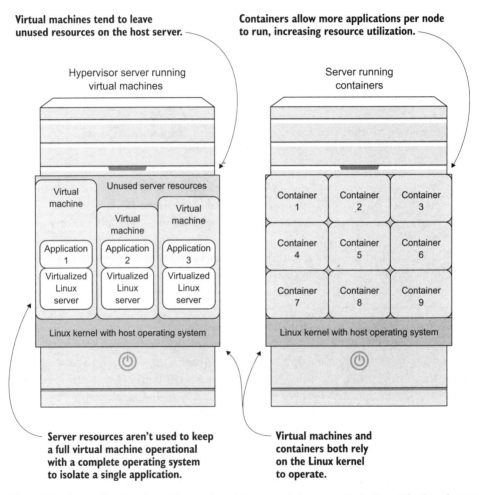

Figure 1.8   Comparing virtual machines and containers: containers provide better utilization of server resources

Even though containers are great tools, and we'll talk about them on every page of this book, they aren't always the best tool for every job. In the next section, we'll discuss a few times when containers aren't the best fit.

1.4.3   When containers aren't the answer

An ever-increasing number of workloads are good fits for containers. The container revolution started with pure web applications but now includes command-line tools, desktop tools, and even relational databases. Even with the massive growth of use cases for containers, in some situations they're not the answer.

WHEN THE RETURN ON INVESTMENT IS TOO LOW

If you have a complex legacy application, be careful when deciding to break it down and convert it to a series of containers. If an application will be around for 18 months, and it will take 9 months of work to properly containerize it, you may want to leave it where it is. It's OK, we promise.

WHEN YOU NEED ACCESS TO EXOTIC HARDWARE

Containers solutions began in the enterprise IT world. They're designed to work with most enterprise-grade storage and networking solutions, but they don't work with all of them easily. When you're using a networking solution like InfiniBand, or a storage solution like Lustre, containers can be a challenge. This is quickly being addressed by the Kubernetes community, with access to devices like GPUs being previewed in OpenShift 3.9 with more to follow.

> **NOTE**   InfiniBand (http://mng.bz/6CMb) is a high-performance networking standard that's often found in high-performance computing (HPC) environments. Lustre (http://lustre.org/) is a high-performance parallel filesystem that's also often found in HPC environments.

WHEN YOUR MONOLITH APPLICATIONS WILL ALWAYS BE MONOLITHS

Some applications are always going to be very large, very resource-intensive monolithic applications. Examples are software used to run HR departments and some very large relational databases. If a single application will take up multiple servers on its own, running it in a container that wants to share resources with other applications on a server doesn't make a lot of sense.

Now that you have a solid idea of how OpenShift uses containers, and where they're good (and not good) fits for applications, let's look at how you can provide containers for applications that need persistent or shared storage.

1.5   Solving container storage needs

Containers are a revolutionary technology, but they can't do everything on their own. Storage is an area where containers need to be paired with another solution to deploy production-ready applications.

This is because the storage created when a container is deployed is ephemeral. If a container is destroyed or replaced, the storage from inside that container isn't reused.

This is by design, to allow containers to be stateless by default. If something goes bad, a container can be removed from your environment completely, and a new one can be stood up to replace it almost instantly.

The idea of a stateless application container is great. But somewhere in your application, usually in multiple places, data needs to be shared across multiple containers, and state needs to be preserved. Here are some examples of these situations:

- Shared data that needs to be available across multiple containers, like uploaded images for a web application
- User state information in a complex application, which lets users pick up where they leave off during a long-running transaction
- Information that's stored in relational or nonrelational databases

In all of these situations, and many others, you need to have persistent storage available in your containers. This storage should be defined as part of your application's deployment and should be available from all the nodes in your OpenShift cluster. Luckily, OpenShift has multiple ways to solve this problem.

In chapter 7, you'll configure an external network storage service. You'll then configure it to interact with OpenShift so applications can dynamically allocate and take advantage of its persistent storage volumes (see figure 1.9).

When you're able to effectively integrate shared storage into your application's containers, you can think about scalability in new ways.

1.6   *Scaling applications*

For stateless applications, scaling up and down is straightforward. Because there are no dependencies other than what's in the application container, and because the transactions happening in the container are atomic by design, all you need to do to scale a stateless application is to deploy more instances of it and load-balance them together.

To make this process even easier, OpenShift proxies the connections to each application through a built-in load balancer. This allows applications to scale up and down with no change in how users connect to the application.

If your applications are *stateful*, meaning they need to store or retrieve shared data, such as a database or data that a user has uploaded, then you need to be able to provide persistent storage for them. This storage needs to automatically scale up and down with your applications in OpenShift. For stateful applications, persistent storage is a key component that must be tightly integrated into your design. At the end of the day, stateful pods are how users will get data in and out of your application.

1.7   *Integrating stateful and stateless applications*

As you begin separating traditional, monolithic applications into smaller services that work effectively in containers, you'll begin to view your data needs in a different way. This process is often referred to as designing applications as *microservices*.

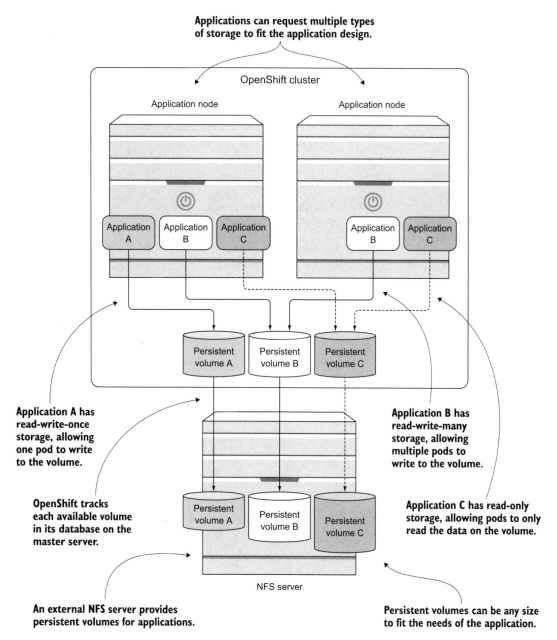

Figure 1.9 OpenShift can integrate and manage external storage platforms and ensure that the best-fit storage volume is matched with the applications that need it.

For any application, you'll have services that you need to be stateful, and others that are stateless. For example, the service that provides static web content can be stateless, whereas the service that processes user authentication needs to be able to write information to persistent storage. These services all go together to form your application.

Because each service runs in its own container, the services can be scaled up and down independently. Instead of having to scale up your entire codebase, with containers you only scale the services in your application that need to process additional workloads.

Additionally, because only the containers that need access to persistent storage have it, the data going into your container is more secure. In figure 1.10, if there was a vulnerability in service B, a compromised process would have a hard time getting access to the data stored in the persistent storage.

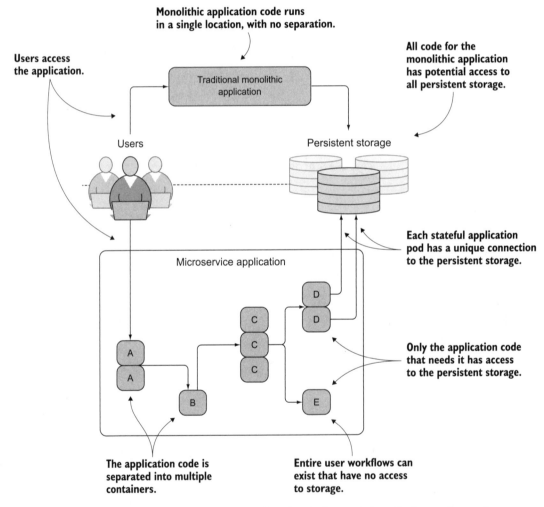

Figure 1.10 Illustrating the differences between traditional and microservice applications: microservice applications scale their components independently, creating better performance and resource utilization

That brings us to the end of our initial walkthrough of OpenShift and how it deploys, manages, and orchestrates applications deployed with containers using docker and Kubernetes. The benefits provided by OpenShift save time for humans and use server resources more efficiently. Additionally, the nature of how containers work provides improved scalability and deployment speed versus virtual machine deployments.

This all goes together to provide an incredibly powerful application platform that you'll work with for the rest of this book. In chapter 2, you'll install and configure OpenShift, and deploy your first applications.

1.8 Summary

- OpenShift is an application platform that uses docker, Kubernetes, and additional services to deploy applications.
- Docker is a container runtime that creates and manages containers on a single host.
- Kubernetes is a container-orchestration engine that's used to orchestrate container engine workloads across multiple servers in a cluster.
- OpenShift expands on the Kubernetes design, adding important components out of the box.
- Containers provide better resource utilization and start up faster than virtual machines.
- Some situations aren't a good fit for running applications in containers.
- OpenShift SDN is a robust, configurable SDN solution that's deployed in OpenShift by default, along with an integrated application routing layer and image registry.
- Containers can easily consume persistent storage in OpenShift.
- OpenShift is able to combine multiple stateless and stateful applications to provide a single application experience for end users.

Getting started

2

This chapter covers

- Accessing your cluster and logging in
- Creating projects and deploying applications
- Accessing your application by creating routes
- Investigating application components
- Comparing command-line and web workflows

There are three ways to interact with OpenShift: the command line, the web interface, and the RESTful API. This chapter focuses on deploying applications using the command line, because the command line exposes more of the process that's used to create containerized applications in OpenShift. In other chapters, the examples may use the web interface or even the API. Our intention is to give you the most real-world examples of using OpenShift. We want to show you the best tools to get the various jobs done.

We'll also try our best not to make you repeat yourself. Almost every action in OpenShift can be performed using all three access methods. If something is limited, we'll do our best to let you know. But we want you to get the best experience possible from using OpenShift. With that said, in this chapter we're going to repeat ourselves. But we have a good reason!

The most common task in OpenShift is deploying an application. Because this is the most common task, we want to introduce you to it as early as practical, using both the command line and the web interface. So please bear with us. This chapter may seem a little repetitive, but we think the repetition will be helpful as you continue to learn how to use OpenShift.

2.1 *Cluster options*

Before you can start using OpenShift, you have to deploy it. Appendix A guides you through a full deployment of OpenShift on multiple servers. Several of the chapter's examples require multiple nodes to function properly or to have enough resources to function properly. But there's a different installer for OpenShift that we'd like to mention here: *Minishift.*

Minishift (https://github.com/minishift/minishift) is a single-node installation of OpenShift that you can stand up in a few minutes on just about any operating system as a virtual machine. As a development platform, it's a very useful tool.

We strongly recommend going through the process of installing a full OpenShift cluster. You can run most of the examples in this book on Minishift, through chapter 6. But you'll run into trouble when you start working with persistent storage, metrics, complex application deployments, and networking. If you're ready to get your full OpenShift cluster up and running, head to appendix A and deploy your cluster before you move on to the examples in this chapter. If you want to dive in to the examples a little faster, Minishift is your path forward. Take a look at its documentation to get it up and running.

When something goes awry

It's almost inevitable. When you're first learning how to use a new tool like OpenShift, you do something, and it doesn't come out quite like you expected. So you start troubleshooting, and that makes things worse. Eventually, you end up with a platform that's full of random weirdness or doesn't work at all.

IT professionals learn by doing. We encourage you to experiment with OpenShift as you go through this book. Give yourself problems to solve, and use OpenShift to solve them. And when one of them doesn't work as expected, use this book as a reference to dig in and figure out what's going on.

We also know that starting from scratch is hard and time-consuming. Toward that end, we've created a GitHub organization: https://github.com/OpenShiftInAction. In this organization, you'll find repositories dedicated to the work and examples for each chapter.

You'll also notice a project called *autoinstaller*. The autoinstaller project uses Ansible (www.ansible.com) to deploy OpenShift with the same configuration you'd deploy by following appendix A. There are also shorter playbooks that do all the work for each chapter in the book. If you break your cluster and need to start over, feel free to use autoinstaller as a quicker path back to where you were before your issues.

> **(continued)**
> Also, please use the issue tracker and other tools in the GitHub organization to com-
> municate with us. Our plan is to continue to work with and update these projects even
> after the book is published. So file issues, submit pull requests, and contribute to
> the *OpenShift in Action* community.

Like most applications, OpenShift requires a little configuration to get going. That's
what the next sections discuss.

2.2 Logging in

In OpenShift, every action requires authentication. This allows every action to be gov-
erned by the security and access rules set up for all users in an OpenShift cluster. We'll
discuss the various methods of managing authentication in chapter 9, but by default
your OpenShift cluster's initial configuration is set to allow any user and password
combination to log in. This is called the *Allow All identity provider*.

The Allow All identity provider creates a user account the first time a user logs in.
Each username is unique, and the password can be anything except an empty field.
This configuration is safe and recommended only for lab and development OpenShift
instances like the one you just set up.

The first user you'll create will be called *dev*. This user will represent any normal
developer or end user in OpenShift. You'll use the dev user for most of the examples
in this book.

> **NOTE** This authentication method is case-sensitive. Although the passwords
> can be anything, dev and Dev are different users and won't be able to see the
> same projects and applications. Be careful when you log in.

2.2.1 Using the oc command-line application

In appendix A, you install oc on your laptop or workstation. This is the tool you'll use
to manage OpenShift on the command line. If you're using an OSX or Linux system,
you can open your favorite terminal application. On Windows, open your command
prompt. From your command line, run the oc login command, using dev for the
username and password and the URL for your master server's API server:

**The syntax for logging in to an OpenShift
cluster, including the username, password,
and URL for your OpenShift master's API server**

```
$ oc login -u dev -p dev https://ocp-1.192.168.122.100.nip.io:8443   ←
Login successful.

You don't have any projects. You can try to create a new project, by running

    oc new-project <projectname>
```

The parameters used here for `oc login` are as follows:

- `-u`, the username to log in with.
- `-p`, the user's password.
- URL for your OpenShift master's API server. By default, it's served over HTTPS on TCP port 8443.

In the example, OpenShift is prompting you to accomplish your next step: creating a project.

2.3 Creating projects

In OpenShift, *projects* are the fundamental way applications are organized. Projects let users collect their applications into logical groups. They also serve other useful roles around security that we'll discuss in chapters 9 and 10. For now, though, think of a project as a collection of related applications. You'll create your first project and then use it to house a handful of applications that you'll deploy, modify, redeploy, and do all sorts of things to over the course of the next few chapters.

> **The default project and working with multiple projects**
>
> The `oc` tool's default action is to execute the command you run using the current working project. If you create a new project, it automatically becomes your working project. The `oc project` command changes among projects that already exist.
>
> To specify a command to be executed against a specific project, regardless of your current working project, use the `-n` parameter with the project name you want the command to run against.
>
> This is a helpful option when you're writing scripts that use `oc` and act on multiple projects. It's also a good habit in general.

To create a project, you need to run the `oc new-project` command and provide a project name. For your first project, use `image-uploader` as the project name:

```
$ oc new-project image-uploader --display-name='Image Uploader Project'
Now using project "image-uploader" on server
➥ "https://ocp-1.192.168.122.100.nip.io:8443".

You can add applications to this project with the 'new-app' command.
➥ For example, try:

    oc new-app centos/ruby-22-centos7~https://github.com/openshift/ruby-ex.git

to build a new example application in Ruby.
```

The output prompts you to deploy your first application.

> **NOTE** You can find documentation for all of the `oc` command's features in the OpenShift CLI Reference documentation at http://mng.bz/dCTv.

In addition to the name for your project, you can optionally provide a *display name*. The display name is a more human-friendly name for your project. The project name has a restricted syntax because it becomes part of the URL for all of the applications deployed in OpenShift. We'll discuss how that works later in this chapter.

Now that you've created your first project, section 2.5 will walk you through deploying your first application, called *Image Uploader*, into your new project. Image Uploader is a web-based PHP application that's used to upload and display graphic files from your computer. But first, let's talk about application components, so you understand how all the parts fit and work together.

2.4   Application components

Applications in OpenShift aren't monolithic structures; they consist of a number of different components in a project that all work together to deploy, update, and maintain your application through its lifecycle. These components are as follows:

- Custom container images
- Image streams
- Application pods
- Build configs
- Deployment configs
- Deployments
- Services

These components all work together to serve your applications to your end users, as shown in figure 2.1. The interactions between the application components can seem a little complex, so next let's walk through what these components do in more detail. We'll start with how OpenShift creates and uses *custom container images* for each application.

2.4.1   Custom container images

Each application deployment in OpenShift creates a custom container image to serve your application. This image is created using the application's source code and a custom base image called a *builder image*. For example, the PHP builder image contains the Apache web server and the core PHP language libraries.

The image build process takes the builder image you choose, integrates your source code, and creates the custom container image that will be used for the application deployment. Once created, all the container images, along with all the builder images, are stored in OpenShift's integrated container registry, which we discussed in chapter 1 (also noted in figure 2.1). The component that controls the creation of your application containers is the *build config*.

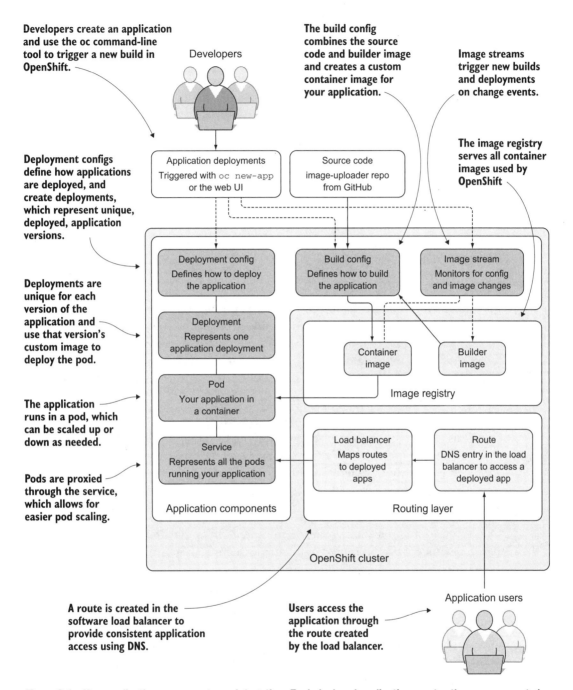

Developers create an application and use the oc command-line tool to trigger a new build in OpenShift.

Developers

The build config combines the source code and builder image and creates a custom container image for your application.

Image streams trigger new builds and deployments on change events.

Deployment configs define how applications are deployed, and create deployments, which represent unique, deployed, application versions.

Application deployments
Triggered with `oc new-app` or the web UI

Source code image-uploader repo from GitHub

The image registry serves all container images used by OpenShift

Deployment config
Defines how to deploy the application

Build config
Defines how to build the application

Image stream
Monitors for config and image changes

Deployments are unique for each version of the application and use that version's custom image to deploy the pod.

Deployment
Represents one application deployment

Container image

Builder image

The application runs in a pod, which can be scaled up or down as needed.

Pod
Your application in a container

Image registry

Service
Represents all the pods running your application

Load balancer
Maps routes to deployed apps

Route
DNS entry in the load balancer to access a deployed app

Pods are proxied through the service, which allows for easier pod scaling.

Application components

Routing layer

OpenShift cluster

A route is created in the software load balancer to provide consistent application access using DNS.

Users access the application through the route created by the load balancer.

Application users

Figure 2.1 How application components work together: Each deployed application creates these components in your OpenShift cluster. This workflow is fully automated and customizable.

2.4.2 Build configs

A build config contains all the information needed to build an application using its source code. This includes all the information required to build the application container image:

- URL for the application source code
- Name of the builder image to use
- Name of the application container image that's created
- Events that can trigger a new build to occur

Figure 2.1 illustrates these relationships. The build config is used to track what's required to build your application and to trigger the creation of the application's container image.

After the build config does its job, it triggers the *deployment config* that's created for your newly created application.

2.4.3 Deployment configs

If an application is never deployed, it can never do its job. The job of deploying and upgrading the application is handled by the deployment config component. In figure 2.1, you see that deployment configs are created as part of the initial application deployment command that you'll run later in this chapter.

Deployment configs track several pieces of information about an application:

- Currently deployed version of the application.
- Number of replicas to maintain for the application.
- Trigger events that can trigger a redeployment. By default, configuration changes to the deployment or changes to the container image trigger an automatic application redeployment
- Upgrade strategy. app-cli uses the default rolling-upgrade strategy.
- Application deployments.

A key feature of applications running in OpenShift is that they're horizontally scalable. This concept is represented in the deployment config by the number of replicas.

MAINTAINING APPLICATION REPLICAS

The number of replicas specified in a deployment config is passed into a Kubernetes object called a *replication controller*. This is a special type of Kubernetes pod that allows for multiple *replicas*—copies of the application pod—to be kept running at all times. All pods in OpenShift are deployed by replication controllers by default.

Another feature that's managed by a deployment config is how application upgrades can be fully automated.

Each deployment for an application is monitored and available to the deployment config component using *deployments*.

Phases of the pod lifecycle

In OpenShift, a pod can exist in one of five phases at any given time in its lifecycle. These phases are described in detail in the Kubernetes documentation at http://mng.bz/NIG1. The following is a brief summary of the five pod phases:

- *Pending*—The pod has been accepted by OpenShift, but it's not yet scheduled on one of the applications nodes.
- *Running*—The pod is scheduled on a node and is confirmed to be up and running.
- *Succeeded*—All containers in a pod have terminated successfully and won't be restarted.
- *Failed*—One or more containers in a pod have failed to start.
- *Unknown*—Something has gone wrong, and OpenShift can't obtain a more accurate status for the pod.

Failed and Succeeded are considered terminal states for a pod in its lifecycle. Once a pod reaches one of these states, it won't be restarted.

You can see the current phase for each pod in a project by running the `oc get pods` command. Pod lifecycles will become important when you begin creating project quotas in chapter 6.

DEPLOYMENTS

Each time a new version of an application is created by its build config, a new deployment is created and tracked by the deployment config. A deployment represents a unique version of an application. Each deployment references a version of the application image that was created, and creates the replication controller to create and maintain the pods to serve the application. In figure 2.1, the deployment is directly linked to the pod that serves an application.

New deployments can be created automatically in OpenShift by managing how applications are upgraded, which is also tracked by the deployment config.

MANAGING UPGRADE METHODS

The default application-upgrade method in OpenShift is to perform a *rolling upgrade*. Rolling upgrades create new versions of an application, allowing new connections to the application to access only the new version. As traffic increases to the new deployment, the pods for the old deployment are removed from the system.

New application deployments can be automatically triggered by events such as configuration changes to your application, or a new version of a container image being available. These sorts of trigger events are monitored by *image streams* in OpenShift.

2.4.4 *Image streams*

Image streams are used to automate actions in OpenShift. They consist of links to one or more container images. Using image streams, you can monitor applications and trigger new deployments when their components are updated.

In figure 2.1, you can see how image streams are linked to the container image for an application, as well as its deployment. We'll discuss image streams in more depth in chapter 6.

Now that we've gone through how applications are built and deployed, it's time for you to deploy your first application.

2.5 *Deploying an application*

Applications are deployed using the `oc new-app` command. When you run this command to deploy the Image Uploader application into the image-uploader project, you need to provide three pieces of information:

- *The type of image stream you want to use*—OpenShift ships with multiple container images called *builder images* that you can use as a starting point for applications. In this example, you'll be using the PHP builder image to create your application.
- *A name for your application*—In this example, use `app-cli`, because this version of your application will be deployed from the command line.
- *The location of your application's source code*—OpenShift will take this source code and combine it with the PHP builder image to create a custom container image for your application deployment.

Here's the new application deployment (we've trimmed the output for clarity):

```
$ oc new-app \                                              Source code for
> --image-stream=php \          Image stream to use         the application
> --code=https://github.com/OpenShiftInAction/image-uploader.git \
> --name=app-cli
...                             Application name
--> Success
    Build scheduled, use 'oc logs -f bc/cli-app' to track its progress.
    Run 'oc status' to view your app.
```

After you run the `oc new-app` command, you'll see a long list of output. This is OpenShift building out all the components needed to make your application work properly, as we discussed at the beginning of this section.

Now that you've deployed your first application, you need to be able to access the newly deployed pod. Figure 2.2 shows that the pod is associated with a component called a *service*, which then links up to provide application access for users. Let's look at services next.

2.5.1 *Providing consistent application access with services*

Chapters 3 and 4 will explore multiple ways to force OpenShift to redeploy application pods. In the course of a normal day, this happens all the time, for any number of reasons:

- You're scaling applications up and down.
- Application pods stop responding correctly.
- Nodes are rebooted or have issues.
- Human error (the most common cause, of course).
- The phase of the moon is out of alignment, one of the many other things that cause computers to not do what you want.

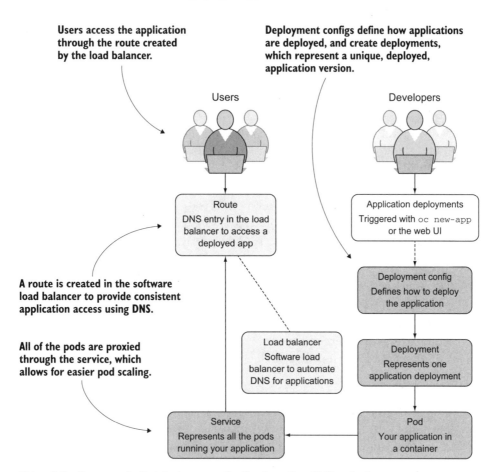

Figure 2.2 Components that deploy an application in an OpenShift project

Although pods may come and go, there needs to be a consistent presence for your applications in OpenShift. That's what a service does. A service uses the labels applied to pods when they're created to keep track of all pods associated with a given application. This allows a service to act as an internal proxy for your application. You can see information about the service for app-cli by running the `oc describe svc/app-cli` command:

```
$ oc describe svc/app-cli
Name:              app-cli
Namespace:          image-uploader
Labels:              app=app-cli
Selector:          app=app-cli,deploymentconfig=app-cli
Type:              ClusterIP
IP:                172.30.90.167
Port:              8080-tcp      8080/TCP
Endpoints:
Session Affinity:    None
No events.
```

IP address for the service ⟶ IP:

Port to connect to the service ⟵ Port:

Each service gets an IP address that's only routable from within the OpenShift cluster. Other information that's maintained includes the IP address of the service and the TCP ports to connect to in the pod.

> **TIP** Most components in OpenShift have a shorthand that can be used on the command line to save time and avoid misspelled component names. The previous command uses `svc/app-cli` to get information about the service for the app-cli application. Build configs can be accessed with `bc/<app-name>`, and deployment configs with `dc/<app-name>`. You can find the rest of the shorthand in the documentation for `oc` at https://docs.openshift.org/latest/cli_reference/get_started_cli.html.

Services provide a consistent gateway into your application deployment. But the IP address of a service is available only in your OpenShift cluster. To connect users to your applications and make DNS work properly, you need one more application component. Next, you'll create a *route* to expose app-cli externally from your OpenShift cluster.

2.5.2 *Exposing services to the outside world with routes*

When you install your OpenShift cluster, one of the services that's created is an *HAProxy* service running in a container on OpenShift. HAProxy is an open source, software load-balancer application. We'll look at this service in depth in chapter 10.

To create a route for the app-cli application, run the following command:

```
oc expose svc/app-cli
```

As we discussed earlier, OpenShift uses projects to organize applications. An application's project is included in the URL that's generated when you create an application route. Each application's URL takes the following format:

```
<application-name>-<project-name>.<cluster-app-domain>
```

When you deploy OpenShift in appendix A, you specify the application domain `apps.192,168.122.101.nip.io`. By default, all applications in OpenShift are served using the HTTP protocol. When you put all this together, the URL for app-cli should be as follows:

```
http://app-cli-image-uploader.apps.192.168.122.101.nip.io
```

You can get information about the route you just created by running the `oc describe route/app-cli` command:

```
$ oc describe route/app-cli
Name:            app-cli
Namespace:        image-uploader
Created:        About an hour ago
Labels:            app=app-cli
Annotations:        openshift.io/host.generated=true
Requested Host:        app-cli-image-uploader.apps.192.168.122.101.nip.io  <───┐
                exposed on router router about an hour ago
```

URL created in HAProxy

```
Path:              <none>
TLS Termination:   <none>
Insecure Policy:   <none>
Endpoint Port:        8080-tcp

Service:    app-cli              ◁── Associated service
Weight:        100 (100%)
Endpoints:     10.129.1.112:8080  ◁── Endpoints for the service
```

The output tells you the host configurations added to HAProxy, the service associated with the route, and the endpoints for the service to connect to when handling requests for the route.

Now that you've created the route to your application, go ahead and verify that it's functional in a web browser. You should be able to browse to your app-cli application using the URL for the route that was created (see figure 2.3).

NOTE You should be able to access your app-cli deployment from anywhere that your test cluster is accessible. If you created the cluster on virtual machines on your laptop, it's most likely accessible only from your laptop. OpenShift is pretty awesome, but it can't overcome the rules of TCP/IP networking.

Figure 2.3 The app-cli application web interface should be up and running and available.

Focusing on the components that deploy and deliver the app-cli application, you can see the relationship between the service, the newly created route, and the end users. We'll cover this in more depth in chapter 10; but in summary, the route is tied to the app-cli service, and users access the application pod through the route (see figure 2.4).

This chapter is about relationships. In OpenShift, multiple components work in concert to build, deploy, and manage applications. We'll spend the rest of this book discussing the different aspects of these relationships in depth. That fundamental knowledge of how container platforms operate is incredibly valuable.

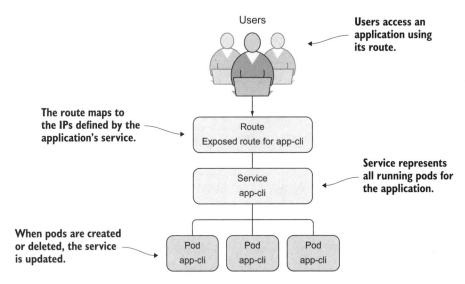

Figure 2.4   Overview of application request routing

2.6   Deploying applications using the web interface

We began this chapter by claiming that we didn't want to repeat ourselves and then warning you that the chapter would be a little repetitive. Well, we've reached the repetitive part. Deploying applications in OpenShift is so fundamental to its purpose that we want to quickly walk you through the same process using the web interface. We'll keep this section as short as possible—the web interface's workflow will help with that.

2.6.1   Logging in to the OpenShift web interface

The OpenShift web interface is served from your master server, using the same URL that you use to log in with the command line. In the example, the web interface is accessible at https://ocp-1.192.168.122.100.nip.io:8443 (see figure 2.5). Go ahead and log in, if you haven't already. Use the same dev user and non-empty password that you used to log in earlier.

After logging in, you'll arrive at a *project overview* page. This page lists all active projects for your user. You should see the image-uploader project that you created earlier in this chapter. Click the Image Uploader name to go to the project details page.

Figure 2.5
Web interface
login page

2.7   Deploying applications with the web interface

The web interface creates the same components that we talked about in the previous section (see figure 2.6). From the project details, you can see the details for the app-cli deployment, including the following:

- Deployment information, including a link to the deployconfig details
- Replica count
- Route information and a link to the application

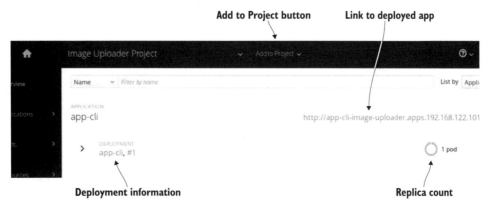

Add to Project button   **Link to deployed app**

Deployment information   **Replica count**

Figure 2.6   App-cli information in the web interface, and the Add to Project button

Also on the project details page, on the top bar, is an Add to Project button. Click Add to Project > Browse Catalog to deploy a new application.

   When you deployed app-cli, you selected the PHP image stream that included the PHP 7.0 builder image. In the web interface, you can follow the same process. The builder image image streams are available in a handy catalog. For your second application, you'll deploy the same Image Uploader application again. Click the PHP option from the catalog to proceed (see figure 2.7).

Figure 2.7   Builder images for multiple languages in the image catalog

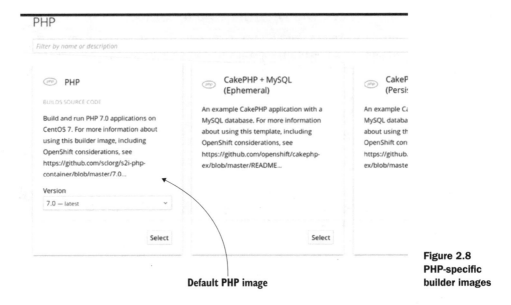

Figure 2.8
PHP-specific
builder images

Default PHP image

The next screen takes you to all the available builder images for the PHP programming language. You should see at least three options at this stage, similar to the information about the app-cli service you saw in section 2.4.2. Because you're deploying the same application, you can select the same default PHP builder image (see figure 2.8).

After selecting the default PHP builder image, you're prompted to provide the same information that was required to deploy app-cli (see figure 2.9):

- *Name*—For your second deployment of the Image Uploader code, call the application *app-gui*.
- *Git Repository URL*—This is the same repository that you supplied to deploy app-cli, https://github.com/OpenShiftInAction/image-uploader.git.

When you've filled in the fields, click Create. This will launch the build and deployment process for your new app-gui application.

Figure 2.9
Create a new PHP
application using
the web interface.

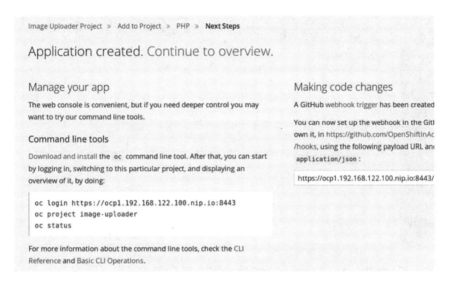

Figure 2.10 **After deploying your app-gui application, you should see the deployment summary page, which offers you a link to the application overview.**

Once the process has started, you're taken to a deployment summary page (see figure 2.10). This page provides you with information about how to log in to the command line, as well as more advanced features like setting application probes, which we'll discuss in chapter 4, and setting resource limits, which we'll discuss in chapter 9.

Click the Continue to Overview link to return to the project details page.

At this point, OpenShift is going through the exact same process we discussed earlier in this chapter. It's taking the source code, creating a custom container image, and building out all the other components that will be used to manage the application's lifecycle. Even though both app-cli and app-gui use the same application source code, OpenShift will create a custom container image for each deployment, along with a unique version of each other component. Doing so allows for fully independent application lifecycles, even if they share the same source code.

Depending on your internet connection speed, the build and deployment process for app-gui may take a couple of minutes. When it completes, you should see both your app-cli and app-gui application deployments up and active (see figure 2.11).

When you deployed app-cli, you had to create a route to access the application. Notice in figure 2.11 that when you deployed app-gui with the web interface, the route was created for you automatically. This is designed to save time for the average user who's using the web interface. Creating routes with the command line isn't automated to allow that workflow to be customized and automated more easily.

And that is, we hope, the last time we'll ask you to do the same thing twice in this book!

This chapter has been all about defining what an application deployment looks like in OpenShift, and how the components that make up an application maintain

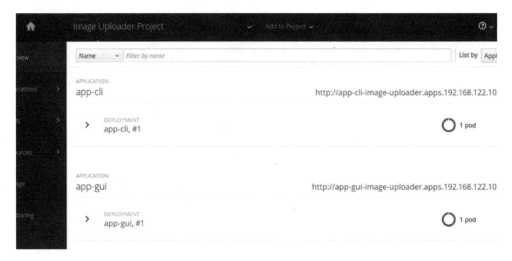

Figure 2.11   Project details page with app-cli and app-gui deployed

their relationships with one another. In the next chapter, we'll discuss how you add persistent storage to applications to make them more flexible and easier to scale.

2.8   Summary

- Application deployments create multiple, tightly orchestrated application components to manage build, deploy, and manage applications.
- All transactions in OpenShift require an authenticated session.
- Projects in OpenShift are used to organize similar applications.
- OpenShift has robust command-line and web-based workflows.
- OpenShift can automatically configure DNS records that route requests to your application when it's deployed.

Containers are Linux

This chapter covers

- How OpenShift, Kubernetes, and docker work together
- How containers isolate processes with namespaces

In the previous chapter, you deployed your first applications in OpenShift. In this chapter, we'll look deeper into your OpenShift cluster and investigate how these containers isolate their processes on the application node.

Knowledge of how containers work in a platform like OpenShift is some of the most powerful information in IT right now. This fundamental understanding of how a container actually works as part of a Linux server informs how systems are designed and how issues are analyzed when they inevitably occur.

This is a challenging chapter—not because you'll be editing a lot of configurations and making complex changes, but because we're talking about the fundamental layers of abstraction that make a container a container. Let's get started by attempting to define exactly what a container is.

3.1 Defining containers

You can find five different container experts and ask them to define what a container is, and you're likely to get five different answers. The following are some of our personal favorites, all of which are correct from a certain perspective:

- A transportable unit to move applications around. This is a typical developer's answer.
- A fancy Linux process (one of our personal favorites).
- A more effective way to isolate processes on a Linux system. This is a more operations-centered answer.

What we need to untangle is the fact that they're all correct, depending on your point of view.

In chapter 1, we talked about how OpenShift uses Kubernetes and docker to orchestrate and deploy applications in containers in your cluster. But we haven't talked much about which application component is created by each of these services. Before we move forward, it's important for you to understand these responsibilities as you begin interacting with application components directly.

3.2 *How OpenShift components work together*

When you deploy an application in OpenShift, the request starts in the OpenShift API. We discussed this process at a high level in chapter 2. To really understand how containers isolate the processes within them, we need take a more detailed look at how these services work together to deploy your application. The relationship between OpenShift, Kubernetes, docker, and, ultimately, the Linux kernel is a chain of dependencies.

When you deploy an application in OpenShift, the process starts with the OpenShift services.

3.2.1 *OpenShift manages deployments*

Deploying applications begins with application components that are unique to OpenShift. The process is as follows:

1. OpenShift creates a custom container image using your source code and the builder image template you specified. For example, app-cli and app-gui use the PHP builder image.
2. This image is uploaded to the OpenShift container image registry.
3. OpenShift creates a build config to document how your application is built. This includes which image was created, the builder image used, the location of the source code, and other information.
4. OpenShift creates a deployment config to control deployments and deploy and update your applications. Information in deployment configs includes the number of replicas, the upgrade method, and application-specific variables and mounted volumes.
5. OpenShift creates a deployment, which represents a single deployed version of an application. Each unique application deployment is associated with your application's deployment config component.

6 The OpenShift internal load balancer is updated with an entry for the DNS record for the application. This entry will be linked to a component that's created by Kubernetes, which we'll get to shortly.

7 OpenShift creates an image stream component. In OpenShift, an image stream monitors the builder image, deployment config, and other components for changes. If a change is detected, image streams can trigger application redeployments to reflect changes.

Figure 3.1 shows how these components are linked together. When a developer creates source code and triggers a new application deployment (in this case, using the `oc` command-line tool), OpenShift creates the deployment config, image stream, and build config components.

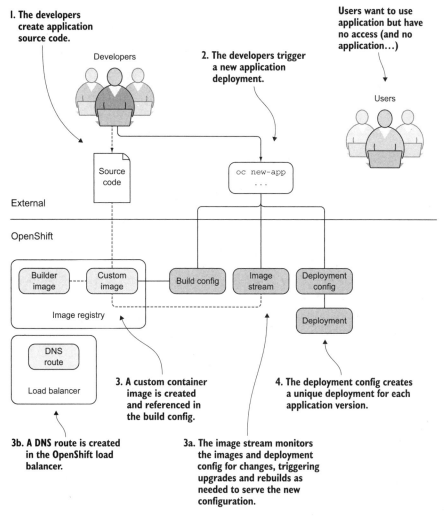

Figure 3.1 Application components created by OpenShift during application deployment

The build config creates an application-specific custom container image using the specified builder image and source code. This image is stored in the OpenShift image registry. The deployment config component creates an application deployment that's unique for each version of the application. The image stream is created and monitors for changes to the deployment config and related images in the internal registry. The DNS route is also created and will be linked to a Kubernetes object.

In figure 3.1, notice that the users are sitting by themselves with no access to the application. There *is* no application. OpenShift depends on Kubernetes, as well as docker, to get the deployed application to the user. Next, we'll look at Kubernetes' responsibilities in OpenShift.

3.2.2   *Kubernetes schedules applications across nodes*

Kubernetes is the orchestration engine at the heart of OpenShift. In many ways, an OpenShift cluster is a Kubernetes cluster. When you initially deployed app-cli, Kubernetes created several application components:

- *Replication controller*—Scales the application as needed in Kubernetes. This component also ensures that the desired number of replicas in the deployment config is maintained at all times.
- *Service*—Exposes the application. A Kubernetes service is a single IP address that's used to access all the active pods for an application deployment. When you scale an application up or down, the number of pods changes, but they're all accessed through a single service.
- *Pods*—Represent the smallest scalable unit in OpenShift.

NOTE   Typically, a single pod is made up of a single container. But in some situations, it makes sense to have a single pod consist of multiple containers.

Figure 3.2 illustrates the relationships between the Kubernetes components that are created. The replication controller dictates how many pods are created for an initial application deployment and is linked to the OpenShift deployment component.

Also linked to the pod component is a Kubernetes service. The service represents all the pods deployed by a replication controller. It provides a single IP address in OpenShift to access your application as it's scaled up and down on different nodes in your cluster. The service is the internal IP address that's referenced in the route created in the OpenShift load balancer.

NOTE   The relationship between deployments and replication controllers is how applications are deployed, scaled, and upgraded. When changes are made to a deployment config, a new deployment is created, which in turn creates a new replication controller. The replication controller then creates the desired number of pods within the cluster, which is where your application is actually deployed.

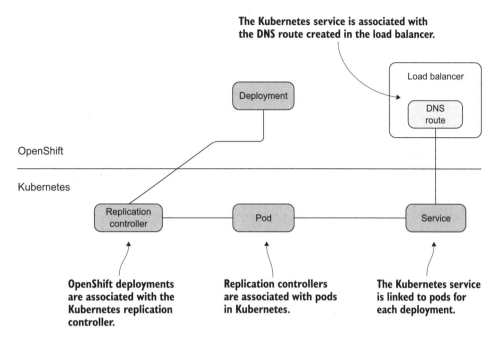

Figure 3.2   Kubernetes components that are created when applications are deployed

We're getting closer to the application itself, but we haven't gotten there yet. Kubernetes is used to orchestrate containers in an OpenShift cluster. But on each application node, Kubernetes depends on docker to create the containers for each application deployment.

3.2.3   Docker creates containers

Docker is a *container runtime*. A container runtime is the application on a server that creates, maintains, and removes containers. A container runtime can act as a standalone tool on a laptop or a single server, but it's at its most powerful when being orchestrated across a cluster by a tool like Kubernetes.

> **NOTE**   Docker is currently the container runtime for OpenShift. But a new runtime is supported as of OpenShift 3.9. It's called cri-o, and you can find more information at http://cri-o.io.

Kubernetes controls docker to create containers that house the application. These containers use the custom base image as the starting point for the files that are visible to applications in the container. Finally, the docker container is associated with the Kubernetes pod (see figure 3.3).

To isolate the libraries and applications in the container image, along with other server resources, docker uses Linux kernel components. These kernel-level resources are the components that isolate the applications in your container from everything else on the application node. Let's look at these next.

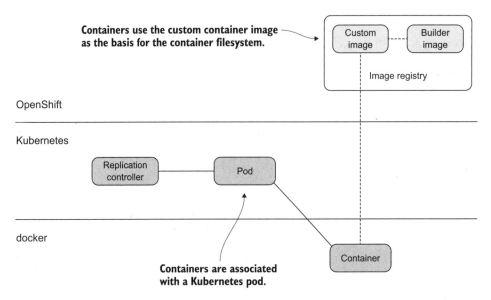

Figure 3.3   Docker containers are associated with Kubernetes pods.

3.2.4   *Linux isolates and limits resources*

We're down to the core of what makes a container a container in OpenShift and Linux. Docker uses three Linux kernel components to isolate the applications running in containers it creates and limit their access to resources on the host:

- *Linux namespaces*—Provide isolation for the resources running in the container. Although the term is the same, this is a different concept than Kubernetes namespaces (http://mng.bz/X8yz), which are roughly analogous to an Open-Shift project. We'll discuss these in more depth in chapter 7. For the sake of brevity, in this chapter, when we reference namespaces, we're talking about Linux namespaces.
- *Control groups (cgroups)*—Provide maximum, guaranteed access limits for CPU and memory on the application node. We'll look at cgroups in depth in chapter 9.
- *SELinux contexts*—Prevent the container applications from improperly accessing resources on the host or in other containers. An SELinux context is a unique label that's applied to a container's resources on the application node. This unique label prevents the container from accessing anything that doesn't have a matching label on the host. We'll discuss SELinux contexts in more depth in chapter 11.

The docker daemon creates these kernel resources dynamically when the container is created. These resources are associated with the applications that are launched for the corresponding container; your application is now running in a container (figure 3.4). Applications in OpenShift are run and associated with these kernel components. They provide the isolation that you see from inside a container. In upcoming sections,

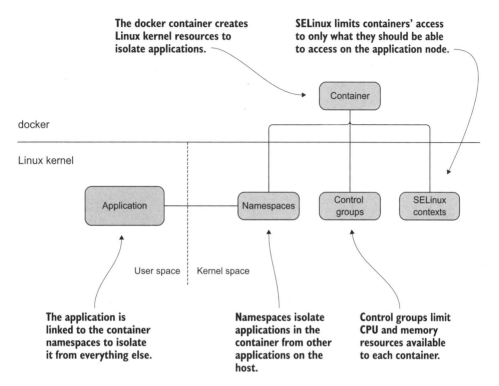

The docker container creates Linux kernel resources to isolate applications.

SELinux limits containers' access to only what they should be able to access on the application node.

The application is linked to the container namespaces to isolate it from everything else.

Namespaces isolate applications in the container from other applications on the host.

Control groups limit CPU and memory resources available to each container.

Figure 3.4   Linux kernel components used to isolate containers

we'll discuss how you can investigate a container from the application node. From the point of view of being inside the container, an application only has the resources allocated to it that are included in its unique namespaces. Let's confirm that next.

Userspace and kernelspace

A Linux server is separated into two primary resource groups: the *userspace* and the *kernelspace*. The userspace is where applications run. Any process that isn't part of the kernel is considered part of the userspace on a Linux server.

The kernelspace is the kernel itself. Without special administrator privileges like those the root user has, users can't make changes to code that's running in the kernelspace.

The applications in a container run in the userspace, but the components that isolate the applications in the container run in the kernelspace. That means containers are isolated using kernel components that can't be modified from inside the container.

In the previous sections, we looked at each individual layer of OpenShift. Let's put all of these together before we dive down into the weeds of the Linux kernel.

3.2.5 *Putting it all together*

The automated workflow that's executed when you deploy an application in Open-Shift includes OpenShift, Kubernetes, docker, and the Linux kernel. The interactions and dependencies stretch across multiple services, as outlined in figure 3.5.

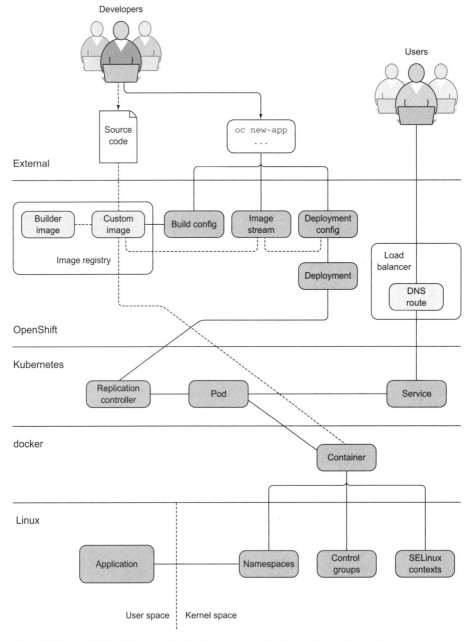

Figure 3.5 OpenShift deployment including components that make up the container

Developers and users interact primarily with OpenShift and its services. OpenShift works with Kubernetes to ensure that user requests are fulfilled and applications are delivered consistently according to the developer's designs.

As you'll recall, one of the acceptable definitions for a container earlier in this chapter was that they're "fancy processes." We developed this definition by explaining how a container takes an application process and uses namespaces to limit access to resources on the host. We'll continue to develop this definition by interacting with these fancy processes in more depth in chapters 9 and 10.

Like any other process running on a Linux server, each container has an assigned process ID (PID) on the application node.

3.3 *Application isolation with kernel namespaces*

Armed with the PID for the current app-cli container, you can begin to analyze how containers isolate process resources with Linux namespaces. Earlier in this chapter, we discussed how kernel namespaces are used to isolate the applications in a container from the other processes on a host. Docker creates a unique set of namespaces to isolate the resources in each container. Looking again at figure 3.4, the application is linked to the namespaces because they're unique for each container. Cgroups and SELinux are both configured to include information for a newly created container, but those kernel resources are shared among all containers running on the application node.

To get a list of the namespaces that were created for app-cli, use the lsns command. You need the PID for app-cli to pass as a parameter to lsns. Appendix C walks you through how to use the docker daemon to get the host PID for a container, along with some other helpful docker commands. Use this appendix as a reference to get the host PID for your app-cli container.

The lsns command accepts a PID with the -p option and outputs the namespaces associated with that PID. The output for lsns has the following six columns:

- NS—Inode associated with the namespace
- TYPE—Type of namespace created
- NPROCS—Number of processes associated with the namespace
- PID—Process used to create the namespace
- USER—User that owns the namespace
- COMMAND—Command executed to launch the process to create the namespace

When you run the command, the output from lsns shows six namespaces for app-cli. Five of these namespaces are unique to app-cli and provide the container isolation that we're discussing in this chapter. There are also two additional namespaces in Linux that aren't used directly by OpenShift. The *user namespace* isn't currently used by OpenShift, and the *cgroup namespace* is shared between all containers on the system.

NOTE On an OpenShift application node, the user namespace is shared across all applications on the host. The user namespace was created by PID 1 on the host, has over 200 processes associated with it, and is associated with the `systemd` command. The other namespaces associated with the app-cli PID have far fewer processes and aren't owned by PID 1 on the host.

OpenShift uses five Linux namespaces to isolate processes and resources on application nodes. Coming up with a concise definition for exactly what a namespace does is a little difficult. Two analogies best describe their most important properties, if you'll forgive a little poetic license:

- Namespaces are like paper walls in the Linux kernel. They're lightweight and easy to stand up and tear down, but they offer sufficient privacy when they're in place.
- Namespaces are similar to two-way mirrors. From within the container, only the resources in the namespace are available. But with proper tooling, you can see what's in a namespace from the host system.

The following snippet lists all namespaces for app-cli with `lsns`:

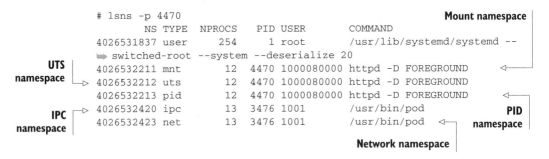

As you can see, the five namespaces that OpenShift uses to isolate applications are as follows:

- *Mount*—Ensures that only the correct content is available to applications in the container
- *Network*—Gives each container its own isolated network stack
- *PID*—Provides each container with its own set of PID counters
- *UTS*—Gives each container its own hostname and domain name
- *IPC*—Shares memory isolation for each container

There are currently two additional namespaces in the Linux kernel that aren't used by OpenShift:

- *Cgroup*—Cgroups are used as a shared resource on an OpenShift node, so this namespace isn't required for effective isolation.

- *User*—This namespace can map a user in a container to a different user on the host. For example, a user with ID 0 in the container could have user ID 5000 when interacting with resources outside the container. This feature can be enabled in OpenShift, but there are issues with performance and node configuration that fall out of scope for our example cluster. If you'd like more information on enabling the user namespace to work with docker, and thus with OpenShift, see the article "Hardening Docker Hosts with User Namespaces" by Chris Binnie (Linux.com, http://mng.bz/Giwd).

> ### What is /usr/bin/pod?
>
> The IPC and network namespaces are associated with a different PID for an application called /usr/bin/pod. This is a pseudo-application that's used for containers created by Kubernetes.
>
> Under most circumstances, a pod consists of one container. There are conditions, however, where a single pod may contain multiple containers. Those situations are outside the scope of this chapter; but when this happens, all the containers in the pod share these namespaces. That means they share a single IP address and can communicate with shared memory devices as though they're on the same host.

We'll discuss the five namespaces used by OpenShift with examples, including how they enhance your security posture and how they isolate their associated resources. Let's start with the mount namespace.

3.3.1 *The mount namespace*

The mount namespace isolates filesystem content, ensuring that content assigned to the container by OpenShift is the only content available to the processes running in the container. The mount namespace for the app-cli container allows the applications in the container to access only the content in the custom app-cli container image, and any information stored on the persistent volume associated with the persistent volume claim (PVC) for app-cli (see figure 3.6).

> **NOTE** Applications always need persistent storage. Persistent storage allows data to persist when a pod is removed from the cluster. It also allows data to be shared between multiple pods when needed. You'll learn how to configure and use persistent storage on an NFS server with OpenShift in chapter 7.

The root filesystem, based on the app-cli container image, is a little more difficult to uncover, but we'll do that next.

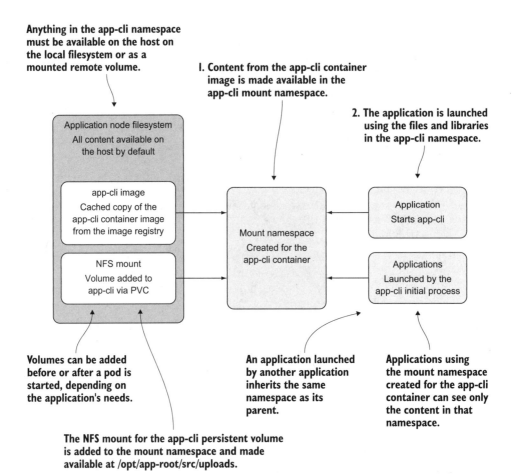

Anything in the app-cli namespace must be available on the host on the local filesystem or as a mounted remote volume.

I. Content from the app-cli container image is made available in the app-cli mount namespace.

2. The application is launched using the files and libraries in the app-cli namespace.

Application node filesystem

All content available on the host by default

app-cli image

Cached copy of the app-cli container image from the image registry

NFS mount

Volume added to app-cli via PVC

Mount namespace

Created for the app-cli container

Application

Starts app-cli

Applications

Launched by the app-cli initial process

Volumes can be added before or after a pod is started, depending on the application's needs.

An application launched by another application inherits the same namespace as its parent.

Applications using the mount namespace created for the app-cli container can see only the content in that namespace.

The NFS mount for the app-cli persistent volume is added to the mount namespace and made available at /opt/app-root/src/uploads.

Figure 3.6   The mount namespace takes selected content and makes it available to the app-cli applications.

ACCESSING CONTAINER ROOT FILESYSTEMS

When you configured OpenShift, you specified a block device for docker to use for container storage. Your OpenShift configuration uses logical volume management (LVM) on this device for container storage. Each container gets its own logical volume (LV) when it's created. This storage solution is fast and scales well for large production clusters.

To view all LVs created by docker on your host, run the `lsblk` command. This command shows all block devices on your host, as well as any LVs. It confirms that docker has been creating LVs for your containers:

```
# lsblk
NAME                               MAJ:MIN RM  SIZE RO TYPE MOUNTPOINT
vda                                253:0    0    8G  0 disk
└─vda1                             253:1    0    8G  0 part /
vdb                                253:16   0   20G  0 disk
```

```
└─vdb1                                    253:17   0   20G   0 part
  ├─docker_vg-docker--pool_tmeta          252:0    0   24M   0 lvm
  | └─docker_vg-docker--pool              252:2    0    8G   0 lvm
  |   ├─docker-253:1-10125-e27ee79f...    252:3    0   10G   0 dm
  |   ├─docker-253:1-10125-6ec90d0f...    252:4    0   10G   0 dm
  ...
  └─docker_vg-docker--pool_tdata          252:1    0    8G   0 lvm
    └─docker_vg-docker--pool              252:2    0    8G   0 lvm
      ├─docker-253:1-10125-e27ee79f...    252:3    0   10G   0 dm
      ├─docker-253:1-10125-6ec90d0f...    252:4    0   10G   0 dm
  ...
```

The LV device that the app-cli container uses for storage is recorded in the information from docker inspect. To get the LV for your app-cli container, run the following command:

```
docker inspect -f '{{ .GraphDriver.Data.DeviceName }}' fae8e211e7a7
```

You'll get a value similar to docker-253:1-10125-8bd64caed0421039e83ee4f1cdc bcf25708e3da97081d43a99b6d20a3eb09c98. This is the name for the LV that's being used as the root filesystem for the app-cli container.

Unfortunately, when you run the following mount command to see where this LV is mounted, you don't get any results:

```
mount | grep docker-253:1-10125-
➥ 8bd64caed0421039e83ee4f1cdcbcf25708e3da97081d43a99b6d20a3eb09c9
```

You can't see the LV for app-cli because it's in a different namespace. No, we're not kidding. The mount namespace for your application containers is created in a different mount namespace from your application node's operating system.

When the docker daemon starts, it creates its own mount namespace to contain filesystem content for the containers it creates. You can confirm this by running lsns for the docker process. To get the PID for the main docker process, run the following pgrep command (the process dockerd-current is the name for the main docker daemon process):

```
# pgrep -f dockerd-current
```

Once you have the docker daemon's PID, you can use lsns to view its namespaces. You can tell from the output that the docker daemon is using the system namespaces created by systemd when the server booted, except for the mount namespace:

```
# lsns -p 2385
        NS TYPE  NPROCS  PID USER COMMAND
4026531836 pid      221    1 root /usr/lib/systemd/systemd --switched-root
➥ --system --deserialize 20
4026531837 user     254    1 root /usr/lib/systemd/systemd --switched-root
➥ --system --deserialize 20
4026531838 uts      223    1 root /usr/lib/systemd/systemd --switched-root
➥ --system --deserialize 20
```

```
4026531839 ipc       221     1 root /usr/lib/systemd/systemd --switched-root
➥ --system --deserialize 20
4026531956 net       223     1 root /usr/lib/systemd/systemd --switched-root
➥ --system --deserialize 20
4026532298 mnt        12  2385 root /usr/bin/dockerd-current --add-runtime
➥ docker-runc=/usr/libexec/docker/docker-runc-current
--default-runtime=docker-runc --exec-opt native.cgroupdriver=systemd
➥ --userland-proxy-p
```

You can use a command-line tool named nsenter to enter an active namespace for another application. It's a great tool to use when you need to troubleshoot a container that isn't performing as it should. To use nsenter, you give it a PID for the container with the --target option and then instruct it regarding which namespaces you want to enter for that PID:

```
$ nsenter --target 2385
```

When you run the command, you arrive at a prompt similar to your previous prompt. The big difference is that now you're operating from inside the namespace you specified. Run mount from within docker's mount namespace and grep for your app-cli LV (the output is trimmed for clarity):

```
mount | grep docker-253:1-10125-8bd64cae...
/dev/mapper/docker-253:1-10125-8bd64cae... on ➥
/var/lib/docker/devicemapper/mnt/8bd64cae... type xfs (rw,relatime,➥
context="system_u:object_r:svirt_sandbox_file_t:s0:c4,c9",nouuid,attr2,inode64,
➥ sunit=1024,swidth=1024,noquota)
```

From inside docker's mount namespace, the mount command output includes the mount point for the root filesystem for app-cli. The LV that docker created for app-cli is mounted on the application node at /var/lib/docker/devicemapper/mnt/8bd64-cae... (directory name trimmed for clarity).

Go to that directory while in the docker daemon mount namespace, and you'll find a directory named rootfs. This directory is the filesystem for your app-cli container:

```
# ls -al rootfs
total 32
-rw-r--r--.  1 root root 15759 Aug  1 17:24 anaconda-post.log
lrwxrwxrwx.  1 root root     7 Aug  1 17:23 bin -> usr/bin
drwxr-xr-x.  3 root root    18 Sep 14 22:18 boot
drwxr-xr-x.  4 root root    43 Sep 21 23:19 dev
drwxr-xr-x. 53 root root  4096 Sep 21 23:19 etc
-rw-r--r--.  1 root root  7388 Sep 14 22:16 help.1
drwxr-xr-x.  2 root root     6 Nov  5  2016 home
lrwxrwxrwx.  1 root root     7 Aug  1 17:23 lib -> usr/lib
lrwxrwxrwx.  1 root root     9 Aug  1 17:23 lib64 -> usr/lib64
drwx------.  2 root root     6 Aug  1 17:23 lost+found
drwxr-xr-x.  2 root root     6 Nov  5  2016 media
drwxr-xr-x.  2 root root     6 Nov  5  2016 mnt
drwxr-xr-x.  4 root root    32 Sep 14 22:05 opt
```

```
drwxr-xr-x.  2 root root    6 Aug  1 17:23 proc
dr-xr-x---.  2 root root  137 Aug  1 17:24 root
drwxr-xr-x. 11 root root  145 Sep 13 15:35 run
lrwxrwxrwx.  1 root root    8 Aug  1 17:23 sbin -> usr/sbin
...
```

It's been quite a journey to uncover the root filesystem for app-cli. You've used information from the docker daemon to use multiple command-line tools, including `nsenter`, to change from the default mount namespace for your server to the namespace created by the docker daemon. You've done a lot of work to find an isolated filesystem. Docker does this automatically at the request of OpenShift every time a container is created. Understanding how this process works, and where the artifacts are created, is important when you're using containers every day for your application workloads.

From the point of view of the applications running in the app-cli container, all that's available to them is what's in the rootfs directory, because the mount namespace created for the container isolates its content (see figure 3.7). Understanding how mount namespaces function on an application node, and knowing how to enter a container namespace manually, are invaluable tools when you're troubleshooting a container that's not functioning as designed.

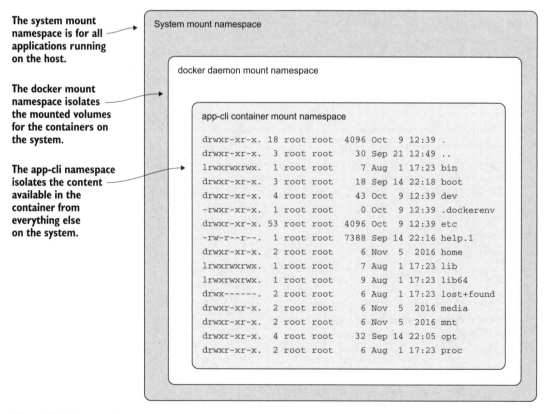

The system mount namespace is for all applications running on the host.

The docker mount namespace isolates the mounted volumes for the containers on the system.

The app-cli namespace isolates the content available in the container from everything else on the system.

```
System mount namespace

  docker daemon mount namespace

    app-cli container mount namespace

    drwxr-xr-x. 18 root root 4096 Oct  9 12:39 .
    drwxr-xr-x.  3 root root   30 Sep 21 12:49 ..
    lrwxrwxrwx.  1 root root    7 Aug  1 17:23 bin
    drwxr-xr-x.  3 root root   18 Sep 14 22:18 boot
    drwxr-xr-x.  4 root root   43 Oct  9 12:39 dev
    -rwxr-xr-x.  1 root root    0 Oct  9 12:39 .dockerenv
    drwxr-xr-x. 53 root root 4096 Oct  9 12:39 etc
    -rw-r--r--.  1 root root 7388 Sep 14 22:16 help.1
    drwxr-xr-x.  2 root root    6 Nov  5  2016 home
    lrwxrwxrwx.  1 root root    7 Aug  1 17:23 lib
    lrwxrwxrwx.  1 root root    9 Aug  1 17:23 lib64
    drwx------.  2 root root    6 Aug  1 17:23 lost+found
    drwxr-xr-x.  2 root root    6 Nov  5  2016 media
    drwxr-xr-x.  2 root root    6 Nov  5  2016 mnt
    drwxr-xr-x.  4 root root   32 Sep 14 22:05 opt
    drwxr-xr-x.  2 root root    6 Aug  1 17:23 proc
```

Figure 3.7 The app-cli mount namespace isolates the contents of the rootfs directory.

Press Ctrl-D to exit the docker daemon's mount namespace and return to the default namespace for your application node. Next, we'll discuss the UTS namespace. It won't be as involved an investigation as the mount namespace, but the UTS namespace is useful for an application platform like OpenShift that deploys horizontally scalable applications across a cluster of servers.

3.3.2 The UTS namespace

UTS stands for *Unix time sharing* in the Linux kernel. The UTS namespace lets each container have its own hostname and domain name.

> **Time sharing**
>
> It can be confusing to talk about time sharing when the UTS namespace has nothing to do with managing the system clock. Time sharing originally referred to multiple users sharing time on a system simultaneously. Back in the 1970s, when this concept was created, it was a novel idea.
>
> The UTS data structure in the Linux kernel had its beginnings then. This is where the hostname, domain name, and other system information are retained. If you'd like to see all the information in that structure, run `uname -a` on a Linux server. That command queries the same data structure.

The easiest way to view the hostname for a server is to run the `hostname` command, as follows:

```
# hostname
```

You could use `nsenter` to enter the UTS namespace for the app-cli container, the same way you entered the mount namespace in the previous section. But there are additional tools that will execute a command in the namespaces for a running container.

> **NOTE** On the application node, if you use the nip.io domain discussed in appendix A, your hostname should look similar to `ocp2.192.168.122.101.nip.io`.

One of those tools is the `docker exec` command. To get the hostname value for a running container, pass `docker exec` a container's short ID and the same `hostname` command you want to run in the container. Docker executes the specified command for you in the container's namespaces and returns the value. The hostname for each OpenShift container is its pod name:

```
# docker exec fae8e211e7a7 hostname
app-cli-1-18k2s
```

Each container has its own hostname because of its unique UTS namespace. If you scale up app-cli, the container in each pod will have a unique hostname as well. The value of this is identifying data coming from each container in a scaled-up system. To confirm that each container has a unique hostname, log in to your cluster as your developer user:

```
oc login -u developer -p developer https://ocp1.192.168.122.100.nip.io:8443
```

The oc command-line tool has functionality that's similar to docker exec. Instead of passing in the short ID for the container, however, you can pass it the pod in which you want to execute the command. After logging in to your oc client, scale the app-cli application to two pods with the following command:

```
oc scale dc/app-cli --replicas=2
```

This will cause an update to your app-cli deployment config and trigger the creation of a new app-cli pod. You can get the new pod's name by running the command oc get pods --show-all=false. The show-all=false option prevents the output of pods in a Completed state, so you see only active pods in the output.

Because the container hostname is its corresponding pod name in OpenShift, you know which pod you were working with using docker directly:

```
$ oc get pods --show-all=false
NAME              READY   STATUS    RESTARTS   AGE       Original app-cli pod
app-cli-1-18k2s   1/1     Running   1          5d    ◁────┘
app-cli-1-9hsz1   1/1     Running   0          42m       ◁──  New app-cli pod
app-gui-1-165d9   1/1     Running   1          5d
```

To get the hostname from your new pod, use the oc exec command. It's similar to docker exec, but instead of a container's short ID, you use the pod name to specify where you want the command to run. The hostname for your new pod matches the pod name, just like your original pod:

```
$ oc exec app-cli-1-9hsz1 hostname
app-cli-1-9hsz1
```

When you're troubleshooting application-level issues on your cluster, this is an incredibly useful benefit provided by the UTS namespace. Now that you know how hostnames work in containers, we'll investigate the PID namespace.

3.3.3 *PIDs in containers*

Because PIDs are how one application sends signals and information to other applications, isolating visible PIDs in a container to only the applications in it is an important security feature. This is accomplished using the PID namespace.

On a Linux server, the ps command shows all running processes, along with their associated PIDs, on the host. This command typically has a lot of output on a busy system. The --ppid option limits the output to a single PID and any child processes it has spawned.

From your application node, run ps with the --ppid option, and include the PID you obtained for your app-cli container. Here you can see that the process for PID 4470 is httpd and that it has spawned several other processes:

```
# ps --ppid 4470
  PID TTY          TIME CMD
 4506 ?        00:00:00 cat
 4510 ?        00:00:01 cat
 4542 ?        00:02:55 httpd
 4544 ?        00:03:01 httpd
 4548 ?        00:03:01 httpd
 4565 ?        00:03:01 httpd
 4568 ?        00:03:01 httpd
 4571 ?        00:03:01 httpd
 4574 ?        00:03:00 httpd
 4577 ?        00:03:01 httpd
 6486 ?        00:03:01 httpd
```

Use oc exec to get the output of ps for the app-cli pod that matches the PID you collected earlier. If you've forgotten, you can compare the hostname in the docker container to the pod name. From inside the container, don't use the --ppid option, because you want to see all the PIDs visible from within the app-cli container.

When you run the following command, the output is similar to that from the previous command:

```
$ oc exec app-cli-1-18k2s ps
  PID TTY          TIME CMD
    1 ?        00:00:27 httpd
   18 ?        00:00:00 cat
   19 ?        00:00:01 cat
   20 ?        00:02:55 httpd
   22 ?        00:03:00 httpd
   26 ?        00:03:00 httpd
   43 ?        00:03:00 httpd
   46 ?        00:03:01 httpd
   49 ?        00:03:01 httpd
   52 ?        00:03:00 httpd
   55 ?        00:03:00 httpd
   60 ?        00:03:01 httpd
   83 ?        00:00:00 ps
```

There are three main differences in the output:

- The initial httpd command (PID 4470) is listed in the output.
- The ps command is listed in the output.
- The PIDs are completely different.

Each container has a unique PID namespace. That means from inside the container, the initial command that started the container (PID 4470) is viewed as PID 1. All the processes it spawned also have PIDs in the same container-specific namespace.

NOTE Applications that are created by a process already in a container automatically inherit the container's namespace. This makes it easier for applications in the container to communicate.

So far, we've discussed how filesystems, hostnames, and PIDs are isolated in a container. Next, let's take a quick look at how shared memory resources are isolated.

3.3.4 *Shared memory resources*

Applications can be designed to share memory resources. For example, application A can write a value into a special, shared section of system memory, and the value can be read and used by application B. The following shared memory resources, documented at http://mng.bz/Xjai, are isolated for each container in OpenShift:

- POSIX message queue interfaces in /proc/sys/fs/mqueue
- The following shared memory parameters:
  - msgmax
  - msgmnb
  - msgmni
  - sem
  - shmall
  - shmmax
  - shmmni
  - shm_rmid_forced
- IPC interfaces in /proc/sysvipc

If a container is destroyed, shared memory resources are destroyed as well. Because these resources are application-specific, you'll work with them more in chapter 8 when you deploy a stateful application.

The last namespace to discuss is the network namespace.

3.3.5 *Container networking*

The fifth kernel namespace that's used by docker to isolate containers in OpenShift is the network namespace. There's nothing funny about the name for this namespace. The network namespace isolates network resources and traffic in a container. The resources in this definition mean the entire TCP/IP stack is used by applications in the container.

Chapter 10 is dedicated to going deep into OpenShift's software-defined networking, but we need to illustrate in this chapter how the view from within the container is drastically different than the view from your host.

The PHP builder image you used to create app-cli and app-gui doesn't have the `ip` utility installed. You could install it into the running container using `yum`. But a faster way is to use `nsenter`. Earlier, you used `nsenter` to enter the mount namespace of the docker process so you could view the root filesystem for app-cli.

The OSI model

It would be great if we could go through the OSI model here. Unfortunately, it's out of scope for this book. In short, it's a model to describe how data travels in a TCP/IP network. There are seven layers. You'll often hear about layer 3 devices, or a layer 2 switch; when someone says that, they're referring to the layer of the OSI model on which a particular device operates. Additionally, the OSI model is a great tool to use any time you need to understand how data moves through any system or application.

If you haven't read up on the OSI model before, it's worth your time to look at the article "The OSI Model Explained: How to Understand (and Remember) the 7 Layer Network Model" by Keith Shaw (*Network World*, http://mng.bz/CQCE).

If you run nsenter and include a command as the last argument, then instead of opening an interactive session in that namespace, the command is executed in the specified namespace and returns the results. Using this tool, you can run the ip command from your server's default namespace in the network namespace of your app-cli container.

If you compare this to the output from running the /sbin/ip a command on your host, the differences are obvious. Your application node will have 10 or more active network interfaces. These represent the physical and software-defined devices that make OpenShift function securely. But in the app-cli container, you have a container-specific loopback interface and a single network interface with a unique MAC and IP address:

```
# nsenter -t 5136 -n /sbin/ip a
1: lo: <LOOPBACK,UP,LOWER_UP> mtu 65536 qdisc noqueue
state UNKNOWN qlen 1
    link/loopback 00:00:00:00:00:00 brd 00:00:00:00:00:00
    inet 127.0.0.1/8 scope host lo
       valid_lft forever preferred_lft forever
    inet6 ::1/128 scope host
       valid_lft forever preferred_lft forever
3: eth0@if12: <BROADCAST,MULTICAST,UP,LOWER_UP> mtu 1450 qdisc noqueue
state UP
    link/ether 0a:58:0a:81:00:2e brd ff:ff:ff:ff:ff:ff link-netnsid 0
    inet 10.129.0.46/23 scope global eth0
       valid_lft forever preferred_lft forever
    inet6 fe80::858:aff:fe81:2e/64 scope link
       valid_lft forever preferred_lft forever
```

Loopback device in the container — lo

eth0 device in the container

IP address for eth0

MAC address for eth0

The network namespace is the first component in the OpenShift networking solution. We'll discuss how network traffic gets in and out of containers in chapter 10, when we cover OpenShift networking in depth.

In OpenShift, isolating processes doesn't happen in the application, or even in the userspace on the application node. This is a key difference between other types of software clusters, and even some other container-based solutions. In OpenShift, isolation and resource limits are enforced in the Linux kernel on the application nodes. Isolation with kernel namespaces provides a much smaller attack surface. An exploit that would let someone break out from a container would have to exist in the container runtime or the kernel itself. With OpenShift, as we'll discuss in depth in chapter 11 when we examine security principles in OpenShift, configuration of the kernel and the container runtime is tightly controlled.

The last point we'd like to make in this chapter echoes how we began the discussion. Fundamental knowledge of how containers work and use the Linux kernel is invaluable. When you need to manage your cluster or troubleshoot issues when they arise, this knowledge lets you think about containers in terms of what they're doing all the way to the bottom of the Linux kernel. That makes solving issues and creating stable configurations easier to accomplish.

Before you move on, clean up by reverting back to a single replica of the app-cli application with the following command:

```
oc scale dc/app-cli --replicas=1
```

3.4 Summary

- OpenShift orchestrates Kubernetes and docker to deploy and manage applications in containers.
- Multiple levels of management are available in your OpenShift cluster that can be used for different levels of information.
- Containers isolate processes in containers using kernel namespaces.
- You can interact with namespaces from the host using special applications and tools.

Part 2

Cloud-native applications

*C*loud native is how the next generation of applications is being created. In this part of the book, we'll discuss the technologies in OpenShift that create the continuously deploying, self-healing, autoscaling behaviors we all expect in a cloud-native application.

Chapter 4 focuses on working with and modifying services in OpenShift. This chapter also walks you through creating probes for your applications to ensure that they're always functioning correctly.

Chapter 5 takes that to the next level: using OpenShift to automatically scale applications based on resource consumption.

Chapter 6 brings everything cloud-native into a single functional example of deploying an entire continuous integration, continuous deployment application, all in OpenShift.

Working with services

4

This chapter covers

- Testing application resiliency
- Working with labels and selectors
- Scaling applications
- Tracking application health and status

In chapter 2, you deployed your first application in OpenShift and reviewed many of the components that were created. You confirmed that all the components worked together to deliver two deployments of the Image Uploader application. In this chapter, we'll discuss those relationships in depth, and how OpenShift recovers when those relationships are altered.

4.1 Testing application resiliency

When you deployed the Image Uploader application in chapter 2, one pod was created for each deployment. If that pod crashed, the application would be temporarily unavailable until a new pod was created to replace it. If your application became more popular, you wouldn't be able to support new users past the capacity of a single pod. To solve this problem and provide scalable applications, OpenShift deploys each application with the ability to scale up and down. The application component that handles scaling application pods is called the *replication controller* (RC).

4.1.1   Understanding replication controllers

The RC's main function is to ensure that the desired number of identical pods is running at all times. If a pod exits or fails, the RC deploys a new one to ensure a healthy application is always available (see figure 4.1).

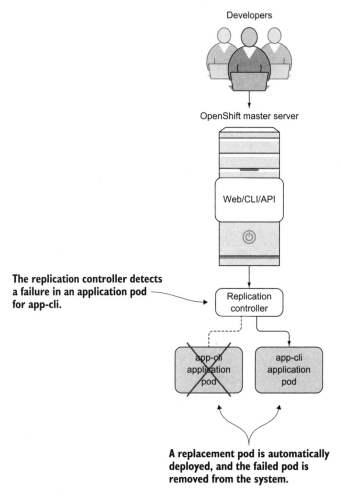

Figure 4.1   If an application pod fails to function correctly, it's automatically replaced by the replication controller.

You can think of the RC as a pod-monitoring agent that ensures certain requirements are met across the entire OpenShift cluster. You can check the current status of the RCs for the app-cli deployment by running the oc describe command (listing 4.1). Note that in listing 4.1, the individual deployment (app-cli-1) is specified, not the name of the application.

The information tracked about the RC helps to establish its relationship to the other components that make up the application:

- Name of the RC, which is the same as the name of the deployment it's associated with
- Image name used to create pods for the RC
- Labels and selectors for the RC
- Current and desired number of pod replicas running in the RC
- Historical pod status information for the RC, including how many pods are waiting to be started or have failed since the creation of the RC

The labels and selectors in the next listing are key-value pairs that are associated with all OpenShift components. They're used to create and maintain the relationships and interactions between applications. We'll discuss them in more depth in the next section.

Listing 4.1 Using `oc describe` to get information about the app-cli RC

Replication controller name

```
$ oc describe rc $(oc get rc -l                              Labels and
  app=app-cli -o=jsonpath='{.items[].metadata.name}')        selectors
  Name:          app-cli-1                                    for the RC
  Namespace:     image-uploader
  Selector: app=app-cli,deployment=app-cli-1,deploymentconfig=app-cli     ◄─
  Labels:        app=app-cli
         openshift.io/deployment-config.name=app-cli
  Annotations:     openshift.io/deployer-pod.name=app-cli-1-deploy
         openshift.io/deployment-config.latest-version=1
         openshift.io/deployment-config.name=app-cli
         openshift.io/deployment.phase=Complete
         openshift.io/deployment.replicas=
         openshift.io/deployment.status-reason=config change
         openshift.io/encoded-deployment-config=
         ➥ {"kind":"DeploymentConfig","apiVersion":"v1","metadata":      Current
         ➥ {"name":"app-cli","namespace":                               running
         ➥ "image-uploader","selfLink":                                 pods, and
         ➥ "/apis/apps.openshift.io/v1/namespaces/image-up...           the desired
  Replicas:    1 current / 1 desired                                    number
  Pods Status:    1 Running / 0 Waiting / 0 Succeeded / 0 Failed   ◄──┘
  Pod Template:
    Labels:      app=app-cli
         deployment=app-cli-1
         deploymentconfig=app-cli
    Annotations:      openshift.io/deployment-config.latest-version=1
         openshift.io/deployment-config.name=app-cli
         openshift.io/deployment.name=app-cli-1
         openshift.io/generated-by=OpenShiftNewApp              Image used
    Containers:                                                 to create the
     app-cli:                                                   pods for the RC
      Image:      docker-registry.default.svc:
      ➥ 5000/image-uploader/app-cli@sha256:
      ➥ cef79b2eaf6bb7bf495fb16e9f720d5728299673dfec1d8f16472f1871633ebc
      Port:    8080/TCP
```

```
    Environment:    <none>
    Mounts:
       /opt/app-root/src/uploads from volume-mddzb (rw)    <--- Mounted volumes
  Volumes:
   volume-mddzb:
    Type:     PersistentVolumeClaim
    ↳ (a reference to a PersistentVolumeClaim in the same namespace)
    ClaimName:    app-cli
    ReadOnly:     false
Events:           <none>
```

NOTE By using the `oc describe` command, you can quickly look at the information about the component, but not all the fields are shown. If you want to see every attribute for the component, use the `oc get` command, which can be output in multiple formats, including YAML syntax. An example is `oc get rc app-cli-1 -o yaml`.

The RC doesn't keep track of a specific list of pods that it manages. This is by design. In keeping with Kubernetes design philosophies, OpenShift API objects are loosely coupled. RCs use label selectors to constantly query the pods that they manage. If pods are created or deleted outside of the normal process, the RC can immediately take action to put the system back into the desired state. Listing 4.1 included the selector field; the RC will manage any pod that has the three labels shown in that selector field. This loosely coupled philosophy is demonstrated throughout OpenShift, including many of the API objects discussed in the first three chapters:

- *Image streams* monitor for changes and trigger new deployments and builds for applications.
- *Build configs* track everything required to build an application deployment.
- *Deployment configs* keep track of all information required to deploy an application.
- *Pods* are the default unit of work. They're where your application code is served.
- *Deployments* are unique deployed versions of an application.
- *Container images* are the template used to deploy application pods.
- *Services* are a consistent interface for all the application pods for a deployment.
- *Routes* are external-facing, DNS-based load-balancer entries that are connected to services.
- *Replication controllers* ensure that the desired number of application pods is running at all times.

TIP The RC and other objects track pods through labels and selectors, and this can be used in troubleshooting. For instance, a pod may exhibit odd behavior that requires extensive debugging. Instead of taking the system offline, an OpenShift administrator can modify the pod's labels so it's no longer included as part of the RC. The old pod is quarantined and can be debugged via a command shell without affecting end users or services. The RC will then notice that the desired number of pods is different from the current number of pods and start a new pod in place of the one that's in quarantine.

4.1.2   *Labels and selectors*

As we go forward, it's important that you understand the following regarding how labels and selectors are used in OpenShift:

- When an application is deployed in OpenShift, every object that's created is assigned a collection of labels. Labels are unique per project, just like application names. That means in Image Uploader, only one application can be named app-cli.
- Labels that have been applied to an object are attributes that can be used to create relationships in OpenShift. But relationships are two-way streets: if something can have a label, something else must be able to state a need for a resource with that label. The other side of this relationship exists in the shape of label selectors (selectors).
- Label selectors are used to define the labels that are required when work needs to happen.

Let's examine this in more depth, using the app-cli application you deployed in chapter 2. In the next example, you'll remove a label from a deployed pod. This is one of the few times we'll ask you to do something to intentionally break an application. Removing a label from a pod will break the relationship with the RC and other application components. The purpose of this example is to demonstrate the RC in action—and to do that, you need to create a condition that it needs to remedy.

Using listing 4.1 as an example, the selectors and labels for the app-cli-1 RC and the app-cli-1 pods are shown in figure 4.2. Selectors in an application component are the labels it uses to interact with other components. The app-cli RC will create and monitor applications pods with the following labels:

- `app=app-cli`
- `deployment=app-cli-1`
- `deploymentconfig=app-cli`

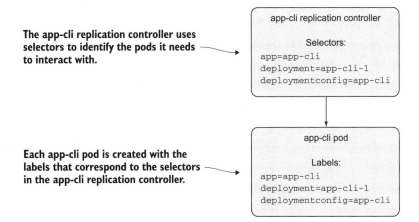

Figure 4.2   The app-cli-1 RC manages pods with labels that match its `Selector` field.

The app-cli-1 RC will always ensure that there is the configured number of replica applications pods with those three labels. When you deployed app-cli, you didn't specify a specific replica count, so the RC ensures that one replica is running. In the next section, you'll manipulate the number of replicas for the app-cli deployment. First, let's discuss what happens when an application pod no longer meets the criteria defined by the RC.

As an exercise, remove the `app=app-cli` label from the app-cli pod:

1 In the web interface, choose Applications > Pods on the left panel of your project view. This takes you to a list of all the pods in the current project. You should see a single running pod at this point.

2 Click the pod to get the full pod view. The three labels appear at the top of the screen, just below the pod name.

3 Choose Actions > Edit YAML, remove the `app=app-cli` label as shown in figure 4.3, and click Save.

4 You're sent back to the pod view. But you want to view all the pods in the project, so click Applications > Pods again. You'll notice that there are now two pods: the pod you from which you removed the `app=app-cli` label, and a newly deployed pod to replace it.

image-uploader » app-cli-1-2wpkj » **Edit YAML**

Edit Pod app-cli-1-2wpkj

```
 1   apiVersion: v1
 2   kind: Pod
 3 ▾ metadata:
 4 ▾   annotations:
 5 ▾     kubernetes.io/created-by: >
 6         {"kind":"SerializedReference","apiVersion":"v1","reference":{"kind":"Replicat:
 7       openshift.io/deployment-config.latest-version: '1'
 8       openshift.io/deployment-config.name: app-cli
 9       openshift.io/deployment.name: app-cli-1
10       openshift.io/generated-by: OpenShiftNewApp
11       openshift.io/scc: restricted
12     creationTimestamp: '2018-04-12T18:45:59Z'
13     generateName: app-cli-1-
14 ▾   labels:
15         app: app-cli                          ◀
16       deployment: app-cli-1
17       deploymentconfig: app-cli
18     name: app-cli-1-2wpkj
19     namespace: image-uploader
20 ▾   ownerReferences:
```

Delete this line

Figure 4.3   Edit pod view

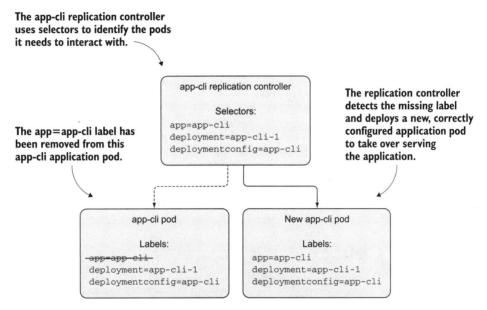

The app-cli replication controller uses selectors to identify the pods it needs to interact with.

app-cli replication controller

Selectors:
```
app=app-cli
deployment=app-cli-1
deploymentconfig=app-cli
```

The app=app-cli label has been removed from this app-cli application pod.

The replication controller detects the missing label and deploys a new, correctly configured application pod to take over serving the application.

app-cli pod

Labels:
```
app=app-cli
deployment=app-cli-1
deploymentconfig=app-cli
```

New app-cli pod

Labels:
```
app=app-cli
deployment=app-cli-1
deploymentconfig=app-cli
```

Figure 4.4   An RC spins up a new pod with labels to match its selectors, after original pod labels are modified.

If you click each pod individually, you'll see that one pod has all three labels, and one pod has only two labels (because you deleted one). The RC immediately detected your label deletion and deployed a new pod that had all the labels to meet its requirement of one pod with the proper labels defined by the selectors in the RC (see figure 4.4). The original pod from which you removed a label is now considered abandoned, because there isn't an RC with matching selectors. If it dies, a new pod won't be started in its place. The new pod is being managed by the app-cli-1 RC, which means if that pod dies or is deleted, then a replacement pod will be started quickly.

The fastest way to delete the pods for the app-cli deployment is through the command line. This process shouldn't be part of your normal application workflow, but it can come in handy when you're troubleshooting issues in an active cluster. From the command line, run the following `oc delete` command to delete all the pods for the app-cli application. The `-l` parameter specifies a label to look for when performing the delete:

```
$ oc delete pod -l app=app-cli
```

Switching back to the web console, you can see that a single pod for app-cli was recreated. By navigating down to the pod details, you can see that the new pod, which was started by the RC in response to you deleting the `app=app-cli` label, has all three labels specified by the RC's selectors.

You may be wondering whether the abandoned pod will still receive traffic from users. It turns out that the service object, responsible for network traffic, also works on the concepts of labels and selectors. To determine whether the abandoned pod would have served traffic, you need to look at the `Selector` field in the service object. You can get the selector information about the app-cli service by running the following `oc` `describe` command. There's a lot of output, so passing it into a `grep` command to look for only the information you want can be helpful:

```
$ oc describe svc app-cli | grep Selector
Selector:          app=app-cli,deploymentconfig=app-cli
```

The output shows that the service component has two selectors:

- app=app-cli
- deploymentconfig=app-cli

Because you deleted the `app=app-cli` label from the original pod, its labels are no longer a match for the app-cli service selectors and would no longer receive traffic requests.

Fundamental Kubernetes design

Kubernetes was born out of many lessons learned at Google from running containers at scale for 10+ years. The main two orchestration engines internally at Google during this time have been Borg and its predecessor, Omega. One of the primary lessons learned from these two systems was that control loops of decoupled API objects were far preferable to a large, centralized, stateful orchestration. This type of design is often called *control through choreography*. Here are just a few of the ways it was implemented in Kubernetes:

- Decoupled API components
- Avoiding stateful information
- Looping through control loops against various microservices

By running through control loops instead of maintaining a large state diagram, the resiliency of the system is considerably improved. If a controller crashes, it reruns the loop when it's restarted, whereas a state machine can become brittle when there are errors or the system starts to grow in complexity. In our specific examples, this holds true because the RC loops through pods with the labels in its `Selector` field as opposed to maintaining a list of pods that it's supervising.

You can find more information about the Kubernetes structure at https://kubernetes.io.

Replication controllers ensure that properly configured application pods are always available in the proper number. Additionally, the desired replica counts can be modified manually or automatically. In the next section, we'll discuss how to scale application deployments.

4.2   Scaling applications

An application can consist of many different pods, all communicating together to do work for the application's users. Because different pods need to be scaled independently, each collection of identical pods is represented by a service component, as we initially discussed in chapter 1. More complex applications can consist of multiple services of independently scaled pods.

A standard application design uses three tiers to separate concerns in the application:

- *Presentation layer*—Provides the user interface, styling, and workflows for the user. This is typically where the website lives.
- *Logic layer*—Handles all the required data processing for an application. This is often referred to as the *middleware* layer.
- *Storage layer*—Provides persistent storage for application data. This is often a database, filesystems, or a combination of both.

Figure 4.5 shows how a three-tier application is deployed in OpenShift. The application code runs in the pods for each application layer. That code is accessed directly from the routing layer. Each application's service communicates with the routing layer and the pods it manages. This design results in the fewest network hops between the user and the application. This design also allows each layer in the three-tier design to be independently scaled to handle its workload effectively without making any changes to the overall application configuration.

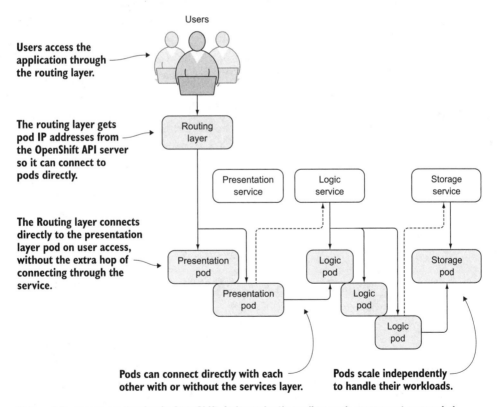

Figure 4.5   A web application in OpenShift, independently scaling each component as needed

Figure 4.5 is a simple example. In a large, enterprise application, dozens (sometimes hundreds) of services often work together to build an application. The design methodology behind building out multiple small, decoupled applications that work together to act together is often called *microservices*. When you start designing applications that are made up of multiple smaller, independent pods, the act of scaling those pods up and down becomes more important. In the next section, we'll discuss different ways to scale application pods in OpenShift.

> **NOTE** Extreme examples of the microservice paradigm exist in large tech companies like Google, Amazon, and Netflix. These companies often connect to hundreds of different services on the backend of a single user session. Not many other IT organizations may need to scale to the level of Netflix, but the need for a platform to handle modern web application designs is nearly universal.

4.2.1   *Modifying the deployment config*

To scale an application, begin at the deployment configuration page. Follow these steps:

1 Choose Applications > Deployments on the left panel of your project overview. This takes you to a list of all your OpenShift deployments in the current project.
2 Click the link for your app-cli deployment. The History tab opens, with a list of changes to the app-cli deployment.
3 Click Configuration to see details of the deployment configuration. On this page, you can change the number of replicas to meet the demands of your application.
4 Click Edit next to the current replica count (see figure 4.6), and change the number of replicas to three. Changing this number will change the deployment config object, which will update the RC behind the scenes.

Figure 4.6   Editing the number of replica pods by editing the deployment config

Changing the number of pods will take a few seconds to complete. When that's done, you'll have scaled the app-cli deployment from one pod to three (see figure 4.6).

> **NOTE** The deployment config component makes changes to the RC in the background. When you instruct the deployment config to add replicas to an application, it in turn tells the RC to create the additional pods.

The same functionality is available on the command line. To scale the number of pods back down to one, run the following `oc scale` command:

```
$ oc scale dc app-cli-1 --replicas=1
```

At this point, you've done the following:

- Deployed app-cli and app-gui versions of the Image Uploader application
- Attached persistent storage to both deployments so uploaded images will be consistent when they're scaled
- Confirmed that OpenShift will automatically replace an application pod if it becomes unhealthy
- Edited the deployment config for app-cli to scale it up to three pods

> **NOTE** The up and down arrows on the project overview page also scale applications by modifying the deployment config component the same way. The only difference is that if you use the arrows, you can add or remove only one pod at a time. If you needed to scale to 20 or even 100 pods, you wouldn't want to click the console for every change in replica count.

In the real world, manually editing deployment configs to scale applications isn't practical for many scenarios. In chapter 5, we'll discuss ways to automate application scaling.

4.3 *Maintaining healthy applications*

In most situations, application pods run into issues because the code in the pod stops responding or begins to respond in ways that aren't desired. The first step in building a resilient application is to run automated health and status checks on your pods, restarting them when necessary without manual intervention. Creating probes to run the needed checks on applications to make sure they're healthy is built into OpenShift. The first type of probe we'll look at is the *liveness probe.*

In OpenShift, you define a liveness probe as a parameter for specific containers in the deployment config. The liveness probe configuration then propagates down to the individual containers created in pods running as part of the DC. A service on each node running the container is responsible for running the liveness probe that's defined in the deployment config. If the liveness probe was created as a script, then it's run inside the container. If the liveness probe was created as an HTTP response or

TCP socket-based probe, then it's run by the node connecting to the container. If a liveness probe fails for a container, then the pod is restarted.

NOTE The service that executes liveness probe checks is called the *kubelet* service. This is the primary service that runs on each application node in OpenShift.

4.3.1 *Creating liveness probes*

In OpenShift, the liveness probe component is a simple, powerful concept that checks to be sure an application pod is running and healthy. Liveness probes can check container health three ways:

- *HTTP(S) checks*—Checks a given URL endpoint served by the container, and evaluates the HTTP response code.
- *Container execution check*—A command, typically a script, that's run at intervals to verify that the container is behaving as expected. A non-zero exit code from the command results in a liveness check failure.
- *TCP socket checks*—Checks that a TCP connection can be established on a specific TCP port in the application pod.

NOTE An HTTP response code is a three-digit number supplied by the server as part of the HTTP response headers in a web request. A 2xx response indicates a successful connection, and a 3xx response indicates an HTTP redirect. You can find a full description of all response codes on the IETF website at http://mng.bz/XfMi.

As a best practice, always create a liveness probe unless your application is intelligent enough to exit when it hits an unhealthy state. Create liveness probes that not only check the internal components of the application, but also isolate problems from external service dependencies. For example, a container shouldn't fail its liveness probe because another service that it needs isn't functional. Modern applications should have code to gracefully handle missing service dependencies. If you need an application to wait for a missing service dependency, you can use readiness probes, which are covered later in this chapter. For legacy applications that require an ordered startup sequence of replicated pods, you can take advantage of a concept called stateful sets, which we'll cover in chapter 8.

To make creating probes easier, a health check wizard is built into the OpenShift web interface. Using the wizard will help you avoid formatting issues that can result from creating the raw YAML template by hand.

To add a new liveness probe to a deployed application, follow these steps:

1 Choose Applications > Deployments on the left panel of your project view.
2 Click your deployment, app-cli.
3 Click the Configuration tab. You should see an alert that shows you haven't yet configured any health checks (see figure 4.7).

Figure 4.7   The Deployments page, showing the app-cli deployment config link

4 Choose Add Health Checks > Add Liveness Probe.
5 On the page that opens, set the following values for your probe, and click Save (see figure 4.8):

   – Type: HTTP Get
   – Use HTTPS: no (unchecked)
   – Path: /
   – Port: 8080
   – Initial Delay: 5
   – Timeout: 1

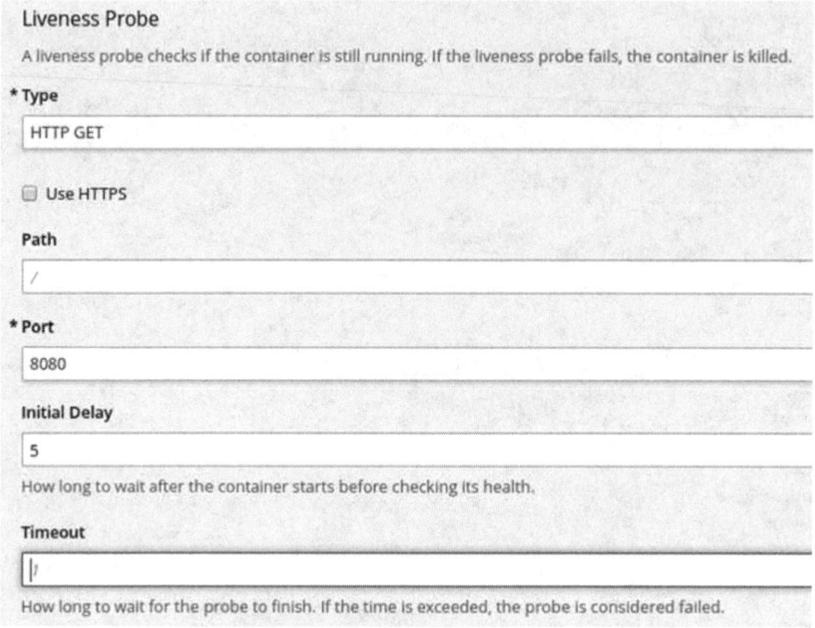

Liveness Probe

A liveness probe checks if the container is still running. If the liveness probe fails, the container is killed.

* Type

HTTP GET

☐ Use HTTPS

Path

/

* Port

8080

Initial Delay

5

How long to wait after the container starts before checking its health.

Timeout

|

How long to wait for the probe to finish. If the time is exceeded, the probe is considered failed.

Figure 4.8   Fields in the liveness probe wizard

The values you specify to create a liveness probe are as follows:

- *Type*—An HTTP(S) check, a container execution check, or a socket check, as discussed earlier in this chapter.
- *Use HTTPS*—Whether to run an HTTP(S) check using HTTP or HTTPS. This depends on how you deployed your application and its route. In chapter 2, when you created the route for app-cli, you didn't specify the use of TLS encryption; that's why you don't tell the liveness probe to use HTTPS.
- *Path*—The path for an HTTP(S) check to look for. Because the Image Uploader application is only a couple of pages, you're using the root context.
- *Port*—The TCP port to connect to.
- *Initial Delay*—An arbitrary value that specifies how long to wait before running the probe for the first time against an application pod. This gives the pod time to start all the needed services and be ready to respond properly. For a simple application like Image Uploader, the time it takes for a pod to be ready is typically less than a second.
- *Timeout*—An arbitrary value that specifies how long to wait for a response before declaring the probe as a failed check. A timeout value of one second is just in case something goes awry in the application pod.

After you create the liveness probe, you'll be redirected back to the Deployments page for app-cli. When you added the liveness probe, the deployment config automatically created a new deployment for app-cli that includes the liveness probe. The deployment config also automatically migrated the app-cli route to the new deployment. Click #2 to access the app-cli deployment config overview for the newly deployed application.

Scroll down to the bottom of the page to see information about the newly deployed pod. If the deployment has failed for some reason, a large error with a link to the events and logs to help begin troubleshooting will appear at the top of the Deployments page.

Click Pod Name. The default pod view should show that there's a liveness probe configured for the app-cli deployment (see figure 4.9).

Containers

CONTAINER: APP-CLI

- **Image:** image-uploader/app-cli **fc168cd** 219.8 MiB
- **Build:** app-cli, #1
- **Source:** Update index.php 549c356 authored by johnfosborneiii
  Ports: 8080/TCP
- **Mount:** volume-wvckc → /opt/app-root/src/uploads read-write
- **Liveness Probe:** GET / on port 8080 (HTTP) 5s delay, 1s timeout

Figure 4.9   Pod liveness probe after the app-cli deployment updates

Using the health check wizard

The OpenShift health check wizard was designed for ease of use to cover most situations, but not all. Other parameters can be passed to the liveness probe that aren't implemented in the web interface, but are available from the command line. One that's useful is `failureThreshold`, which defaults to three attempts. As we discussed in the previous section, `failureThreshold` for a readiness probe (discussed in the next section) or a liveness probe sets the number of times a probe will be attempted before it's considered a failure.

Imagine a situation where a liveness probe's initial delay was run before the application started up. You wouldn't want the container to be killed right away. `failureThreshold` allows the liveness probe to try again in `periodSeconds`, another liveness probe parameter that can be manually set. In the current release of OpenShift, `periodSeconds` defaults to 10 seconds.

To create a probe on the command line, you use the `oc set probe` command, which we'll discuss in chapter 5.

You can find the documentation for all probes at http://mng.bz/Yh16.

Liveness probes are a good way to ensure that application pods are functioning properly. For app-cli, a new deployment should take less than a minute on your system. But some applications may not be ready to receive traffic that soon after the pod is deployed.

4.3.2 Creating readiness probes

Many applications need to perform any combination of the following before they're able to receive traffic, which increases the amount of time before an application is ready to do work. Some common tasks include

- Loading classes into memory
- Initializing a dataset
- Performing internal checks
- Establishing a connection to other containers or external services
- Finishing a startup sequence or other workflow

Fortunately, OpenShift also supports the concept of *readiness probes*, which ensures that the container is ready to receive traffic before marking the pod as active. Similar to a liveness probe, a readiness probe is run at the container level in a pod and supports the same HTTP(S), container execution, and TCP socket-based checks. Unlike a liveness probe, though, a failed readiness check doesn't result in a new pod being deployed. If a readiness check fails, the pod remains running while not receiving traffic.

Let's run through an example of adding a readiness probe to the app-cli application using the command line. For this readiness probe, you'll tell OpenShift to look for a non-existent endpoint.

Looking for a URL that doesn't exist in your app-cli deployment will cause the readiness probe to fail. This exercise illustrates how an OpenShift probe works when it runs into an undesired condition. Until a deployment passes a readiness probe, it won't receive user requests. If it never passes the readiness probe, as in this example, the deployment will fail and never be made available to users.

To create the readiness probe, use the command line and run the `oc set probe` command:

```
$ oc set probe dc/app-cli \
  --readiness \
  --get-url=http://:8080/notreal \
  --initial-delay-seconds=5
deploymentconfig "app-cli" updated
```

The output includes a message that the deployment configuration was updated. Just like a liveness probe, creating a readiness probe triggers the creation of a new app-cli deployment. Check to see whether the new pods were deployed by running the `oc get pods` command:

```
$ oc get pods
NAME              READY    STATUS       RESTARTS   AGE
app-cli-1-build   0/1      Completed    0          17d
app-cli-2-js7z9   1/1      Running      0          38m
app-cli-3-6snpl   0/1      Running      0          1m
app-cli-3-deploy  1/1      Running      0          2m
app-gui-1-build   0/1      Completed    0          15d
app-gui-1-x6mvw   1/1      Running      1          15d
```

The pod for the previous deployment is still running and ready.

The pod for the new deployment is running but not marked as ready.

The new app-cli pod is running but not ready, which means it isn't yet receiving traffic. The previous pod is still running and receiving any incoming requests. Eventually, the readiness probe will fail two more times and will meets the readiness probe `failure-Threshold` metric, which is set to 3 by default. As we discussed in the previous section, `failureThreshold` for a readiness or liveness probe sets the number of times a probe will be attempted before it's considered a failure.

> **NOTE** The readiness probe will take 10 minutes to trigger a failed deployment. When this happens, the pod will be deleted, and the deployment will roll back to the old working configuration, resulting in a new pod without the readiness probe. You can modify the default timeout parameters by changing the `timeoutSeconds` parameter as part of `dc.spec.strategy.*params` in the deployment config object. Deployment strategies are covered in greater detail at the end of chapter 6.

Once all three failures occur, the deployment is marked as failed, and OpenShift automatically reverts back to the previous deployment:

```
$ oc get pods
NAME              READY    STATUS       RESTARTS   AGE
app-cli-1-build   0/1      Completed    0          17d
app-cli-2-js7z9   1/1      Running      0          47m
app-cli-3-deploy  0/1      Error        0          10m
app-gui-1-build   0/1      Completed    0          15d
app-gui-1-x6mvw   1/1      Running      1          15d
```

The previous deployment is still active and serving requests.

The deployment pod errored out after the readiness probe failed three times.

The reason for the failure appears as an event in OpenShift that can be shown from the command line or the web console. Because events are easier to read through the web console, let's check it out there. Click the Overview tab on the left panel to go to your project's home page. There you'll see a warning showing that the previous deployment configuration failed (see figure 4.10).

Expand the panel by clicking the down arrow, and then click View Events, as shown in figure 4.11. You'll see all the events for the current project, including one that says, "Readiness probe failed: HTTP probe failed with statuscode: 404." HTTP response code 404 means "Page Not Found." This makes sense, because the readiness probe was configured to check for a nonexistent URL.

APPLICATION
app-cli   http://app-cli-image-uploader.apps.192.168.1.

> DEPLOYMENT
  app-cli, #3   ⊗ 1 Error   ◯ 1 pod

Figure 4.10   Pod readiness probe

Figure 4.11   Failed readiness probe

TIP   In the last example, the readiness probe failed, and after the deployment config time was reached, OpenShift automatically rolled back the application to the previous working development. To manually trigger rollbacks, you can use the console or the command line. An example of using the command line for rollback is executing the following command:

```
$ oc rollback app-cli
```

In this chapter, we've discussed how replication controllers work and are managed by their corresponding deployment configs. By replicating pods across your OpenShift cluster, you can ensure that your applications are resilient and highly available, and that multipod applications have independently scaling components.

4.4   *Summary*

- OpenShift deploys resilient pods using replication controllers for all applications by default.
- OpenShift uses labels and selectors for all components to define relationships between application components.
- Deployment configs interact with RCs to maintain multiple pods for application deployments.
- Services provide a consistent IP address and access path for applications, whereas pods scale up and down as needed.
- Applications are scaled up and down by modifying the deployment config component.
- Liveness probes check to be sure application pods are responding to requests properly, restarting them if they don't respond properly.
- Readiness probes check to be sure applications are ready to receive traffic, not allowing requests to be routed to the application pods until they pass the readiness probe.
- Deployments can be rolled back when needed with a single OpenShift command.

Autoscaling with metrics

This chapter covers

- Using container metrics
- Creating a Horizontal Pod Autoscaler
- Setting resource requests and limits
- Autoscaling applications
- Load testing with the Apache HTTP server benchmarking tool

In the last chapter, you learned about the health and status of an application. You learned that OpenShift deployments use replication controllers (RCs) under the covers to ensure that a static number of pods is always running. Readiness probes and liveness probes make sure running pods start as expected and behave as expected. The number of pods servicing a given workload can also be easily modified to a new static number with a single command or the click of a button.

This new deployment model gives you much better resource utilization than the traditional virtual machine (VM) model, but it's not a silver bullet for operational efficiency. One of the big IT challenges with VMs is resource utilization. Traditionally, when deploying VMs, developers ask for much higher levels of CPU and RAM than are actually needed. Not only is making changes to VM resources challenging, but many developers typically have no idea what types of resources are needed to run the application. Even at large companies like Google and Netflix, predicting application workload demand is so challenging that tools are often used to scale the applications as needed.

5.1 *Determining expected workloads is difficult*

Imagine that you deployed a new application, and it unexpectedly exploded in popularity. External monitoring tools notify you that you need more pods to run your application. Without any historical context, there's no data to indicate how many pods are needed tomorrow, next week, or next month. A great example is Pokémon GO, a popular mobile application that runs on Kubernetes. Within minutes of its release, demand spiked well past expectations; and over the opening weekend it became an international sensation. Without the ability to dynamically provision pods on demand, the game likely would have crashed, as millions of users started to overload the system.

In OpenShift, triggering horizontal pod scaling without human intervention is called *autoscaling*. Developers can set objective measures to scale pods up and down on demand, and administrators can limit the number of pods to a defined range. The indicators that OpenShift uses to determine whether the application needs more or fewer pods are based on pod metrics such as CPU and memory. But those pod metrics aren't available out of the box; to use metrics in OpenShift, the administrator must deploy the OpenShift *metrics stack*. This metrics stack comprises several popular open source technologies including Hawkular, Heapster, and Apache Cassandra. Once the metrics stack is installed, OpenShift autoscaling has the objective measures it needs to scale pods up and down on demand.

> **TIP** The metrics stack can also be deployed with the initial OpenShift installation by using the advanced installation option.

> **TIP** The latest versions of OpenShift also have the option to deploy Prometheus, a popular open source monitoring and altering solution, to provide and visualize cluster metrics. In the future, Prometheus may be used as the default metrics solution, but more engineering work needs to be done. You can learn more about Prometheus at https://prometheus.io/.

5.2 *Installing OpenShift metrics*

Installing the OpenShift metrics stack is straightforward. By default, the pods that are used to collect and process metrics run in the openshift-infra project that was created by default during the installation. Switch to the openshift-infra project from the command line:

```
$ oc project openshift-infra
Now using project "openshift-infra"...
```

OpenShift provides an Ansible playbook called openshift-metrics.yml to install the OpenShift metrics stack. The playbook comes with reasonable default settings but can also be customized by passing environment variables on the command line. Switch to the ocp-1 VM that you used to install OpenShift, and then run the openshift-metrics.yml playbook as follows:

OpenShift metrics Ansible playbook

Deploys the metrics stack

Number of days to retain metrics

```
$ ansible-playbook -i /root/hosts \
    /usr/share/ansible/openshift-ansible/playbooks/byo/openshift-cluster/
    openshift-metrics.yml \
    -e openshift_metrics_install_metrics=True \
    -e openshift_metrics_start_cluster=True \
    -e openshift_metrics_duration=1 \
    -e openshift_metrics_hawkular_hostname=hawkular-metrics.apps.192.168.
    122.101.nip.io
```

Starts gathering metrics after the components are deployed

Route for the metrics endpoint

NOTE For a full listing of environment variables that can be passed to the openshift-metrics.yml Ansible playbook, visit http://mng.bz/TRyO.

If all the tasks run properly, the end of the output should show zero failed tasks, as in the following example:

```
...
TASK [openshift_metrics : Delete temp directory] ***************************
ok: [192.168.122.100 -> localhost]

PLAY RECAP ****************************************************************
192.168.122.100            : ok=181   changed=33   unreachable=0    failed=0
192.168.122.101            : ok=1     changed=0    unreachable=0    failed=0
localhost                  : ok=10    changed=0    unreachable=0    failed=0
```

If the deployment fails, double-check that the environment variables you passed to openshift-metrics.yml are accurate. Pay especially close attention to the openshift _metrics_hawkular_hostname variable to be sure it's correct for your installation.

After the playbook completes, check from the command line that the metrics stack is running. Similar to other features in OpenShift, the stack is deployed as several different pods. You may have to wait a couple of minutes for the system to pull down the metrics container images. You can use the watch command to check the results of oc get pods every two seconds:

```
$ watch oc get pods
Every 2.0s: oc get pods

NAME                          READY     STATUS     RESTARTS   AGE
hawkular-cassandra-1-fk86b    1/1       Running    0          20m
hawkular-metrics-cg4cz        1/1       Running    0          20m
heapster-jg8wf                1/1       Running    0          20m
```

Once the pods are deployed, you need to make an additional configuration change. Although the metrics stack is functional and publishing metrics at the HTTP endpoint that you set with the openshift_metrics_hawkular_hostname environment variable, it's doing so with self-signed certificates. OpenShift allows its administrators to bring their own certificates, but that's not necessary for this exercise.

Although most modern browsers such as Chrome and Firefox allow for self-signed certificates, they require an extra approval step before they will serve the endpoint. Luckily, the approval step is as easy as navigating to the URL you set with `openshift _metrics_hawkular_hostname` and manually accepting the certificate. Navigate to the `hawkular-metrics` route in your browser, and accept the self-signed certificate. Once you do so, the OpenShift console will be able to make direct calls to the Hawkular endpoint. Verify this by logging in to the OpenShift console and selecting the Image Uploader Project, as shown in figure 5.1. You'll see metrics on the overview page. OpenShift metrics is now installed!

> **TIP** For instructions on how to accept self-signed certificates for various browsers, visit https://support.solarwinds.com/Success_Center/Virtualization _Manager_(VMAN)/Accept_a_self-signed_certificate.

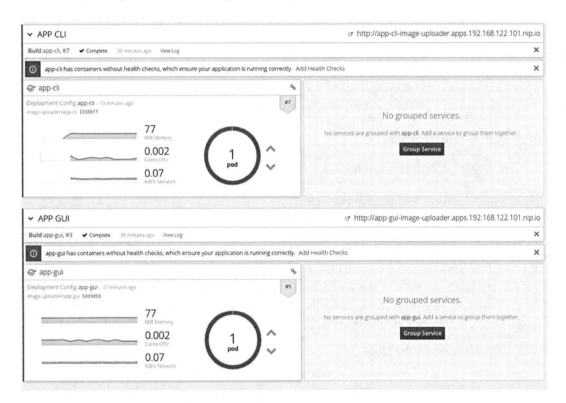

Figure 5.1 Project overview page displaying metrics

5.2.1 Understanding the metrics stack

In the previous section, you successfully deployed the OpenShift metrics stack. Three types of pods were deployed to make this happen, each with a different purpose, using technologies including Hawkular, Heapster, and Cassandra.

But none of the pods generate metrics themselves. Those come from *kubelets*. A kubelet is a process that runs on each OpenShift node and coordinates which tasks the node should execute with the OpenShift master. As an example, if an RC requests that a pod be started, the OpenShift scheduler, which runs on the master, eventually tasks an OpenShift node to start the pod. The command to start the pod is passed to the kubelet process running on the assigned OpenShift node. One of the additional responsibilities of the kubelet is to expose the local metrics available to the Linux kernel through an HTTPS endpoint. The OpenShift metrics pods use the metrics exposed by the kubelet on each OpenShift node as their data source.

Although the kubelet exposes the metrics for individual nodes through an HTTPS endpoint, no built-in tools are available to aggregate this information and present a cluster-wide view. This is where Heapster comes in handy. Heapster acts as the backend for the metrics deployment. It queries the API server for the list of nodes and then queries each individual node to get the metrics for the entire cluster. It stores the metrics in an Apache Cassandra database. On the frontend, the Hawkular pod processes the metrics by connecting directly to Heapster. Hawkular exposes all the metrics in the cluster through a common REST API to enable further custom integration. OpenShift uses the Hawkular REST API to pull metrics into the OpenShift console; the API can also be used for integration into other third-party tools or other monitoring solutions. You can find documentation about connecting directly to the Hawkular API at http://mng.bz/Vf3H.

> **NOTE** Apache Cassandra is a NoSQL database that was originally designed at Facebook. It's often used for large datasets that need to scale horizontally.

5.3 *Using pod metrics to trigger pod autoscaling*

To implement pod autoscaling based around metrics, you need a couple of simple things. First, you need a metrics stack to pull and aggregate metrics from the entire cluster and then make those metrics easily available. So far, so good. Second, you need an object to monitor the metrics and trigger the pods up and down. This object is called a Horizontal Pod Autoscaler (HPA), and its main job is to define when OpenShift should change the number of replicas in an application deployment.

5.3.1 *Creating an HPA object*

OpenShift provides a shortcut from the CLI to create the HPA object. This shortcut is available through the `oc autoscale` command. Switch to the CLI, and use the following command:

```
$ oc autoscale dc/app-cli \        ⬅── Specifies the deployment
--min 2                                config to update
--max 5                            ⬅── Defines the maximum number of pods
--cpu-percent=75
deploymentconfig "app-cli" autoscaled
```

Defines the minimum number of pods ⟶ `--min 2`

Defines the pod CPU percentage threshold ⟶ `--cpu-percent=75`

A couple of things happen when you run that command. First, you trigger an automatic scale-up to two app-cli pods by setting the minimum number of pods to 2. Run the following command to verify the number of app-cli pods:

```
$ oc get pods -l app=app-cli
NAME              READY   STATUS    RESTARTS   AGE
app-cli-1-6vskd   1/1     Running   0          8m
app-cli-1-9c12j   1/1     Running   0          8m
```

Second, the HorizontalPodAutoscaler object was created for you. By default, it has the same name as DeploymentConfig (app-cli). This command gets the name of the HPA object created by oc autoscale:

```
$ oc get hpa
NAME       REFERENCE                 TARGET   CURRENT   MINPODS   MAXPODS
⇒ AGE
app-cli    DeploymentConfig/app-cli  75%      0%        2         5
⇒ 10m
```

And this command lets you inspect the HPA object:

```
$ oc describe hpa app-cli
Name:                    app-cli
Namespace:               image-uploader
Labels:                  <none>
Annotations:             <none>
CreationTimestamp:       Tue, 08 Aug 2017 15:20:10 -0400
Reference:               DeploymentConfig/app-cli
Target CPU utilization:        75%
Current CPU utilization:   0%
Min replicas:            2
Max replicas:            5
Events:
  FirstSeen    LastSeen    Count    From
⇒ SubObjectPath
⇒ Type         Reason                Message
  ---------    --------    -----    ----
⇒ -------------
⇒ --------     ------                -------
  11m          11m         3        {horizontal-pod-autoscaler }   Normal
⇒ SuccessfulRescale  New size: 2; reason: Current number of replicas
⇒ below Spec.MinReplicas
  10m          8m          7        {horizontal-pod-autoscaler }   Normal
⇒ MetricsNotAvailableYet  missing request for cpu on container app-cli
⇒ in pod image-uploader/app-cli-1-6vskd
  7m           14s         16       {horizontal-pod-autoscaler }   Warning
⇒ FailedGetMetrics  missing request for cpu on container app-cli
⇒ in pod image-uploader/app-cli-1-6vskd
```

The description displays a couple of errors because you aren't finished. If you were to log in to the OpenShift console, you'd see a similar error on the overview page, as shown in figure 5.2.

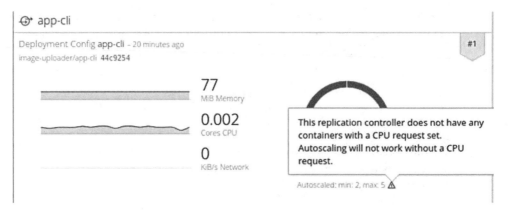

Figure 5.2   HPA error on the OpenShift console overview page

The error occurs because some information is missing. You've set the HPA object to scale up to five pods when the CPU reaches 75% of an undetermined threshold. You need to set that threshold, which is called a resource request.

REQUESTS AND LIMITS

In OpenShift, a resource *request* is a threshold you can set that affects scheduling and quality of service. It essentially provides the minimum amount of resources guaranteed to the pod. For example, a user can set a CPU request of four-tenths of a core, written *400 millicores* or *400m*. This tells OpenShift to schedule the pod on nodes that can guarantee that there will always be at least 400m of CPU available to it.

> **NOTE**   CPU is measured in units called *millicores* (one-thousandth of a core). By default, pods don't get individual cores; they get timeslices of CPU, sharing the cores on the node with other pods. If a particular node has four CPUs assigned to it, then 4,000 millicores are available to all the running pods on that node.

Resource requests also can be combined with a resource *limit*, which is similar to a request but sets the maximum amount of resources guaranteed to the pod. Setting requests and limits also allows the user to set a quality of service level by default:

- BestEffort—Neither a resource nor a limit is specified. This is for low-priority applications that can live with very low amounts of CPU and memory.
- Burstable—A request is set, indicating a minimum amount of resources allocated to the pod.
- Guaranteed—A request and a limit are both set to the same number. This is for the highest-priority applications that need the most consistent amount of computing power.

Setting a lower quality of service gives the scheduler more flexibility by allowing it to place more pods in the cluster. Setting a higher quality of service limits flexibility but gives applications more consistent resources. Because choosing the quality of service is about finding reasonable defaults, most applications should fall into the `Burstable` tier.

> **TIP** You can view the resource capacity on a node along with the requests and limits of the running pods on the node by running the command `oc describe node <node name>`.

SETTING A CPU REQUEST

You can set a CPU request for all the pods in the app-cli application by changing the deployment config with the following command:

```
oc set resources dc app-cli --requests=cpu=400m
```

As with other changes to the deployment config, this results in a new deployment config object that will, in turn, create new pods. Once running, these new pods' CPU request is set to 400m. The OpenShift scheduler places the pods only on nodes that can guarantee 400 millicores available to the application. Figure 5.3 shows the new pod description in the OpenShift console, indicating that the 400m request has propagated to the new pods

> **NOTE** Requests and limits can also be set by default on a project-wide basis by creating a `LimitRange` object. The `LimitRange` object removes the need to set requests and limits manually for each deployment as well as define the range of the request and limit values. You can find more information at http://mng.bz/tB5m.

Figure 5.3 New pods have a 400m CPU request.

The previous error is now resolved. An HPA event appears, indicating a normal status. Run the `oc describe` command again to confirm that the output is healthy:

```
$ oc describe hpa app-cli
...
Events:
...
  1m  12s  4  {horizontal-pod-autoscaler }  Normal  DesiredReplicasComputed
➥ Computed the desired num of replicas: 0 (avgCPUutil: 0, current replicas: 2)
```

No errors are shown, so autoscaling is successfully enabled!

5.3.2   *Testing your autoscaling implementation*

To demonstrate that autoscaling works as expected, you need to trigger the CPU threshold that you previously set. To help reach this mark, use the Apache benchmark instance (ab) that comes preinstalled with CentOS and is already available in your path. Before you run the benchmarking test, make sure you're logged in to the Open-Shift console in another window, so you can switch over to see pods being spun up. Then, go to the overview page for the image-uploader project and run the command in the following snippet, updating the route for the app-cli application:

Sets the number of concurrent requests

Sets the total number of HTTP requests

Application route

```
ab \
-n 50000 \
-c 500 \
http://app-cli-route-image-uploader.apps.192.168.122.101.nip.io/
...
Benchmarking app-cli-route-image-uploader.apps.192.168.122.101.nip.io
➥ (be patient)
Completed 5000 requests
Completed 10000 requests
Completed 15000 requests
Completed 20000 requests
Completed 25000 requests
Completed 30000 requests
Completed 35000 requests
Completed 40000 requests
Completed 45000 requests
Completed 50000 requests
Finished 50000 requests
...
Concurrency Level:      500
Time taken for tests:   14.101 seconds
Complete requests:      50000
Failed requests:        0
Write errors:           0
...
```

```
Percentage of the requests served within a certain time (ms)
   50%    134
   66%    146
   75%    155
   80%    161
   90%    176
   95%    195
   98%    221
   99%    237
  100%   3122 (longest request)
```

Now, quickly switch over to the OpenShift console, and see whether OpenShift has spun up more pods. It should have scaled up your application, but your mileage may vary. If your application is still running two pods, try increasing the number of total or concurrent requests sent to the route with the Apache Benchmark.

5.3.3 Avoiding thrashing

When the Apache benchmark tests kicked off, the OpenShift autoscaler detected very high CPU usage on the deployed pods, which violated the HPA constraints. This caused new pods to be spun up on demand. Behind the scenes, the deployment was modified, creating a new number of replicas. After the tests were completed, the CPU usage on the pods went back down close to zero, because the pods were finished processing requests. But unlike when the CPU spiked and the new pods spun up quickly, it took several minutes for new pods to spin down.

> **TIP** By default, the HPA synchronizes with the Heapster metrics every 30 seconds. You can modify this sync period in master-config.yaml in the `horizontalPodAutoscalerSyncPeriod` field under `controllerArguments`.

This time window is by design, to avoid something called *thrashing*: in OpenShift, that's the constant starting and stopping of pods unnecessarily. Thrashing can cause wasted resource consumption, because deploying new pods uses resources to schedule and deploy a pod on a new node, which often includes things like loading application libraries into memory. After OpenShift triggers an initial scale, there's a *forbidden window* to prevent thrashing. During the forbidden window, no autoscaling options can occur. This prevents thrashing. The rationale is that in practice, if there's a need to constantly scale up and scale down within a matter of minutes, it's probably less expensive to keep the pods running than it is to continuously trigger scaling changes.

In versions of OpenShift up to 3.6, the forbidden window is hardcoded at 5 minutes to scale down the pods and 3 minutes to scale up the pods. In OpenShift 3.7 and higher, the default values are still 5 minutes and 3 minutes, respectively, but they can be modified via the `controllerManagerArgs` field in the master-config.yaml file as `horizontal-pod-autoscaler-upscale-delay` and `horizontal-pod-autoscaler-downscale-delay`.

5.4   Summary

- Determining the size and number of pods required to run an application is difficult and error-prone.
- OpenShift can autoscale the number of pods in a service based on metric consumption.
- The OpenShift metrics stack is easy to deploy and provides end users with performance and monitoring capabilities.
- You can set resource limits and quality-of-service tiers in OpenShift.
- You can use the Apache benchmarking tool to test OpenShift autoscaling.
- OpenShift has a built-in forbidden window to avoid constant thrashing.

Continuous integration and continuous deployment

This chapter covers

- Promoting images
- Invoking object triggers
- Service discovery
- Protecting sensitive data with secrets
- Altering applications with config maps

Deploying software into production is difficult. One major challenge is adequately testing applications before they make it into production. And adequate testing requires one of the longest-standing challenges in IT: consistent environments. For many organizations, it's time-consuming to stand up new environments for development, testing, QA, and more. When the environments are finally in place, they're often inconsistent. These inconsistencies develop over time due to poor configuration management, partial fixes, and fixing problems upstream, such as directly making a patch in a production environment. Inconsistent environments can lead to unpredictable software. To eliminate risk, organizations often schedule maintenance windows during software deployments and then cross their fingers.

Over the last 15 years, there have been many attempts to improve software processes. Most notable has been the industry-wide effort to move from the waterfall method of deploying software to flexible approaches such as Agile that attempt to eliminate risk by performing many small, iterative deployments as opposed to the massive software rollouts common with the waterfall method. But Agile falls short in several areas, because it focuses on software development and doesn't address the efficiency of the rest of the stakeholders in the organization. For example, code may get to operations more quickly, but a massive bottleneck may result because operations now has to deploy code more frequently.

Many organizations are trying to solve these problems with a modern DevOps approach that brings together all the stakeholders to work jointly throughout the software-development lifecycle. DevOps is now almost synonymous with automation and *continuous integration* (CI) and *continuous deployment* (CD), often shortened to CI/CD. The delivery mechanism for implementing CI/CD is often called a *software-deployment pipeline* or *CI/CD pipeline*. Although DevOps methodologies involve people and processes in addition to technology, this chapter focuses largely on the technology aspect and how it relates to containers.

> **TIP** You can find an explanation of DevOps in the article "What Is DevOps?" (Ernest Mueller, *The Agile Admin*, https://theagileadmin.com/what-is-devops). For a more in-depth read on DevOps principles, practices, and tools being implemented at high-flying IT companies, see "DevOps Cookbook" (Gene Kim, www.realgenekim.me/devops-cookbook).

6.1 Container images as the centerpiece of a CI/CD pipeline

From a technology perspective, containers are becoming the most important technology in the software-deployment pipeline. Developers can code applications and services without the need to design or even care about the underlying infrastructure. Operations teams can spend fewer resources designing the installation of applications. Applications and services can easily be moved not only between environments like dev, QA, testing, and so on in the software-development pipeline but also between on-premises and public cloud environments, such as Amazon Web Services, Microsoft Azure, and Google Compute Platform.

When applications need to be modified, developers package new container images, which include the application, configuration, and runtime dependencies. The container then goes through the software-deployment pipeline, automated testing, and processing. Using container images in a software-deployment pipeline reduces risk because the exact same binary (container image) is run in every environment. If a change needs to be made, then it begins in the sandbox or development environment, and the entire deployment process starts over. Because running containers are created from container images, there's no such thing as fixing things upstream. If a developer or operator attempted to circumvent the deployment pipeline and patch directly into production, the change wouldn't persist. The change must be made to the underlying container image.

By making the container the centerpiece of the deployment pipeline, system stability and application resiliency are greatly increased. When failures occur, identifying issues and rolling back software is quicker because the container can be rolled back to a previous version. This is much different than in previous approaches, where entire application servers and databases may need to be reconfigured in parallel to the application rollback—often a manual process.

In addition, containers let developers run more meaningful testing earlier in the development cycle, because they have environments that mimic production on their laptops. A developer can reasonably simulate production load and performance testing on the container during development. The result is higher-quality, more-reliable software updates. Better, more-efficient testing also leads to less work in progress and fewer bottlenecks, which means faster updates.

6.2 *Promoting images*

In this chapter, you'll build a CI/CD pipeline in OpenShift. To keep the promise of using the same binary in every environment, you'll build your image just once in your development environment. You'll then use *image tagging* to indicate that the image is ready to be promoted to other projects. To facilitate this process, you'll use Jenkins and some additional OpenShift concepts, which you'll learn about as you go. Jenkins is an open source automation server that's commonly used as the backbone for CI/CD pipelines because it has many plugins for existing tools and technologies. Jenkins often becomes a Swiss army knife that's used to integrate disparate technologies into a CI/CD pipeline.

> **NOTE** Container images typically have *image tags* associated with them when they're built. By default, container images built with docker are tagged as `latest`. To list the container images and their tags, run the following command as root on one of the VMs: $ `docker images`.

6.3 *CI/CD part 1: creating a development environment*

The first part of any CI/CD pipeline is the development environment. Here, container images are built, tested, and then tagged if they pass their tests. All container builds happen in this environment. You'll use a prebuilt template to spin up a simple ToDo application that runs on Python and uses MongoDB as a database. The template also provides an open source Git repository called Gogs, which comes preinstalled with the application already in it. PostgreSQL is also provided as a database for Gogs. Figure 6.1 shows the pods that are created during instantiation of the template. (There's also a builder pod for the Python application, and a Gogs installation pod that will exit when completed, but these aren't shown in the figure.)

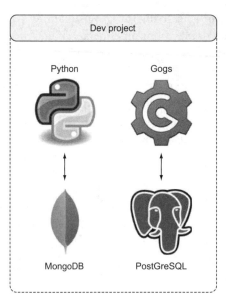

Figure 6.1   Dev project pods

Working with OpenShift templates

This chapter makes heavy use of OpenShift templates to install applications. An OpenShift *template* is essentially an array of objects that can be parameterized and spun up on demand. In most cases, the API objects created as part of the template are all part of the same application, but that is not a hard requirement. Using Open-Shift templates provides several features that aren't available if you manually import objects, including the following:

- Parameterized values can be provided at creation time.
- Values can be created dynamically based on regex values, such as randomly generated database passwords.
- Messages can be displayed to the user in the console or on the CLI. Typical messages include information on how to use the application.
- You can create labels that can be applied to all objects in the template.
- Part of the OpenShift API allows templates to be instantiated programmati-cally and without a local copy of the template.

OpenShift comes with many templates out of the box that you can see through the service catalog or by running `oc get templates -n openshift`. To see the raw template files, navigate to /usr/share/openshift/examples/ on the OpenShift mas-ter node.

For more information on how to author and use templates, visit http://mng.bz/1LTp.

At the command line, create your development environment by running the following command:

```
$ oc new-project dev --display-name="ToDo App - Dev"
```

Next, import the ToDo application template in the dev project:

```
$ oc create -f \                          Creates a resource from file
    https://raw.githubusercontent.com/OpenShiftInAction/
  chapter6/master/openshift-cicd-flask-mongo/OpenShift/templates/
  dev-todo-app-flask-mongo-gogs.json \       Raw JSON template for this chapter
    -n dev                  Installs the template into the dev project
```

Now, instantiate the template:

```
$ oc new-app --template="dev/dev-todo-app-flask-mongo-gogs"
--> Deploying template "dev/todo-app-flask-mongo-gogs" to project dev
    Flask + MongoDB (Ephemeral)
    ---------
    An example Flask application with a MongoDB database. For more
    information about using this template, including OpenShift considerations
    ,see https://github.com/sclorg/mongodb-container/blob/master/3.2/README.md

    WARNING: MongoDB instance is ephemeral so any data will be lost on pod
    destruction.

    The following service(s) have been created in your project:
    todo-app-flask-mongo, mongodb.
```

Password to access the MongoDB instance →
```
    mongodb Connection Info:           Username to access the
        Username: userImE     ←        MongoDB instance
        Password: mPO37nup
```
Database name for the application →
```
        Database Name: tododb
        Connection URL: mongodb://userImE:mPO37nup@mongodb/tododb   ←
```
Full connection string for an application to access the created MongoDB database
```
  * With parameters:
      * Application Name=todo-app-flask-mongo
      * Mongodb App=mongodb
      * Application route=
      * Git source repository=https://github.com/
```
Git repository for the Python ToDo application →
```
      OpenShiftInAction/chapter6
      * Context Directory=openshift-cicd-flask-mongo   ←
```
Git context directory in the Git repository
```
      * Git branch/tag reference=master
      * Database name=tododb
      * Database user name=userImE # generated
      * Database user password=mPO37nup # generated
      * Database admin password=mDsUVISh # generated
```
Max memory for the ToDo application, covered further in chapter 5 →
```
      * Memory Limit (Flask)=128Mi
      * Memory Limit (MongoDB)=128Mi   ←
```
Max memory for the MongoDB database

Password for the default Gogs user in the Gogs application
...

```
* Gogs Password=password
* Gogs version=0.11.29
* Gogs' PostgreSQL Password=EqLiXiUqoHCtl0dc # generated
* GitHub Trigger=F2v00WoE # generated
* Generic Trigger=GGg1KqHl # generated
```

Token to trigger automated builds

The pods will take a few minutes to deploy. First, the Gogs, PostgreSQL, and Mon-goDB pods are deployed. A separate pod called install-gogs also automates the instal-lation of Gogs by initializing PostgreSQL and cloning the remote Git repository locally. When Gogs is fully installed with a local copy of the remote Git repository, the install-gogs pod configures a *webhook*: an event-drive HTTP callback that you'll use to automate new builds in OpenShift. More specifically, every time there's a new Git commit, Gogs will recognize the event and send an HTTP POST to the OpenShift API, telling OpenShift to start a new source-to-image (S2I). Every time there's a new commit, the ToDo application will be rebuilt. Once the install-gogs pod finishes its task, it exits.

TIP If the pod deployments fail, verify that your network connection is fast enough to pull the new container images required for this application.

Next, open the OpenShift console in your browser, and navigate to the ToDo applica-tion by choosing Applications > Routes > todo-app-flask-mongo. You'll see the applica-tion's home page, as shown in figure 6.2.

Bootstrap/Python/Flask/Mongo   Powered by OpenShift

ToDo App

Task	Priority	Action
	Low ▾	Add

OpenShift In Action

Figure 6.2   The home page for the ToDo application in the dev project

Verify that Gogs is running properly by navigating to the gogs route. If the install-gogs pod isn't finished and marked completed, you'll see the database-initialization page shown in figure 6.3. Once the pod has completed the installation process, you'll see the Gogs home page and will be ready to proceed.

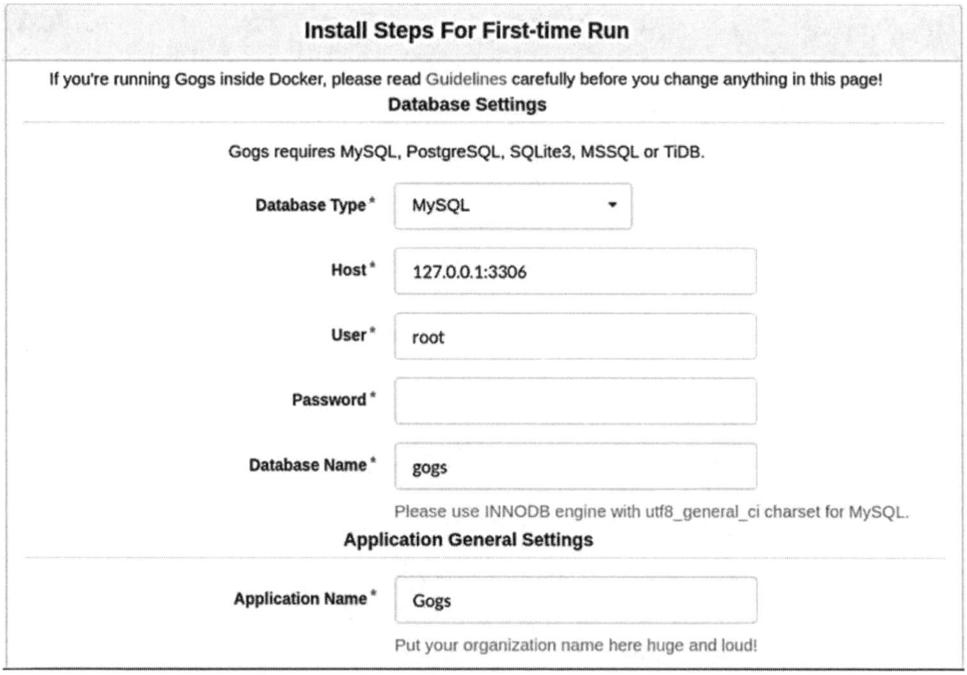

Install Steps For First-time Run

If you're running Gogs inside Docker, please read Guidelines carefully before you change anything in this page!

Database Settings

Gogs requires MySQL, PostgreSQL, SQLite3, MSSQL or TiDB.

Database Type* [MySQL ▾]

Host* [127.0.0.1:3306]

User* [root]

Password* [ ]

Database Name* [gogs]

Please use INNODB engine with utf8_general_ci charset for MySQL.

Application General Settings

Application Name* [Gogs]

Put your organization name here huge and loud!

Figure 6.3 The Gogs database-initializing page

TIP Because the application is using Python, an interpreted language, the build process is very fast. For languages like Java that may take a while to build using tools like Maven, you can enable *incremental builds* that allow the build pod to reuse build artifacts such as Maven JARs and Maven POMs that were imported during the build process. This avoids the redundancy of having to install the same dependencies multiple times for every build. You can find more information at http://mng.bz/262s.

You now have a full development environment. By making some application code changes, you can see the environment in action and demonstrate many of the Open-Shift automation features. Here, you'll edit the main landing page of the application. Follow these steps:

1 Switch back to the Gogs home page, and click the sign-in link at upper right. Log in using the username/password combination *gogs/password*.

2 Click the openshift-cicd-flask-mongo repository on the right of the page. You're now in the master directory of your git repository.

3 Navigate to openshift-cicd-flask-mongo > Templates > todo.html.

4 Click the Edit icon shown in figure 6.4. In the text editor, scroll down to the h1 HTML tag on line 32, and change the text to the following:

```
<h1 class="text-center">OIA ToDo App</h1>
```

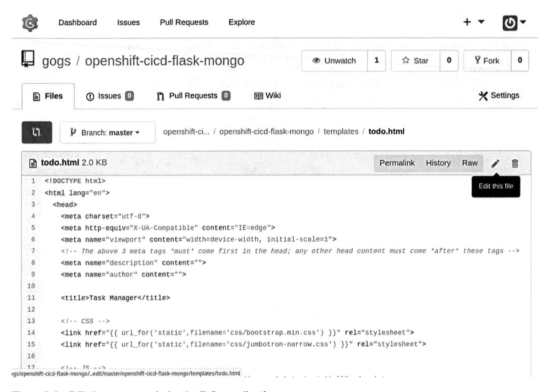

Figure 6.4   Edit the source code for the ToDo application.

5 Scroll to the bottom, and click Commit Changes. The source code for the application is modified and committed into the Git repository.

Verify that the Gogs webhook successfully started a new build by going back to the OpenShift console and clicking Builds in the panel on the left and then clicking Builds again. You should see that a new build was created. When the S2I process completes again, your application will be updated with the new HTML heading.

Take a minute to go back to the route for the ToDo application, and verify that it's up to date with the new code. If the browser still shows the old code, try clearing your browser cache and then refreshing the route.

TIP   Most browsers allow you to clear your cache by pressing Ctrl-Shift-Delete on a Windows or Linux machine. If you're using a Mac, press Command-Shift-Delete.

6.3.1   *Invoking object triggers*

In the previous example, you configured a trigger of type webhook to automatically start a new OpenShift build. The webhook trigger is an HTTP URL that can be accessed via HTTP POST and includes a token for security. When called, the webhook can trigger new actions such as starting new builds. Often, webhooks are used in conjunction with source code repositories such as GitHub and GitLab to automatically trigger new Open-Shift builds when the application source code has changed.

The template you installed for the dev project automatically generated the web-hook for you. In most scenarios, such as using the `oc new-app` command, webhook triggers are generated automatically by OpenShift. These webhooks can be used by any external system to trigger builds in OpenShift. Some examples of common systems that are used to trigger OpenShift builds include the following:

- Git-based source control systems like GitHub and Gogs
- Configuration-management systems
- Ticketing systems
- Automation tools like Jenkins

To see the webhooks that were automatically created for you by the template you installed, go to the OpenShift console and navigate back to the build's landing page, and then click the todo-app-flask-mongo Build > Configuration tab. You'll see the triggers listed for the build and the webhooks that were generated for the trigger, as shown in figure 6.5. These webhooks are specific triggers that can be used by any external system to start a new todo-app-flask-mongo build.

Triggers are an important part of automation in OpenShift, and they can be used in several ways. In addition to initiating new builds, they can automate things such as new application deployments and statefulset rollouts (covered in chapter 8). In the context of CI/CD, external systems triggering new builds are only a piece of the puzzle. For example, in a container landscape, live applications aren't patched in a traditional way like VMs. If they were patched live, the changes wouldn't persist, because when the container died, a new container would be spun up from the previous known container image—which wouldn't contain the patch. Therefore, the proper way to apply a patch is to rebuild the container image when a new patch needs to be applied.

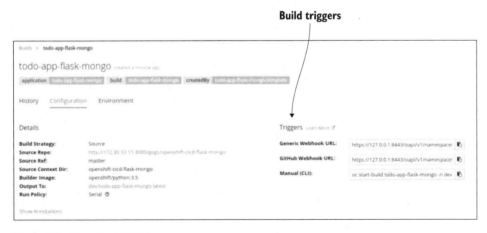

Figure 6.5 View the build triggers

Similarly, in a CI/CD context, the same container image is used in many different environments. When a new container is built in dev, the test environment needs to have an automated way to trigger a redeployment and run its tests.

Automating container image promotion between environments is difficult for several reasons. First, most container image registries have very little built-in automation features. Second, keeping versions of container image tags aligned between different environments can be challenging. Finally, because container images can be overridden, there needs to be another mechanism to ensure consistency of container images. A good example can be during development. Suppose, for instance, you have 10 pods in your dev environment running from the same image, todo-app-flask-mongo:latest. When you build a new container image with the same image and tag, you want to be guaranteed that all 10 pods have the new image and not the old one.

6.3.2   *Enabling automated and consistent deployments with image streams*

To solve these challenges, OpenShift has the concept of an *image stream*. This is often one of the most difficult concepts for new users of OpenShift to understand. Essentially, an image stream is an interface for one or more container images; it's treated the same as a container registry.

For example, a docker pull pointed to an image stream pulls down a docker image, just as it would if the pull was issued directly to the container registry. But having the image stream allows for two key features versus a regular container registry. First, as mentioned in chapter 2, the image stream enables automation, such as providing triggers. For example, it's easy to issue a new build or deployment every time a dependency image has changed. Second, the image stream ensures additional consistency. Docker image tags can be overwritten, so containers running from the same image tag can be inconsistent. An image stream tracks the sha256 hash of the images it's pointing at, to ensure consistency. By using an image stream, OpenShift ensures that when pods are replicated, they're the same binary.

> **TIP** You can read about the consistency of container image tags and image streams in the article "Docker Tag vs. Hash: A Lesson in Deterministic Ops" (Tariq Islam, *Medium*, May 7, 2017, http://mng.bz/adCf).

Image streams are a perfect mechanism to use to build a test environment for the ToDo application. Every time the image stream is updated, a new deployment can be triggered in the test environment. Because image streams also support tagging, the test environment can be configured to trigger new deployments only when the image stream with a certain tag is updated.

Switch to the command line, and find the specific image that the image stream is currently referencing with the sha256 hash:

```
$ oc describe imagestream todo-app-flask-mongo | grep sha256
  * docker-registry.default.svc:5000/dev/todo-app-flask-mongo@sha256:55f29
  ➥ 438305f9d8b6baf7ac0df8ee17965bb62a1dba8ac01190ad88e0ca18843
```

The output of the command shows the exact image the image stream is currently referencing. Copy the full image string to your clipboard, and tag that image as promoteToTest, as shown next. The test environment will pull only images that are ready for the test environment as referenced by the new imagestream tag:

```
$ oc tag todo-app-flask-mongo@sha256:55f29438305f9d8b6baf7ac0df8ee17965bb6
⮑ 2a1dba8ac01190ad88e0ca18843 \
    dev/todo-app-flask-mongo:promoteToTest
Tag todo-app-flask-mongo:promoteToTest set to todo-app-flask-mongo@sha256:55
⮑ f29438305f9d8b6baf7ac0df8ee17965bb62a1dba8ac01190ad88e0ca18843.
```

The same container image now has two tags, latest and promoteToTest. Having multiple tags for the same container image is helpful when you're using the same image for different environments, because environments aren't always in sync. By having multiple tags, you can use the tags to manage the images in each environment. Although you'll eventually promote this container image into a test environment, you're likely to come back later and add new code, features, enhancements, and so on. Doing so will generate new container images tagged as todo-app-flask-mongo:latest in dev but won't impact what's running in the test environment. Eventually, when the latest image is ready to be promoted to the test environment, the promoteToTest tag can be updated to point to the new container image.

6.4 *CI/CD part 2: promoting dev images into a test environment*

In the last section, you built a development environment and then tagged the image stream for the ToDo application as promoteToTest to indicate that it's ready to be run in the test environment. Before you pull down the application, you need to create a new project called test, deploy an instance of MongoDB, and modify a security setting for the test environment.

In the OpenShift CLI, run the following commands to create a new test environment and deploy a new instance of MongoDB:

```
$ oc new-project test --display-name="ToDo App - Test"
...
$ oc new-app \
    -e MONGODB_USER=oiatestuser \
    -e MONGODB_PASSWORD=password \
    -e MONGODB_DATABASE=tododb \
    -e MONGODB_ADMIN_PASSWORD=password mongodb:3.2
--> Found image 5540f1c (10 days old) in image stream "openshift/mongodb"
    under tag "3.2" for "mongodb:3.2"
...
--> Success
   Run 'oc status' to view your app.
```

Next, you'll deploy the same image that you built in the dev environment into your test environment. By default, image streams in the OpenShift project can be seen by all other projects. But image streams created in other projects, such as those in the dev project, aren't visible outside those individual projects. The image streams have limited scope in order to provide increased security. It's recommended that users and teams who want to share images with other projects, such as in a CI/CD context, should modify this behavior using the OpenShift CLI. Run this command to allow the test project to pull images from the dev project:

Applies the change to serviceaccounts in the test project

```
$ oc policy add-role-to-group \
    system:image-puller \
    system:serviceaccounts:test \
    -n dev
```

The system:image-puller role allows users/groups to pull images from projects.

The test project can now access images in the dev project. Next, deploy the image tagged `promoteToTest` in the dev project into your test project:

```
$ oc new-app dev/todo-app-flask-mongo:promoteToTest
--> Found image 8bd4599 (22 hours old) in image stream
    "dev/todo-app-flask-mongo" under tag "promoteToTest"
    for "development/todo-app-flask-mongo:promoteToTest"
...
    * Port 8080/tcp will be load balanced by service "todo-app-flask-mongo"
      * Other containers can access this service through the hostname
        "todo-app-flask-mongo"

--> Creating resources ...
    deploymentconfig "todo-app-flask-mongo" created
    service "todo-app-flask-mongo" created
--> Success
    Run 'oc status' to view your app.
```

By default, the Python image that you used to create your application is configured for applications listening on port 8080—but the actual application listens on port 5000. Run this command to update to the correct port:

```
$ oc patch svc todo-app-flask-mongo --type merge \
    --patch '{"spec":{"ports":[{"port": 8080, "targetPort": 5000 }]}}'
service "todo-app-flask-mongo" patched
```

Now that the service has been correctly updated, create a route for the ToDo application:

```
$ oc expose svc todo-app-flask-mongo
route "todo-app-flask-mongo" exposed
```

Normally, everything would be good to go at this point. But if you double-check your pods, you'll notice that the pod isn't running as expected:

```
$ oc get pods
NAME                            READY   STATUS             RESTARTS   AGE
mongodb-1-61z9p                 1/1     Running            0          19h
todo-app-flask-mongo-1-4xzj6    0/1     CrashLoopBackOff   6          10m
```

The ToDo application pod has a status of `CrashLoopBackOff`, which usually means the pod is starting and then immediately exiting. This behavior is also confirmed by the high number of restarts.

In this case, the `CrashLoopBackOff` status indicates that although you've deployed a MongoDB instance for the ToDo application to use, the application has no way to discover it. One of the challenges with promoting the same container image to multiple environments is that the application must dynamically find the dependencies it needs. We'll look at this next.

6.4.1 *Service discovery*

In chapter 4, you learned that a service object provides a single IP address and port for all identical pods. Unlike pod IP addresses, which are ephemeral, the service provides a static IP address and port that don't change for the life of the service object. The service object becomes even more critical as you try to maintain one of the underlying promises of containers: the same binary that runs on the developer's laptop runs in production. To make this promise a reality, you need a dynamic discovery mechanism so the container can use different systems and different data sets as images move between environments. The most common example is a database. Your application container may process dummy data on a laptop and then process more robust, targeted data sets as it moves from various environments into production. As it does so, it needs a discovery mechanism to find the databases services it will use. In OpenShift, service discovery works with both environment variables and DNS.

When you create applications in OpenShift, the service object is usually generated for you behind the scenes to avoid the manual process of creating API objects. In most cases, there is a single service object per deployment, but many service objects can be used when multiple ports need to be exposed.

In the example, the MongoDB exposes only a single port: the database connections port. The ToDo application needs to find the service used to expose this port. In the console, view the MongoDB service object that OpenShift automatically created for you by choosing Applications > Services > Mongodb. You should see a screen similar to figure 6.6.

The service type is listed as ClusterIP, which means you have a cluster-wide IP address. Typically, this is automatically generated by OpenShift. ClusterIP is the most common service type. The IP is a private IP address that was automatically generated by OpenShift and isn't available from outside the OpenShift cluster. The ClusterIP can be identified in OpenShift using either DNS or environment variables, each of which come with its own advantages and disadvantages.

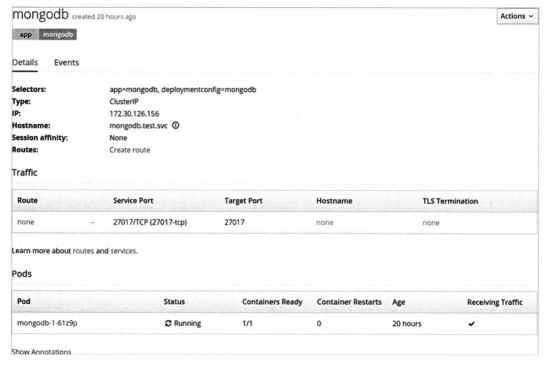

Figure 6.6   Viewing the service object that was automatically generated by the `oc new-app` command

DNS

OpenShift runs *SkyDNS* for internal discovery of services. SkyDNS is a distributed name-server specifically designed to run with etcd, the Kubernetes API server backend, as its data store. It runs on the master on port 8053 by default. When a container initially starts up, the nameserver on the master(s) is added to the container configuration (in /etc/resolv.conf in the container). When this happens, the container uses the master for all DNS queries ending in .cluster.local.

TIP SkyDNS is covered in greater detail in chapter 10.

In OpenShift, DNS is often the preferred choice for service discovery. These DNS entries normally take the form <service>.<pod_namespace>.svc.cluster.local, but the format can be shortened to <service>.<pod_namespace>.svc or even <service> if you're looking for a service local to the current namespace. The main benefit of using DNS as the service-discovery mechanism is that it's consistent and less brittle than using environment variables, as we'll demonstrate in the next section.

ENVIRONMENT VARIABLES

Services can also be discovered using environment variables. Many developers who use docker are probably using environment variables in some capacity. They're easy to use with containers, even without a platform. They have the benefit of being injectable at runtime, thus increasing application portability across environments. Unfortunately, they also have a significant disadvantage: the backend services need to be up and running before other services can discover them with environment variables. If the backend services are created after the consuming services are spun up, service discovery won't work properly unless the backend service is redeployed. For this reason, using DNS is often the preferred method for service discovery in OpenShift. Some reasons you may want to use environment variables anyway include the following:

- Consistency with the way you run the containers using the docker CLI
- Portability outside of Kubernetes-based platforms
- Ability to run dynamic smoke tests
- Support for older applications pre-configured for environment variables
- Ease of use

In the next section, you'll fix the ToDo application by providing a service-discovery mechanism for the Python frontend to find the MongoDB instance.

FIXING TODO BY INJECTING ENVIRONMENT VARIABLES

It turns out that the ToDo application uses both DNS and environment variables to look for the database. In the template you deployed for your development environment, this is handled automatically for you by injecting an environment variable into the todo-app-flask-mongo deployment. The environment variable that the application is looking for has the following format:

```
mongodb://${MONGODB_USER}:${MONGODB_PASSWORD}@${MONGODB_HOSTNAME}/
➥ ${MONGODB_DATABASE}
```

The MongoDB hostname is a DNS entry for the MongoDB service. Because the ToDo application is looking for the MongoDB service in the same namespace, you'll use the short format of *service*. Based on the variables you used to create the MongoDB application in section 6.4, inject the environment variable into the todo-app-flask-mongo deployment:

```
MONGO_CONNECTION_URI=mongodb://testuser:password@mongodb/tododb
```

Adding environment variables to your deployment configuration will propagate down to the pod level. This can be done either through the CLI or through the OpenShift console, but adding them via the console is easiest. Go back to your Deployments page, and click the Environment tab. Then add the environment variable as shown in figure 6.7.

As with any changes to a deployment configuration, OpenShift will version-control the change and then roll out the latest deployment configuration, which will propagate the changes down to the pods. Test this by navigating to your pod and choosing Applications > Pods. You should have only one pod running, so click that pod. Click the Environment Variable tab to see the MONGO_CONNECTION_URI environment variable. To

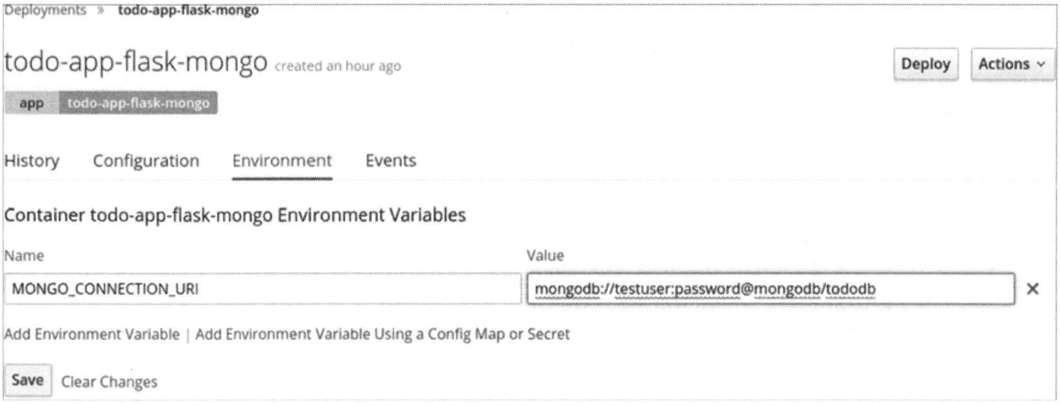

Figure 6.7   Injecting the `MONGO_CONNECTION_URI` environment variable into the todo-app-flask-mongo deployment

double-check that the container in the pod can see the change, navigate to the Terminal tab on the pod view, and check the environment variable from the command prompt:

```
$ echo $MONGO_CONNECTION_URI
mongodb://testuser:password@mongodb/tododb
```

Adding `MONGO_CONNECTION_URI` will prevent the pod from immediately exiting and causing the pod status to be set to `CrashLoopBackOff`. Verify through the browser that the ToDo application is working.

Only one problem remains: there's still no automation between environments. If you were to go back to Gogs in the development environment and make a code change, doing so would trigger a new source-to-image build of the ToDo application in the development environment. The output of that source-to-image would be another container image called todo-app-flask-mongo:latest. Even when todo-app-flask-mongo:promoteToTest was updated to point to the new image, nothing would propagate to the test environment. Although you can manually trigger a new deployment in the test environment, you want this to be automated. To create this automation, you need to add a trigger for the image stream.

Manually triggering builds

You can manually trigger builds from the web console or the command line. In the web console, there's a Deploy button on the landing page for each deployment.

To manually trigger builds from the command line, use the `rollout` subcommand. For example, to roll out a new deployment of the todo-app-flask-mongo app in the test environment, you'd run this command:

```
$ oc rollout latest dc/todo-app-flask-mongo -n test
```

6.4.2 Automating image promotion with image stream triggers

In this section, you'll create an image stream trigger that will cause the todo-app-flask-mongo application in the test environment to be redeployed every time there's a new image in the dev environment tagged as `todo-app-flask-mongo:promoteToTest`. The triggers for the image stream object are included in the deployment config object. You can add an image stream trigger through both the web console and the command line.

Configure the todo-app-flask-mongo deployment to redeploy every time a new image is available in the dev/todo-app-flask-mongo:promoteToTest image stream by running the following command:

```
$ oc patch dc todo-app-flask-mongo --patch '{"spec":{"triggers": [{
            "imageChangeParams": {
                "automatic": true,
                "containerNames": [
                    "todo-app-flask-mongo"
                ],
                "from": {
                    "kind": "ImageStreamTag",
                    "name": "todo-app-flask-mongo:promoteToTest",
                    "namespace": "dev"
                }
            },
            "type": "ImageChange"
        }
    ]
}}'
deploymentconfig "todo-app-flask-mongo" patched
```

> **TIP** There's a shortcut to create triggers using the command-line tool `oc set triggers`. You can find more information at http://mng.bz/8LFv.

You now have a CI/CD pipeline that consists of a dev environment and a test environment. When code is committed into the Git repository, it will be automatically built and deployed in the dev environment. To promote the image into the test environment, the user is still required to tag the image as `promoteToTest`, as shown in figure 6.8.

Verify that this is automated by making an additional edit to the source code. Switch back to the Gogs UI, and edit the todo.html file again. In the text editor, modify the HTML tag on line 32 to this:

```
<h1 class="text-center">Ready For Test - ToDo App</h1>
```

After the text is updated, scroll to the bottom of the page, and click Commit Changes. Doing so will cause a webhook from Gogs to trigger a new application build. When the build completes, your application will be updated and can be tested through the route. Take a minute to go back to the route for the ToDo application and verify that it's up to date with the new code.

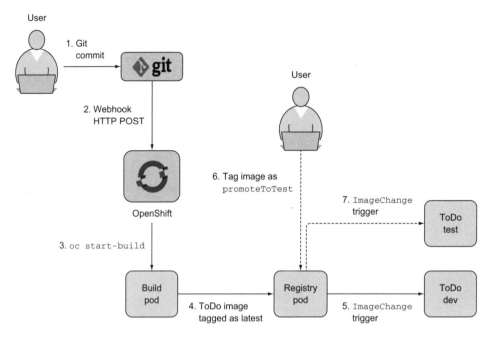

Figure 6.8   Images are automatically promoted to test once they're tagged as `promoteToTest`.

At this point, the test environment is still running the older code. The new build generated a new container image of todo-app-flask-mongo with the tag `latest`, and the deployment in the test environment is configured to redeploy the application only when there's a new container image of todo-app-flask-mongo with the tag `promote-ToTest`. Review the image streams by switching to the dev project and describing the image streams in that project:

```
$ oc project dev
Now using project "dev" on server "https://ocp-1.192.168.122.100.nip.io:8443"
$ oc describe is todo-app-flask-mongo
Name:           todo-app-flask-mongo
Namespace:      dev
...
Unique Images:       3
Tags:           2

latest
  pushed image

  * docker-registry.default.svc:5000/dev/todo-app-flask-mongo@sha256:85
  ➥ 01f5a2b7cdd8650ffb69975f512af23f681e0cb01c5bef41def890ba7925a7
    About a minute ago
  docker-registry.default.svc:5000/dev/todo-app-flask-mongo@sha256:ce
  ➥ ee1ea5bfca8beed8c34411af2dccef19c32364933971fe0623303a45201074
    About an hour ago
  docker-registry.default.svc:5000/dev/todo-app-flask-mongo@sha256:55
```

```
➥ f29438305f9d8b6baf7ac0df8ee17965bb62a1dba8ac01190ad88e0ca18843
    25 hours ago

promoteToTest
    tagged from todo-app-flask-mongo@sha256:ceee1ea5bfca8beed8c34411af2dccef
    ➥ 19c32364933971fe0623303a45201074


    * docker-registry.default.svc:5000/dev/todo-app-flask-mongo@sha256:ceee1
    ➥ ea5bfca8beed8c34411af2dccef19c32364933971fe0623303a45201074
       About an hour ago
      docker-registry.default.svc:5000/dev/todo-app-flask-mongo@sha256:55f29
       ➥ 438305f9d8b6baf7ac0df8ee17965bb62a1dba8ac01190ad88e0ca18843
        25 hours ago
```

Notice that the active images for `latest` and `promoteToTest` both have an asterisk in front of them. The image you just built was tagged as `latest` and has a different hash value string than the one marked `promoteToTest`. Grab the full string so that you can tag it as `promoteToTest`, which will automate deployment into the test environment. Do this to tag the image as `promoteToTest`:

```
$ oc tag todo-app-flask-mongo@sha256:8501f5a2b7cdd8650ffb69975f512af23f681
➥ e0cb01c5bef41def890ba7925a7 \
    todo-app-flask-mongo:promoteToTest
Tag todo-app-flask-mongo:promoteToTest set to todo-app-flask-mongo@sha256:
➥ 8501f5a2b7cdd8650ffb69975f512af23f681e0cb01c5bef41def890ba7925a7
```

Now, open the OpenShift Console and go to the pod overview page in the test project. The pod's age will indicate that a new image was pulled from the development environment. Refresh the application again in the browser, making sure you're looking at the test version. You'll see that the application change was automatically deployed from dev to test! The process of tagging the image may have seemed a little awkward, but at the end of the chapter you'll learn how to automate this process with Jenkins.

> **NOTE** Normally, many other processes would be involved to test an application before promoting it to production, often including unit tests, load tests, code quality inspections, security scans, and even manual approval processes. That information isn't in the scope of this chapter, but you can find more information in the article "CI and CD With OpenShift" (Siamak Sadeghianfar, *DevOps Zone*, February 24, 2017, https://dzone.com/articles/cicd-with-openshift).

6.5 CI/CD part 3: masking sensitive data in a production environment

In this section, you'll quickly build an environment for production that's similar to the one you built for the test environment, but you'll use a template and some shortcuts to avoid duplicating the work. You'll then learn how to mask sensitive information.

To get started, switch to your dev project and create a new tag named `promoteTo-Prod`:

```
$ oc tag todo-app-flask-mongo@sha256:8501f5a2b7cdd8650ffb69975f512af23f681
➥ e0cb01c5bef41def890ba7925a7 \
    todo-app-flask-mongo:promoteToProd
Tag todo-app-flask-mongo:promoteToProd set to todo-app-flask-mongo@sha256:
➥ 8501f5a2b7cdd8650ffb69975f512af23f681e0cb01c5bef41def890ba7925a7
```

Create a new project named prod by running the following command:

```
$ oc new-project prod --display-name="ToDo App - Prod"
```

Now, import the template:

```
$ oc create -f \
https://raw.githubusercontent.com/OpenShiftInAction/chapter6/master/]opensh
➥ ift-cicd-flask-mongo/OpenShift/templates/prod-todo-app-flask-mongo.json \
    -n prod
template "prod-todo-app-flask-mongo" created
```

Instantiate the template by running the following command. The template assumes that your development project is called dev and your production project is called prod. If you made any changes to the default values, initialize the template through the OpenShift console and modify the default parameters:

```
$ oc new-app --template="prod/prod-todo-app-flask-mongo"
--> Deploying template "prod/prod-todo-app-flask-mongo" to project prod
...
    mongodb Connection Info:                   Template auto-
        Username: userqOe           ◁――――――    generated username
        Password: PNG7YEVF
        Database Name: tododb
        Connection URL: mongodb://userqOe:PNG7YEVF@mongodb/tododb   ◁――
...
--> Creating resources ...                                    Full connection URL
    rolebinding "image-puller-prod" created    ◁――――          for MongoDB clients
    service "mongodb" created
    deploymentconfig "mongodb" created                    Role binding gives the
    imagestream "todo-app-flask-mongo" created            prod project access to
    deploymentconfig "todo-app-flask-mongo" created       dev project images.
    service "todo-app-flask-mongo" created
    route "todo-app-flask-mongo" created
--> Success
    Run 'oc status' to view your app.
```

Labels: *Template auto-generated password* points to the Password line.

TIP Many users want their environments to run on dedicated OpenShift nodes. For example, a user may want all development projects to run on older hardware, and all production projects to run on newer, fast hardware. When running in a public cloud, production environments often have their own VMs with higher quality of service (QoS) tiers for disks and networking. For instance, Amazon Web Services (AWS) allows users to upgrade their network bandwidth and latency in addition to upgrade to solid-state drives (SSDs) for local disk storage. It's easy in OpenShift to match environments to dedicated machines by using OpenShift labels to match nodes to projects. You can find more information at http://mng.bz/FmM6 and http://mng.bz/f02E.

Earlier in the chapter, you set up your test project manually and ran the `oc policy` command to allow the test project to access images from the dev project. In setting up the prod environment, this was handled for you by the template. At this point, the dev project is the only project with a build config. All projects are built in dev. The test and prod projects have access to pull these images but not modify or push new ones, as shown in figure 6.9.

In the examples up to this point, you've used environment variables to dynamically configure the MongoDB instance and then pass the credentials (username, password, hostname, database) to the ToDo application. From a security perspective, using environment variables for sensitive data is a significant drawback: it's easy to accidentally expose an environment variable. For example, it's common for application frameworks to automatically print environment variables and other configuration data during a server error (returning an HTTP 500 response). Printing environment variables during a server error usually happens when an application is accidentally left in development mode or is poorly configured for error handling. In addition, many application frameworks print environment variables to log files, which are available to users who aren't supposed to have access to sensitive information. When environment variables are printed in log files, that also means the sensitive information will likely be printed in clear text on disk.

Fortunately, OpenShift has the concept of *secrets*: API objects that can be used to mask data better than environment variables. We'll discuss them next.

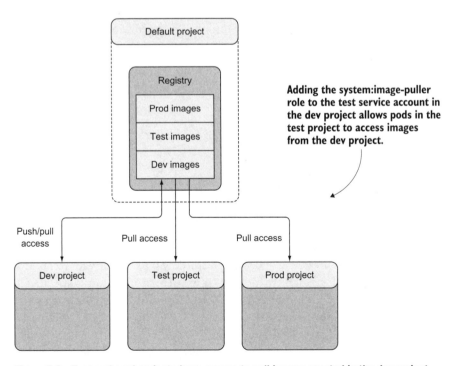

Figure 6.9   Test and prod projects have access to pull images created in the dev project.

6.5.1   *Protecting sensitive data with secrets*

Secrets can be used to make sensitive information dynamically available to a container in OpenShift. They're encoded/decoded and kept in memory only on the OpenShift nodes that require them and only for the period during which they're needed. Secrets can be used in many ways, including as better-protected environment variables.

In the example, you want to avoid using an environment variable, so you'll create a secret and mount the data as files in the container. Follow these steps:

1 Navigate to the prod project in the OpenShift console, and choose Applications > Deployments > Mongodb.

2 Click the Environment tab, and update the username and password to *oiauser* and *SecretPwd12*, respectively.

3 Click *save* to deploy a new MongoDB instance with the updated username and password.

4 Create a new secret:

```
oc create secret generic \          Secret name
    oia-prod-secret \         ←
    --from-literal=mongodb_user=oiauser \      ←      MongoDB username
    --from-literal=mongodb_password=SecretPwd12 \    ←—  MongoDB password
    --from-literal=mongodb_hostname=mongodb \      ←
    --from-literal=mongodb_database=tododb         MongoDB service name
```

MongoDB database

NOTE Like other Kubernetes platforms, OpenShift uses etcd as the database for the API Server. You can learn more about securing secrets in etcd at http://mng.bz/Qa46.

1 OpenShift provides a shortcut through the command-line tool to mount the literals to files in the container. Run this command to mount the secret literals as files in the ToDo application pods:

```
$ oc set volumes dc/todo-app-flask-mongo \       Adds a new volume
    --add \                                       and volume mount
    --name=secret-volume \                        to the container
    --mount-path=/opt/app-root/mongo/ \      ←  Container directory where
    --secret-name=oia-prod-secret      ←          files will be mounted
```

Arbitrary volume name

Creates files from the secret named oia-prod-secret

The secret used to mask the Mongo connection information is now mounted as a local file in the container. The ToDo application will use these files to determine how to find and access MongoDB. By default, the ToDo application is specifically configured to look first in files located in the /opt/app-root/mongo directory. If the files aren't there, it looks for the MONGO_CONNECTION_URI environment variable, which was initially configured for you by the template.

Ensure that the application is configured to use the secret you created by running the following command:

```
$ oc logs $(oc get pods -l deploymentconfig=todo-app-flask-mongo \
    -o=jsonpath='{.items[].metadata.name}')
---> Running application from Python script (app.py) ...
Using files in /opt/app-root/mongo/ for MongoDB connection
Successful connection to MongoDB instance
 * Running on http://0.0.0.0:5000/ (Press CTRL+C to quit)
```

> **TIP** When secrets are mounted as volumes, any update to the secret will automatically be pushed to the volumes that use that secret. This also goes for config maps (covered in the next section). This functionality allows you to update your applications without restarting them. In order for this to work properly, though, the application must be configured to look for updates and reload them. Many applications only look for files at startup and never reload them, so be careful about relying on live updates for secrets and config maps.

The output should indicate that the application is using the files in the /opt/app-root/directory. If that isn't the case, double-check that you ran the previous two commands correctly. If you did, but problems still occur, navigate to the Deployment page in the OpenShift console and ensure that the secret is properly configured as a volume in the container

Secrets can be used for other sensitive information, as well. OpenShift by default creates and manages many secrets for you behind the scenes, to make a better user experience. One example is the `dockercfg` secret, which is used internally so that OpenShift can automate updates to the container registry. Other common use cases for secrets are SSL/TLS certificates and private Git repository credentials.

Secrets provide a secure mechanism to dynamically pass sensitive information to containers. By passing this information at runtime, the credentials aren't in the actual container image, which is a security best practice. Secrets are a powerful tool for making dynamic container images that can be promoted between environments, although they often have additional administrative or configuration overhead.

There may be times when you need a simple mechanism to get different settings to your application at runtime. If the configuration file doesn't contain sensitive data, it makes more sense to use a *config map*.

6.5.2 *Using config maps for environment-specific settings*

Similar to secrets, config maps are API objects. A config map object holds key-value pairs, typically configuration data. The data can be individual strings or entire properties files. Config maps are an important component in using container images for a CI/CD pipeline which allow for environment-specific configuration artifacts to be decoupled from the image. Config map objects can be exposed as environment variables, mounted as files in a container, or even configured as command-line arguments on application startup. By presenting environment-specific configurations at runtime, the container image becomes truly portable across environments.

The most common use case for a configuration map is an application that is pre-configured to look at a properties or settings file upon startup. Often times, applications may look for this file on its local filesystem. Before containers became the backbone of CI/CD pipelines, these configuration files were typically bundled with the application. In the next section, you will make such a change to modify the ToDo application.

IMPLEMENTING A CONFIG MAP

The ToDo application is configured to look for a file called style.properties in the /opt/app-root/ui directory. If the file exists, the application checks for a usebuttons property in the file. If the usebuttons property exists, then ToDo displays buttons instead of text for adding and removing tasks from the application. Because this configuration isn't sensitive, you can use a config map to make sure the property isn't hardcoded in the image. Follow these steps:

1 Switch to the dev project on the command line. Create a style.properties file with the value usebuttons:

```
echo "usebuttons" > style.properties
```

2 Use the command line to create a config map from the style.properties file:

```
$ oc create configmap \
    ui-config \
    --from-file=style.properties
```

3 Patch the deployment to mount the config map to the expected directory:

```
$ oc set volumes dc/todo-app-flask-mongo \
  --add \
  --name=configmap-volume \
  --mount-path=/opt/app-root/ui/ \
  -t configmap --configmap-name=ui-config
```

TIP You can use the previous command to point to a directory instead of an individual file. This is a handy shortcut if you have many configuration files that you want to be included in the same configmap object.

Because the deployment you patched has a ConfigChange trigger, a new todo-app-flask-mongo pod will be immediately started that has the style.properties file mounted in the /opt/app-root/directory. Navigate to the ToDo application in the browser, and refresh the page. Double-check that the application is using buttons instead of text, as shown in figure 6.10. If the application is still showing the old button-style, then first verify that the config map is mounted properly as a file at /opt/app-root/ui/style.properties. If the file is not at that location, go back and ensure that the command to create the config map was run properly. If the file is in the right place, but the app is not functioning properly, then try refreshing your browser or clearing your browser cache.

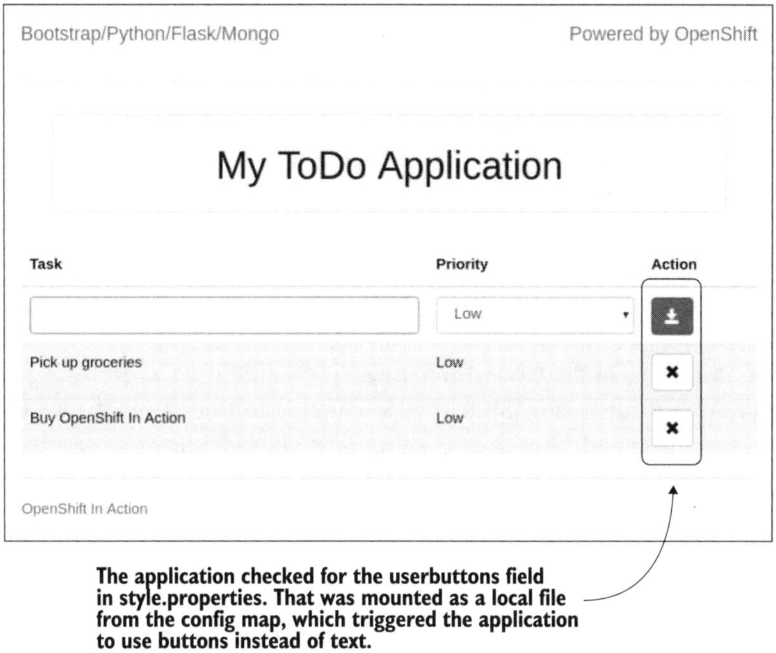

The application checked for the userbuttons field in style.properties. That was mounted as a local file from the config map, which triggered the application to use buttons instead of text.

Figure 6.10   ToDo application using buttons instead of text

NOTE   Some use cases require that many different pod types have the same environment variables, secrets, config maps, and so on. In this scenario, you can use pod presets to inject these constructs into pods, using labels as opposed to modifying individual deployments separately. A common example is many different applications in a project having their own deployments but needing to access the same secret. If you use pod presets, the application deployments don't all need to be modified separately. You can learn more about how to use pod presets at http://mng.bz/H909.

So far in this chapter, you've built a development environment and then used OpenShift native features and API objects to promote the same image from your development environment to your production environment. You use image streams to enable automation; image tagging to trigger image promotion; and environment variables, secrets, and config maps to ensure that the image worked in every environment. Although enabling this automation is useful, it lacks some key features. First, there's no macro view of what's happening in the environment. The OpenShift console provides a project-based view, but it doesn't provide a multiproject view to track images being promoted among various environments. Second, some of the steps require manual effort, such as using the oc tag to tag an image stream as being ready to promote. Finally, it's unclear how to integrate third-party tools such as code scanning and testing tools. For these reasons, many OpenShift users use Jenkins to promote container images to different environments in a fully automated fashion.

6.6   *Using Jenkins as the backbone of a CI/CD pipeline*

Jenkins is a popular, easy-to-use automation tool, and many OpenShift users already have a working knowledge of it. In many ways, Jenkins has become the de facto industry standard to automate a CI/CD pipeline, mainly because it has a large ecosystem of plugins for third-party tools. Typically, when a vendor wants to get a product or technology out to a large audience, creating a plugin for Jenkins is at the top of the priority list.

OpenShift provides Jenkins container images as well as several Jenkins plugins to facilitate integrating Jenkins with OpenShift and building CI/CD pipelines. The following are some common ways to use Jenkins and OpenShift together:

- *Jenkins-as-a-service on OpenShift*—In this scenario, you spin up a Jenkins pod in OpenShift to facilitate CI/CD pipelines in OpenShift. The Jenkins pod can be deployed from the OpenShift service catalog and comes with the OpenShift plugins preinstalled. This can be set up on a cluster-wide or per-project basis.
- *External Jenkins*—Users who already have an existing Jenkins installation and CI/CD pipeline can install the OpenShift plugins into their existing instance to facilitate OpenShift automation.
- *Hybrid*—Typically, this involves running an external Jenkins instance but running Jenkins slaves in OpenShift pods as needed.

You'll deploy Jenkins-as-a-service in this section because it's easy and doesn't require new infrastructure. In many OpenShift environments, each project has its own instance of Jenkins. But in this case, the Jenkins instance will be coordinating across multiple projects, so you'll create a Jenkins instance in a dedicated project. You'll use the same Jenkins instance for your development, test, and production environments. Follow these steps:

1 Allow the the Jenkins Service Account to edit your existing dev, test, and prod projects:

```
$ oc policy add-role-to-user edit \
    system:serviceaccount:cicd:jenkins -n dev
$ oc policy add-role-to-user edit \
    system:serviceaccount:cicd:jenkins -n test
$ oc policy add-role-to-user edit \
    system:serviceaccount:cicd:jenkins -n prod
```

2 Create a new project:

```
$ oc new-project cicd --display-name="ToDo App - CI/CD with Jenkins"
Now using project "cicd" on server "https://ocp-1.192.168.122.100.nip.io
➥ :8443"
. . .
```

3 Import the Jenkins template for this chapter:

```
$ oc create -f \
   https://raw.githubusercontent.com/OpenShiftInAction/chapter6/master/
   ➥ jenkins-s2i/jenkins-s2i-template.json \
   -n cicd
template "jenkins-oia" created
```

4 Run the following command to process the template. It installs Jenkins and uses the OpenShift S2I image, which will pull three preconfigured Jenkins jobs to automate building a new image in dev, tagging it as `promoteToTest`, and then tagging it again as `promoteToProd`. In other words, the preconfigured Jenkins pod in the template will automate the manual steps you had to perform earlier:

```
$ oc new-app --template="cicd/jenkins-oia"
--> Deploying template "openshift/jenkins-ephemeral" to project cicd

    Jenkins (Ephemeral)
    ---------
    Jenkins service, without persistent storage.

    WARNING: Any data stored will be lost upon pod destruction.
    Only use this template for testing.

    A Jenkins service has been created in your project.
    Log into Jenkins with your OpenShift account.  The tutorial at
    https://github.com/openshift/origin/blob/master/examples/jenkins/
    ➥ README.md
    contains more information about using this template.
...
--> Success
    Run 'oc status' to view your app.
```

When the build is finished and the custom Jenkins pod is deployed, open your browser and navigate to the route that was created for you automatically by the template. You can log in with your OpenShift credentials. Choose Dev Build Job > Configure to bring up the job; you should see a page similar to figure 6.11. Note that the template you instantiated created a service account called jenkins with permissions to edit images from the dev project. This allows you to skip providing your login session token, which will expire periodically.

TIP You can find your login token by running *oc whoami -t* from the command line.

If you scroll to the bottom, you'll see that the job is configured to automatically trigger the Promote to Test job (see figure 6.12). Take a couple minutes to explore the Promote To Test and Promote To Prod jobs. They're simple, but they eliminate the need for you to manually find the image ID and tag it as you did earlier in the chapter.

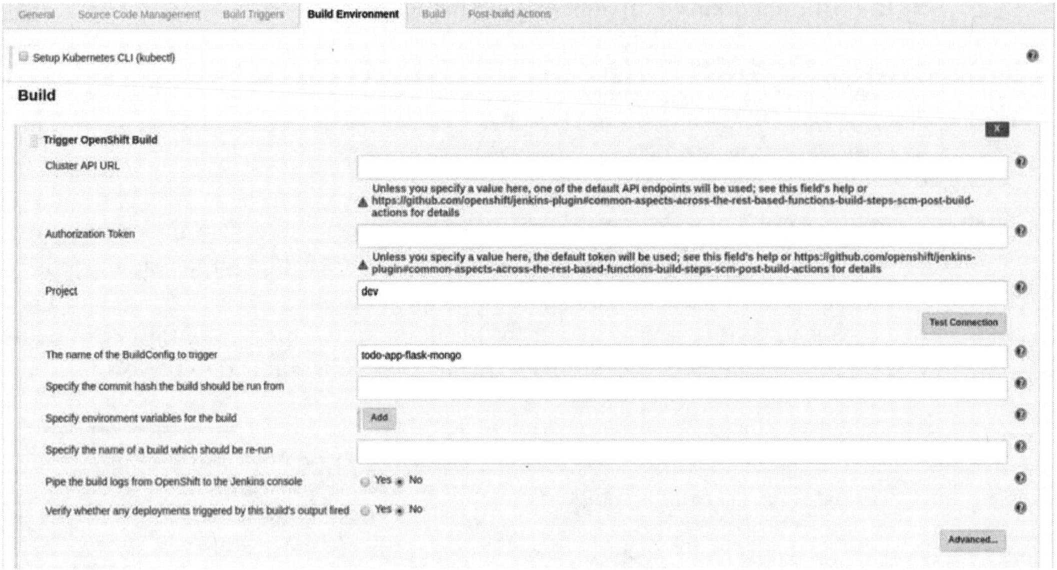

Figure 6.11   Jenkins triggering an OpenShift build

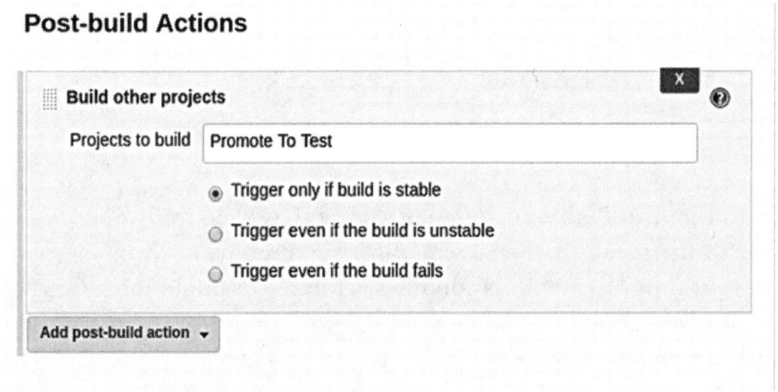

Figure 6.12   Jenkins Promote to Test job

Eventually, the container image is fully promoted to the prod environment, as shown in figure 6.13, by Jenkins automating the image tagging process.

If you go back to the Dev Build job and click Build Now, a new image will be built and promoted all the way to your production environment. In the real world, you'll have many other software testing and code- and image-scanning tools that run in this pipeline. For most customers, there may be manual checkpoints as well. One of the benefits of using Jenkins is that it's easy to integrate external systems like Service Now or Jira, which can trigger Jenkins jobs through an HTTP call.

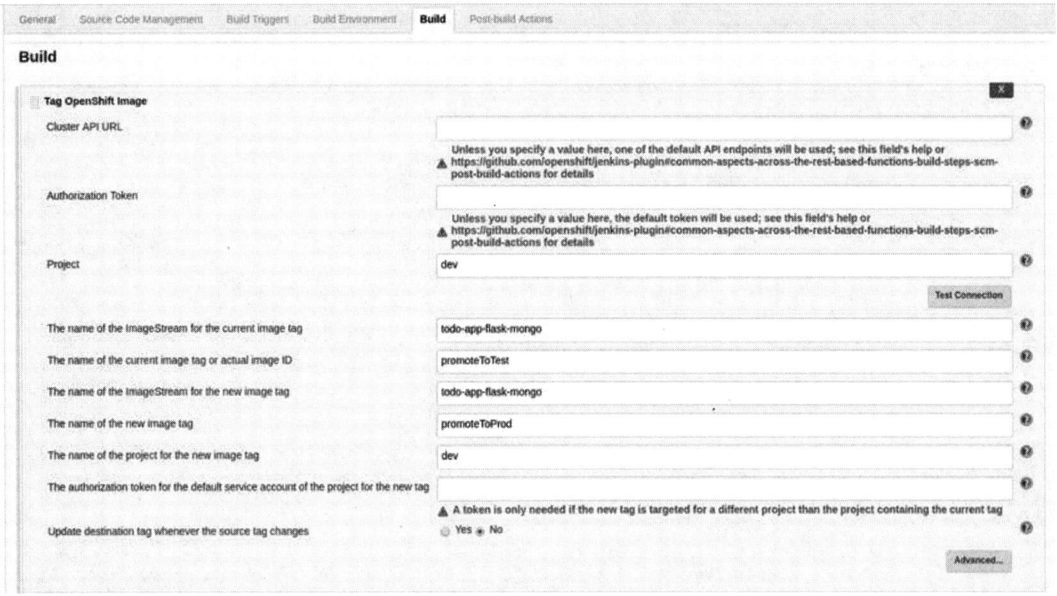

Figure 6.13   Jenkins tagging an image for prod

> **TIP** You can find more about how to trigger Jenkins jobs remotely on the Jenkins wiki at http://mng.bz/4aI6.

6.6.1 *Triggering Jenkins from Gogs*

Earlier in the chapter, you spun up a development environment from a template that included Gogs as the Git source repository. New code commits in Gogs configured an OpenShift build in the dev project. Because you've configured Jenkins as the backbone of your CI/CD, it makes sense to reconfigure Gogs to kick off the pipeline through Jenkins. This will automate the entire pipeline process, not just a single build.

First, configure the Dev Build job to allow remote triggers:

1 In the console, click Dev Build Job > Configure > Build Triggers.
2 Toggle the Trigger Builds Remotely check box, and add an authentication token with the value `cicdtrigger=oia`, as shown in figure 6.14.
3 Click Save.

Now, navigate to the Gogs web interface using the route created in your dev project. Log in, and then follow these steps:

1 Click the the openshift-cicd-flask-mongo repository, and choose Setting > Webhooks.
2 Delete the previous webhook, which was automatically installed for you.
3 Click Add Webhook and Gogs.
4 Configure a new webhook, as shown in figure 6.15. Be sure to update the URL to the correct URL of your Jenkins route.
5 Choose Update Webhook > Test Delivery to trigger a new complete pipeline build.

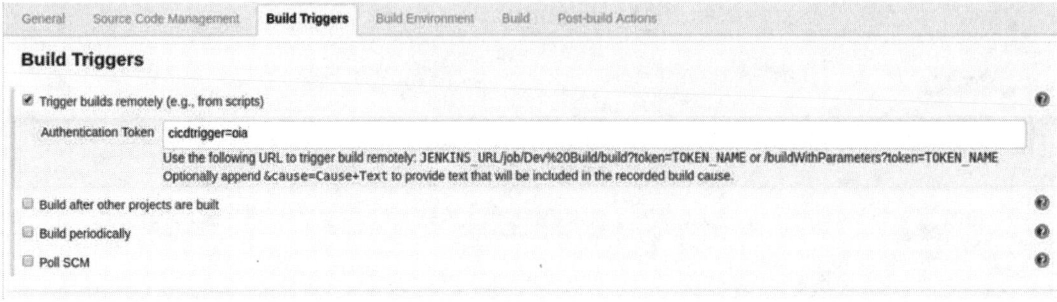

General   Source Code Management   **Build Triggers**   Build Environment   Build   Post-build Actions

Build Triggers

☑ Trigger builds remotely (e.g., from scripts)   ❷

   Authentication Token | cicdtrigger=oia |

   Use the following URL to trigger build remotely: JENKINS_URL/job/Dev%20Build/build?token=TOKEN_NAME or /buildWithParameters?token=TOKEN_NAME
   Optionally append &cause=Cause+Text to provide text that will be included in the recorded build cause.

☐ Build after other projects are built   ❷
☐ Build periodically   ❷
☐ Poll SCM   ❷

Figure 6.14   Allowing a Jenkins job to be triggered remotely

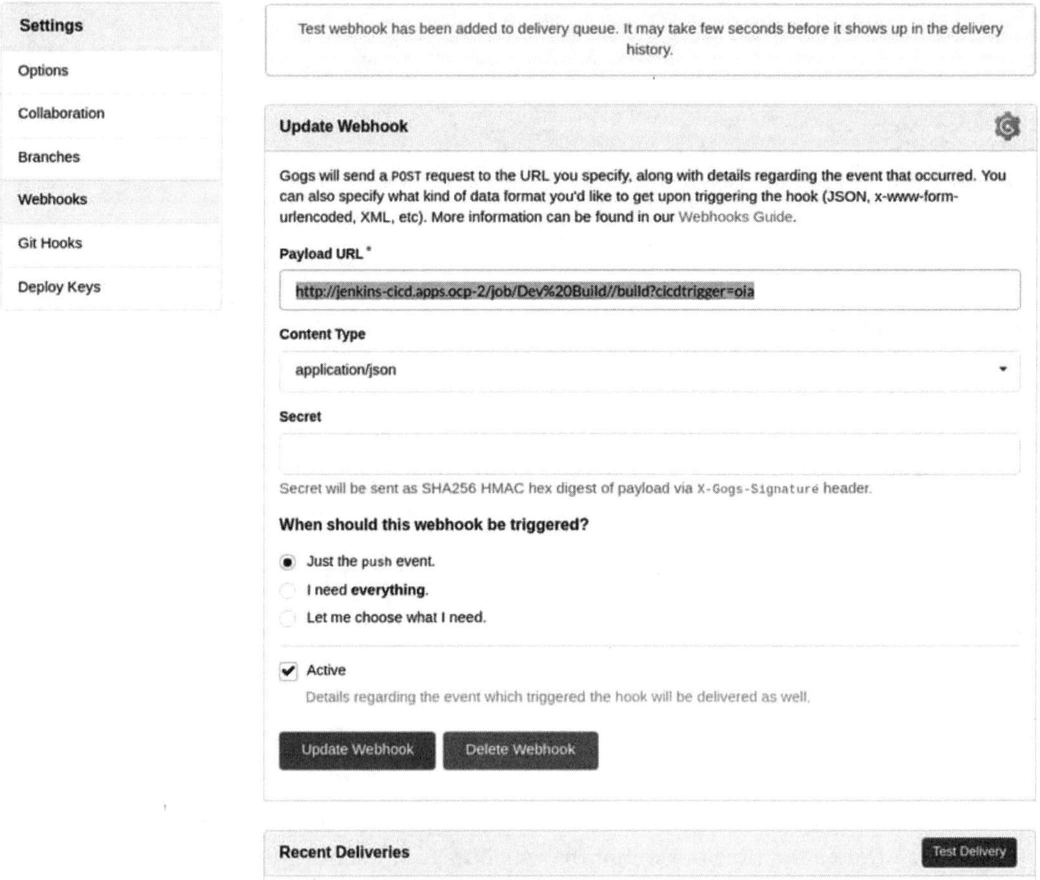

Settings	Test webhook has been added to delivery queue. It may take few seconds before it shows up in the delivery history.
Options	
Collaboration	**Update Webhook** ⚙
Branches	
Webhooks	Gogs will send a POST request to the URL you specify, along with details regarding the event that occurred. You can also specify what kind of data format you'd like to get upon triggering the hook (JSON, x-www-form-urlencoded, XML, etc). More information can be found in our Webhooks Guide.
Git Hooks	**Payload URL** *
Deploy Keys	http://jenkins-cicd.apps.ocp-2/job/Dev%20Build//build?cicdtrigger=oia

Content Type

| application/json   ▾ |

Secret

| |

Secret will be sent as SHA256 HMAC hex digest of payload via X-Gogs-Signature header.

When should this webhook be triggered?

⦿ Just the push event.
◯ I need **everything**.
◯ Let me choose what I need.

☑ Active
   Details regarding the event which triggered the hook will be delivered as well.

[Update Webhook]   [Delete Webhook]

Recent Deliveries   [Test Delivery]

Figure 6.15   Configuring Gogs to trigger a Jenkins job

TIP The username/password credentials for Gogs are *gogs* and *password*, respectively.

You now have a fully automated end-to-end CI/CD pipeline with Jenkins!

6.6.2 *Native integration with a Jenkinsfile*

OpenShift integration with Jenkins has one last important piece of functionality in addition to the plethora of available plugins, single-sign-on capability using OpenShift credentials, and S2I capability: it can natively integrate with Jenkins pipelines. This scriptable approach to building a pipeline allows Jenkins to run truly customizable workflows by using a special file for scripting called a *Jenkinsfile*. Users can create a pipeline with a script that OpenShift extends by providing many OpenShift-specific functions that can be called. This approach is popular in the CI/CD community.

TIP For a list of OpenShift functions that can be called in the Jenkinsfile, check out the documentation at http://mng.bz/7L8Y.

The result of the script is a full pipeline. In OpenShift, this pipeline can be built using a build config for Jenkins. In the OpenShift console, the pipeline can be executed and monitored, providing a deep integration for Jenkins in OpenShift. The Jenkins template that you deployed earlier comes with an example called oia-pipeline, which you likely noticed as the fourth Jenkins job in the browser. This Jenkins job calls the OpenShift Jenkinsfile function to automate the CI/CD pipeline the same way, but it provides several benefits:

- The pipeline can be executed from the OpenShift console.
- The pipeline can be monitored from the OpenShift console.
- The duration of each stage in the job is shown, to allow for better visibility.
- The script is easily extensible.

Let's kick off the oia-pipeline build from the OpenShift console. Navigate to the cicd project in the OpenShift console and, in the Builds panel, choose Pipelines > Start Pipeline. The pipeline includes a manual step before the application is built and promoted to production. You'll see output similar to figure 6.16, indicating a successful CI/CD pipeline in OpenShift through integration with Jenkinsfile builds!

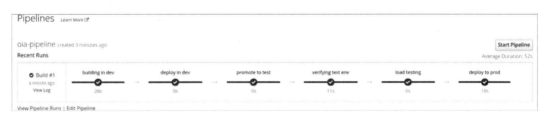

Figure 6.16 Viewing a Jenkins pipeline build in the OpenShift console

6.7   *Deployment strategies*

So far in this chapter, you've learned how to build a container image and automate the promotion of that image across different environments using native OpenShift automation in addition to Jenkins integration. But we haven't discussed the exact sequence for how the new version of the application is rolled out. The way you update your application in OpenShift is called a *deployment strategy*; it's a critical component of supporting a wide variety of applications in the platform. OpenShift supports several deployment strategies, including the following:

- *Rolling*—The default strategy. When pods consisting of the new image become ready by passing their readiness checks, they slowly replace the old images, one by one. Setting this deployment strategy is done in the deployment configuration object.
- *Re-create*—Scales down to zero pods consisting of the old image, and then begins to deploy the new pods. This strategy has the cost of a brief downtime while waiting for the new pods to be spun up. Similar to rolling, in order to use this strategy it must be set in the deployment configuration object.
- *Blue/Green*—Focuses on reducing risk by standing up the pods consisting of new images while the pods with the old images remain running. This allows the user to test their code in a production environment. When the code has been fully tested, all new requests are sent to the new deployment. OpenShift implements this strategy using routes.
- *Canary*—Adds checkpoints to the blue/green strategy by rolling out a fraction of the new images at a time and stopping. The user can test the application adequately before rolling out more pods. As with blue/green deployments, this strategy is implemented using OpenShift routes.
- *Dark launches*—Rolls out new code but doesn't make it available to users. By testing how the new code works in production, the user can then later enable the features when its determined to be safe. This strategy has been made popular at places like Facebook and Google. To accomplish dark launches, the application code must have checks for certain environment variables that are used to enable or disable new features. In OpenShift, you can take advantage of that code by toggling the new features on or off by setting the appropriate environment variables for the application deployment.

> **TIP** OpenShift also includes a way to provide custom deployment strategies. Although seldom used, it's a powerful way to extend the platform. You can find more information at http://mng.bz/SPEt.

There are many considerations for choosing a deployment strategy. The rolling strategy upgrades your application the most quickly while avoiding downtime, but it runs your old code side-by-side with your new code. For many stateful applications, such as clustered applications and databases, this can be problematic. For example, imagine that your new deployment has any of the following characteristics:

- It's rolling out a new database schema.
- It uses clustering to dynamically discover other pods (chapter 8 covers clustering and other stateful-applications in greater detail).
- It has a long-running transaction.
- It shares persistent storage among all the pods in the deployment.

In these cases, it makes sense to use a re-create strategy instead of a rolling upgrade. Databases almost always use the re-create strategy.

You can check the strategy for the MongoDB pod and the ToDo application pod in your deployments by running the following command:

```
echo $(oc get dc todo-app-flask-mongo -o=jsonpath='{.spec.strategy.type}'
⮕ -n dev)
Rolling
```

You can check the strategy for the mongodb deployment the same way:

```
$ echo $(oc get dc mongodb -o=jsonpath='{.spec.strategy.type}' -n dev)
Recreate
```

As expected, a stateless Python application is a good fit for a rolling upgrade, whereas MongoDB makes more sense to run using the re-create strategy. Both the rolling and re-create strategies have extensible options, including various parameters to determine the timing of the rollouts; they also provide *lifecycle hooks,* which allow code to be injected during the deployment process.

TIP You can learn more about lifecycle hooks at http://mng.bz/b351.

Many users also choose to add blue/green- and canary-style deployment strategies by combining the power of OpenShift routes with a rolling or re-create deployment strategy. For applications using rolling deployment, adding a blue/green- or canary-style deployment allows the OpenShift user to reduce risk by providing a more controlled rollout using checkpoints. For applications using the re-create deployment strategy, adding blue/green or canary features lets the application avoid downtime.

Both blue/green and canary deployments use OpenShift routes to manage traffic across multiple services. To implement these deployment strategies, an entire copy of the application is created with the new code. This copy includes the API objects to run the application: the deployment, service, replication controller, pods, and so on. When adequate testing has been performed on the new code, the OpenShift route is patched to point to the service containing the new code. A blue/green deployment has the added benefit of testing code in production—and because the old code is still running, the application can be rolled back to the old code if something breaks. One downside to using blue/green deployments is that they require more infrastructure, because your application needs double the resources while both versions of the code are running. A canary deployment is similar to a blue/green deployment except that whereas blue/green switches the route between services all at once, canary uses weights to determine what percentage of traffic should go to the new and old service. You can modify the weights for the rollout using the OpenShift CLI or console.

TIP You can read a good example of both blue/green and canary deployments in "Colorful Deployments: An Introduction to Blue-green, Canary, and Rolling Deployments" (Maciej Szulik, *Opensource.com*, May 2, 2017, http://mng.bz/64a9).

Cleaning up your projects

This chapter creates four new projects and many new pods. Depending on your environment, you may run out of CPU or memory going forward. If so, you can remove these projects through the command line by running the following commands:

```
$ oc delete project dev
project "dev" deleted
$ oc delete project test
project "test" deleted
$ oc delete project prod
project "prod" deleted
$ oc delete project cicd
project "cicd" deleted
```

6.8 Summary

- Image streams enable automation and consistency for container images.
- You can use OpenShift triggers for event-based image builds and deploys.
- You can use DNS for service discovery.
- You can use environment variables for service discovery if dependencies are installed first.
- Image tagging automates the promotion of images between environments.
- Secrets mask sensitive data that needs to be decoupled from an image.
- Config maps provide startup arguments, environment variables, or files mounted in an image.
- OpenShift provides a Jenkins source-to-image capability, which builds Jenkins with custom jobs and other artifacts.
- OpenShift provides a Jenkins instance with many useful plugins preinstalled.
- Jenkinsfile pipelines can be executed and monitored from the OpenShift console.
- OpenShift supports many types of deployment strategies for a wide variety of applications.

Part 3

Stateful applications

Part 2 of the book focused on how cloud-native applications work in Open-Shift. Part 3 covers more traditional applications that need stateful storage.

In chapter 7, you'll set up an external NFS server and use it to provide persistent storage volumes to OpenShift. You'll then take that persistent storage and attach volumes that have already been deployed in OpenShift.

Chapter 8 focuses on how stateful applications work in OpenShift. We'll go through examples using applications that require session persistence and specific startup and shutdown sequences.

Creating and managing persistent storage

This chapter covers

- Using the system:admin user to administer your cluster
- Attaching persistent storage to applications
- Making remote storage available in containers
- Removing persistent storage from applications
- Cleaning up persistent storage volumes

We haven't discussed what your first application deployed in OpenShift does. We noted that the application you deployed using the image-uploader source code was written in PHP. Here are a few additional application features:

- Uploads images from your workstation
- Shows you those images as thumbnails on the application page
- Verifies that what you're uploading is a standard image format
- Shows you the full-size image when you click it

It's not the next Instagram, but it's simple enough to live in a couple of files of source code and be easy to edit and manipulate in OpenShift. You'll use that simplicity to your advantage in this chapter.

If you haven't already, go ahead and test out the Image Uploader app, and upload an image or two (or three or four or more!) into the app-cli deployment. After you do, your application should look similar to figure 7.1. For the examples, I uploaded a meme, a picture of my super-cute daughter, and a photo of Dan Walsh.

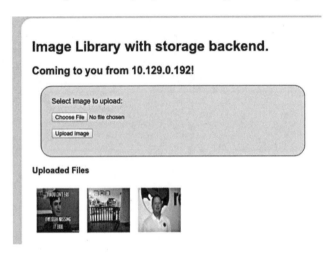

Figure 7.1   Image Uploader after a few pictures have been uploaded. I (Jamie) uploaded a meme, a picture of my daughter, and a photo of Dan Walsh.

Who is Dan Walsh?

Dan is a consulting engineer at Red Hat who joined the company in 2001. Since 2013, Dan has been the lead engineer for Red Hat's container engineering teams. He's also the lead engineer for most of the development around SELinux.

In addition to being a pretty smart guy and a key voice in how containers are changing IT, he's funny, massively sarcastic, and a bit of a hero to both authors. You can find Dan on Twitter at @rhatdan.

When you deploy an application in OpenShift, you can specify the minimum number of replicas (instances of the application) to keep running at all times. If you don't specify a number (you didn't for app-gui or app-cli), OpenShift will always keep one instance of your application running at all times. We initially discussed this in chapter three, and used the feature in chapters four, five, and six. None of these application replicas had persistent storage. If one of the application pods was deleted or scaled down, any data it had written would be gone as well. Let's test this out.

7.1   *Container storage is ephemeral*

After logging in to your OpenShift cluster from the command line with the `oc` command-line tool, you can use the `oc get pods` command to get a list of all of your running pods:

```
$ oc login -u dev -p dev https://ocp-1.192.168.122.100.nip.io:8443
Login successful.

You have one project on this server: "image-uploader"

Using project "image-uploader".
$ oc get pods
NAME              READY     STATUS       RESTARTS   AGE
app-cli-1-2162x   1/1       Running      1          23h
app-cli-1-build   0/1       Completed    0          23h
app-gui-1-build   0/1       Completed    0          23h
app-gui-1-gk5j4   1/1       Running      1          23h
```

Logging in to OpenShift successfully from the command line

The app-cli application container

The app-gui application container

The output shows the app-cli and app-gui application containers. It also lists the completed pods created by the build config and used to create the custom image for each deployment. The pod for the app-cli application is app-cli-1-2162x.

Let's put this idea to the test. You can use the `oc delete pod` command to delete the app-cli pod. To do so, use the command followed by the name of the pod you want to delete:

```
$ oc delete pod app-cli-1-2162x
pod "app-cli-1-2162x" deleted
```

After deleting the pod, check back using the `oc get pods` command. Here you can see that OpenShift created a new pod with a new name for app-cli almost immediately:

```
$ oc get pods
NAME              READY     STATUS       RESTARTS   AGE
app-cli-1-build   0/1       Completed    0          1d
app-cli-1-d2mcd   1/1       Running      0          11s
app-gui-1-build   0/1       Completed    0          1d
app-gui-1-gk5j4   1/1       Running      1          1d
```

Newly created app-cli pod, which has been up for 11 seconds according to the AGE data column

As we mentioned earlier in this chapter, OpenShift always makes sure the desired number of copies of your application are running. When you delete a pod, OpenShift detects that the desired state (one pod running at all times) isn't being met, so it creates a pod using the application image created when you deployed app-cli. In this case, the AGE field indicates that the pod had already been up and running for 11 seconds by the time the `oc get pods` command was run again.

This would seem to be the answer to just about everything, wouldn't it? Applications automatically restart themselves when they go down. But before we close up shop, take another look at your app-cli application's web page.

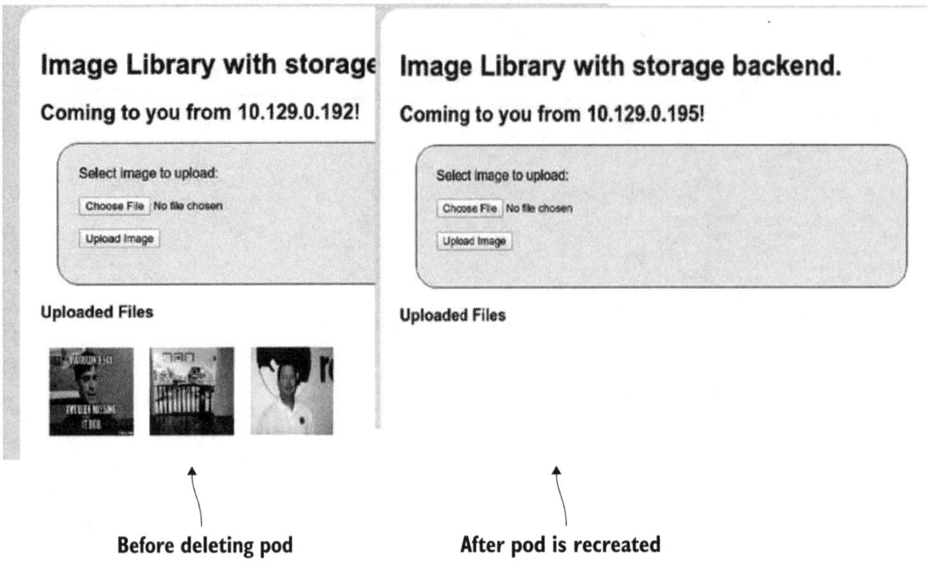

Figure 7.2   After app-cli was automatically redeployed by OpenShift, the isolated storage for the new container didn't include the uploaded images from the previous deployment, because containers don't have persistent storage by default.

In figure 7.2, you can see that the images uploaded earlier are nowhere to be found. When a pod is deployed in OpenShift, the storage that's used for the filesystem is ephemeral: it doesn't carry over from one instance of the application to the next. When applications need to be more permanent, you need to set up *persistent storage* for use in OpenShift.

7.2   *Handling permanent data requirements*

In OpenShift, persistent storage is available for data that needs to be shared with other pods or needs to persist past the lifetime of any particular pod. Creating such permanent storage in pods is handled by persistent volumes (PVs). PVs in OpenShift use industry standard network-based storage solutions to manage persistent data. OpenShift can use a long list of storage solutions to create PVs, including the following:

- Network File System (NFS)
- HostPath (local directories on the OpenShift nodes)
- Gluster
- Ceph RBD
- OpenStack Cinder
- AWS Elastic Block Storage (EBS)
- Google Cloud Platform (GCP) Persistent Disk
- iSCSI
- Fibre Channel
- Azure Disk
- Azure File

In the next section, you'll configure a PV in OpenShift using NFS.

7.3   *Creating a persistent volume*

PVs in OpenShift rely on one of the listed types of network storage to make the storage available across all nodes in a cluster. For the examples in the next few chapters, you'll use a PV built with NFS storage. Appendix B takes you through setting up and exporting an NFS volume on your OpenShift master. It also offers up pointers if you prefer to use a different NFS server. If you haven't already, go ahead and walk through that now.

As we discussed early in chapter 2, your OpenShift cluster is currently configured to allow any user to log in to the system, as long as their password isn't empty. Each new username is added to a local database at first login. You created a user named dev and used that user to create a project and deploy the app-cli and app-gui versions of the Image Uploader application. The dev user can create projects and deploy applications, but it doesn't have the proper permissions to make cluster-wide changes like attaching a PV. We'll take a much deeper look at how users are managed in OpenShift in chapter 9, but to create a PV, you need administrator-level access to your OpenShift cluster.

7.3.1   *Logging in as the admin user*

When an OpenShift cluster is installed, it creates a configuration file for a special user named *system:admin* on the master server. The system:admin user is authenticated using a specific SSL certificate, regardless of the authentication provider that's configured. System:admin has full administrative privileges on an OpenShift cluster. The key and certificate for system:admin are placed in a Kubernetes configuration file when the OpenShift cluster is installed; this makes it easier to run commands as system:admin. To run commands as system:admin, you need to copy this configuration file to the local system where you've been running `oc` commands.

COPYING THE ADMIN USER CONFIGURATION

The configuration file for system:admin is created on the master server at /etc/ origin/master/admin.kubeconfig. You can copy this file into your home directory on your workstation; this process will vary slightly depending on your workstation's operating system. Your admin.kubeconfig file should look similar to the example in the following listing.

> **Listing 7.1   Example admin.kubeconfig file (certificate and key fields trimmed)**

```
apiVersion: v1
clusters:
- cluster:
    certificate-authority-data:
    LS0tLS1CRUdJTiBDRVJUSUZJQ0FURS0tL...
    server: https://ocp-1.192.168.122.100.nip.io:8443
  name: ocp-1-192-168-122-100-nip-io:8443
contexts:
- context:
    cluster: ocp-1-192-168-122-100-nip-io:8443
    namespace: default
    user: system:admin/ocp-1-192-168-122-100-nip-io:8443
  name: default/ocp-1-192-168-122-100-nip-io:8443/system:admin
```

```
current-context: default/ocp-1-192-168-122-100-nip-io:8443/system:admin
kind: Config
preferences: {}
users:
- name: system:admin/ocp-1-192-168-122-100-nip-io:8443
  user:
    client-certificate-data:
    LS0tLS1CRUdJTiBDRVJUSUZJQ0FURS0tL...
    client-key-data: LS0tLS1CRUdJTiBSU0EgUFJJVkFURSBLR...
```

The system:admin user is a special user account in OpenShift. Instead of relying on the configured identity provider, it uses a TLS certificate for authentication. This certificate was generated when you deployed your cluster. The certificate and user information are stored in /etc/origin/master/admin.kubeconfig—that's why copying this file to your workstation allows you to run administrator-level commands on your OpenShift cluster. The root user on your master server also has this configuration file as its default OpenShift setup, which means any user who has root access to your master server can administer your entire OpenShift cluster.

After you've copied admin.kubeconfig to your workstation, you can use it with the oc command to create a PV, as we'll discuss in the next section.

7.3.2 *Creating new resources from the command line*

OpenShift makes extensive use of configuration files written in *YAML* format. YAML is a human-readable language that's often used for configuration files and to serialize data in a way that's easy for both humans and computers to consume. YAML is the default way to push data into and get data out of OpenShift.

> **NOTE** If you'd like to dig a little deeper into what YAML is and how it works, a great place to start is www.yaml.org/start.html.

In chapter 2, we talked about the OpenShift resources that are created when an application is built and deployed. These resources have documented, YAML-formatted templates so you can create and manage the resources easily. In later chapters, you'll use several of these templates to create or change resources in OpenShift. For the application deployments you created in chapter 2, these templates were automatically generated and stored in the OpenShift database when you ran the oc new-app command.

In this chapter, you'll use a template to create a PV. To make this a little easier, we've created an organization on GitHub with repositories for each chapter: https://github.com/OpenShiftInAction. You can download the chapter 7 repository from https://github.com/OpenShiftInAction/chapter7; other chapters have similar names. If you haven't already, clone this repository on to your workstation. It contains ready-made templates that you can use for the rest of the examples in this chapter.

> **NOTE** The source code that you used to create the Image Uploader application is also in this GitHub organization, at https://github.com/OpenShiftInAction/image-uploader. In addition, it's posted on the book's website at www.manning.com/books/openshift-in-action.

The template to create your first PV is detailed in listing 7.2. It contains several key pieces of information about the PV you'll create with it, including the following:

- The type of resource the template will create. Different resources have different template configurations. In this case, you're creating a PV.
- A name for the resource to be created. This example is pv01. In the next section, you'll create pv01 through pv05.
- Storage capacity for the PV that will be created, measured in GB in this example. Each of the PVs you create in this chapter will be 2 GB.
- Access mode for the PV that will be created.
- NFS path for this PV.
- NFS server for this PV. If you used another IP address for your master, or used another server, you'll need to edit this value.
- Recycle policy for the PV that will be created. These policies dictate how data will be disposed of once it's no longer being used by an application. We'll discuss this in the next section.

Listing 7.2 Template to create a PV using the NFS volume created in appendix B

```
apiVersion: v1
kind: PersistentVolume        <--- Type of resource template
metadata:
  name: pv01                  <--- Name of the PV
spec:
  capacity:
    storage: 2Gi              <--- Capacity for this PV
  accessModes:
  - ReadWriteMany
  nfs:                                   Mount path for the NFS
    path: /var/nfs-data/pv01   <---      volume on the NFS server
    server: 192.168.122.100
  persistentVolumeReclaimPolicy: Recycle   <--- Volume reclaim policy
```

Access mode for the PV → accessModes

NFS server address → server: 192.168.122.100

In the next section, you'll create several PVs using the NFS volumes that you created in appendix B.

7.3.3 Creating a physical volume

To create a resource from a YAML template, use the `oc create` command along with the `-f` parameter, which specifies the template file you want to process. To create the PV for this example, you'll use the template named pv01.yaml, which is in the chapter7 repository you cloned onto your workstation earlier in this chapter.

> **NOTE** Creating PVs is one of the few tasks that isn't available in the current OpenShift web interface. To create and manage PVs, the command line is the place to start.

Because PVs are cluster-wide resources, you can also use the `--config` parameter to specify the admin.kubeconfig file that you copied from your master server earlier. You can put all of this together by running the following command:

```
$ oc --config ~/admin.kubeconfig create -f pv01.yaml
persistentvolume "pv01" created
```

In appendix B, you created five NFS exports. Each of these will be mapped to a PV; there are templates for these additional PVs in the chapter7 repository.

To create the other PVs, you can repeat the previous step for each pvX.yaml file in the repository. Or you can run them all as a quick Linux one-liner like the following:

```
for i in $(seq 2 5);do oc --config ~/admin.kubeconfig create -f pv0$i.yaml;done
```

You can confirm that the parameters from your template were correctly interpreted by running the `oc get pv` command using the admin.kubeconfig configuration to get information about all active PVs:

```
$ oc --config ~/admin.kubeconfig get pv
NAME   CAPACITY ACCESSMODES RECLAIMPOLICY   STATUS     CLAIM  REASON  AGE
pv01   2Gi      RWX         Recycle         Available                 15s
pv02   2Gi      RWX         Recycle         Available                 9s
pv03   2Gi      RWX         Recycle         Available                 8s
pv04   2Gi      RWX         Recycle         Available                 8s
pv05   2Gi      RWX         Recycle         Available                 8s
```

Next, let's look at some of those parameters, to help better understand their options and benefits.

DECIDING ON A STORAGE ACCESS MODE

Each PV's template specifies an *access mode*. An access mode for a PV describes how it can be used by other OpenShift resources. There are three options for the access mode:

- *Read/Write once (RWO)*—This volume can be mounted as read/write by a single node in the OpenShift cluster. This is useful when you have workloads where a single application pod will be writing data. An example is a relational database, when you know that all the writes to the persistent data will come from a single pod.
- *Read-only many (ROX)*—Volumes with this access mode can be mounted as read-only by multiple OpenShift nodes. An example of where this type of access mode is useful is when a horizontally scalable web application needs access to the same static content, such as images.
- *Read/Write many (RWX)*—The RWX access mode is the option you'll use for the PV in this chapter. It allows multiple nodes to mount this volume, read from it, and write to it. The Image Uploader application is a good example. When you scale up the Image Uploader application in the next chapter, multiple nodes will need to be able to read and write to the persistent storage you're about to create.

Currently, only GlusterFS and NFS support the RWX access mode.

SELECTING A RECLAIM POLICY

A *reclaim policy* dictates how a PV handles reclaiming space after a storage claim on the PV is no longer required. Two options are available:

- *Retain*—With this reclaim policy, all data is retained in the PV. Reclaiming space is a manual process.
- *Recycle*—This reclaim policy automatically removes data when the claim is deleted. You'll use this option for the PV created in this chapter. This policy is available only for NFS and HostPath PVs.

> **TIP** In OpenShift 3.7 and above, the recycler for NFS has been deprecated in favor of dynamic provisioners. More information about using dynamic provisioners to create storage on demand is available at https://docs.openshift.org/latest/install_config/persistent_storage/dynamically_provisioning_pvs.html.

You've now created persistent storage that can be used with your applications in OpenShift. In the next section, you'll configure your applications to take advantage of this storage.

7.4 *Using persistent storage*

Now that you have PVs configured, it's time to take advantage of them. In OpenShift, applications consume persistent storage using *persistent volume claims* (PVCs). A PVC can be added into an application as a volume using the command line or through the web interface. Let's create a PVC on the command line and add it to an application.

How persistent volume claims match up with persistent volumes

First, you need to know how PVs and PVCs match up to each other. In OpenShift, PVs represent the available storage. PVCs represent an application's need for that storage.

When you create a PVC, OpenShift looks for the best fit among the available PVs and reserves it for use by the PVC. In the example environment, matches are based on two criteria:

- *PV size vs. PVC need*—OpenShift tries to take best advantage of available resources. When a PVC is created, it reserves the smallest PV available that satisfies its need.
- *Access mode*—When a PVC is created, OpenShift looks for an available PV with at least the level of access required. If an exact match isn't available, it reserves a PV with more privileges that still satisfies the requirements. For example, if a PVC is looking for a PV with an RWO access mode (read/write once), it will use a PV with an RWX (read/write many) access mode if one is available.

Because all the PVs in your environment are the same size, matching them to PVCs will be straightforward. Next, you'll create a PVC for your application to use.

7.4.1   *Creating a persistent volume claim using the command line*

Listing 7.3 shows an example PVC template, which you can find in the chapter7 repository on GitHub. The file is named pvc-app-cli.yaml. Some of the important template parameters include the following:

- The name of the PVC to be created.
- The access mode for the PVC. In this example, the PVCs will request the RWX access mode. This aligns with the PVs you created earlier in this chapter.
- The size of the storage request. This example creates a 2 GB storage request, which matches the size of the PVs that you created in the previous section.

Listing 7.3   Example PVC template from the chapter7 repository on GitHub

```
apiVersion: v1
kind: PersistentVolumeClaim
metadata:
  name: app-cli          ◁── Name of the PVC
spec:
  accessModes:
    - ReadWriteMany         ◁── Access mode for the PVC
  resources:
    requests:
      storage: 2Gi      ◁── Requested storage size
```

To create a PVC on the command line, you use the same `oc create` command syntax that you used to create a PV:

```
$ oc create -f pvc-app-cli.yaml
persistentvolumeclaim "app-cli" created
```

Note that this example doesn't use the system:admin user to create the PVC. By default, any user can create a PVC in their project. The one rule to remember is that a PVC needs to be created in the same project as the project for which it will provide storage.

When the PVC is created, it queries OpenShift to get all the available PVs. It uses the criteria described to find the best match and then reserves that PV. Once that's done, it can take a minute or so, depending on the size of your cluster, for the PVC to become available to be used in an application as persistent storage.

The following command shows how you can use `oc` to provide information about all the active PVCs in an OpenShift project:

```
$ oc get pvc
NAME      STATUS    VOLUME    CAPACITY    ACCESSMODES    AGE
app-cli   Bound     pv05      2Gi         RWX            1h
```

A PVC represents reserved storage available to the applications in your project. But it isn't yet mounted into an active application. To accomplish that, you need to mount your newly created PVC into an application as a volume.

7.4.2 *Adding a volume to an application on the command line*

In OpenShift, a *volume* is any filesystem, file, or data mounted into an application's pods to provide persistent data. In this chapter, we're concerned with persistent storage volumes. Volumes also are used to provide encrypted data, application configurations, and other types of data, as you saw in chapter 6.

To add a volume, you use the `oc volume` command. The following example takes the newly created PVC and adds it into the app-cli application (the command is broken into multiple lines to make it a little easier to understand, and to fit on the page):

```
$ oc volume dc/app-cli --add \
--type=persistentVolumeClaim \
--claim-name=app-cli \
--mount-path=/opt/app-root/src/uploads
info: Generated volume name: volume-14dz0        ◄──┐  The volume name
deploymentconfig "app-cli" updated                     was automatically
                                                       created.
```

By applying the volume to the deployment config for app-cli, you can trigger a redeployment of the application automatically to incorporate the new PV. The following parameters are required:

- dc—The deployment config, in this case app-cli
- --add—Tells `oc` that you want to add a new component
- --type—The type of component you want to add, in this case a `persistentVolumeClaim`
- --claim-name—The PVC to use as the mounted volume
- --mount-path—The mount point in the pod

Optionally, you can also specify a name for the volume with the `--name` parameter. If this isn't set, OpenShift creates one dynamically.

Using the `oc describe dc/app-cli` command, you can confirm that this volume is mounted into your application:

```
$ oc describe dc/app-cli              Version of the currently active
Name:          app-cli                deployment. Attaching the volume
Namespace:     image-uploader         caused a new deployment to be
Created:       2 hours ago            created for the application.
Labels:          app=app-cli
Annotations:     openshift.io/generated-by=OpenShiftNewApp
Latest Version:    2                ◄─────────────
Selector:      app=app-cli,deploymentconfig=app-cli
Replicas:      1
Triggers:      Config, Image(app-cli@latest, auto=true)
Strategy:      Rolling
Template:
  Labels:      app=app-cli
        deploymentconfig=app-cli
  Annotations:     openshift.io/generated-by=OpenShiftNewApp
  Containers:
  app-cli:
```

```
Image:      172.30.52.103:5000/image-uploader/
↪ app-cli@sha256:f5ffe8c1...
Port:    8080/TCP
Volume Mounts:
   /opt/app-root/src/uploads from volume-14dz0 (rw)
Environment Variables:     <none>
Volumes:
 volume-14dz0:
   Type:     PersistentVolumeClaim (a reference to a PersistentVolumeClaim in
↪ the same namespace)
   ClaimName:    app-cli
   ReadOnly:    false
...
```

Volumes mounted into the application, including the newly mounted PVC

Because you created the PV and PVC to allow for multiple reads and writes by using the RWX access mode, when this application scales horizontally, each new pod will mount the same PVC and be able to read data from and write data to it. To sum up, you just modified your containerized application to provide horizontally scalable persistent storage.

In the next section, you'll create the same result using the OpenShift web interface. In the web interface, you'll focus on creating a PVC and associating it with an active application, because to create a PV you must use the command line.

7.4.3 *Adding persistent storage to an application using the web interface*

Creating PVCs and associating them as persistent volumes in applications is easy to do using the web interface.

CREATING A PERSISTENT VOLUME CLAIM WITH THE WEB INTERFACE

You don't need administrator-level privileges to create a PVC, so log in as your dev user, if you haven't already done so. Select the Image Uploader project when you log in, and you should see the Storage link in the left menu bar of the project overview page (see figure 7.3).

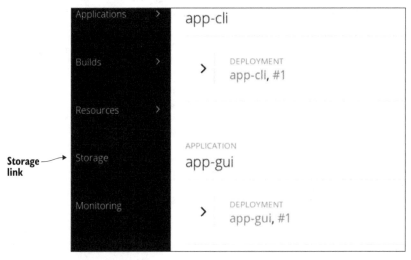

Figure 7.3   The Storage link to create PVCs in the web interface

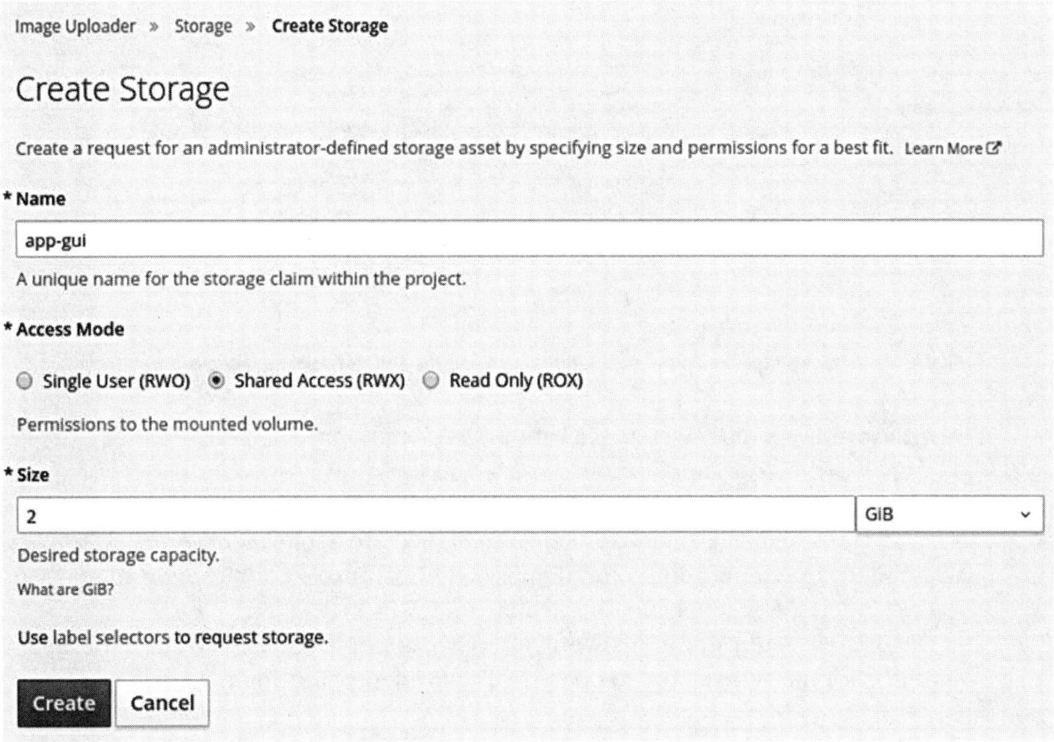

Image Uploader » Storage » **Create Storage**

Create Storage

Create a request for an administrator-defined storage asset by specifying size and permissions for a best fit. Learn More ☐

* Name

```
app-gui
```

A unique name for the storage claim within the project.

* Access Mode

○ Single User (RWO) ◉ Shared Access (RWX) ○ Read Only (ROX)

Permissions to the mounted volume.

* Size

```
2                                                              GiB        ⌄
```

Desired storage capacity.

What are GiB?

Use label selectors to request storage.

[**Create**] [Cancel]

Figure 7.4 Creating a PVC using the web interface

Click the link to go to the Storage page. You should see the PVC that you created on the command line, which is currently mounted as a PV in app-cli. On the right side of the page, click the Create Storage button to open the dialog shown in figure 7.4, where you can create a PVC.

The required parameters for the web interface are as follows:

- *Name*—The name for your PVC. For this example, use the name of your application, app-gui.
- *Access Mode*—Use the same RWX mode that you used to create the PVC for app-cli.
- *Size*—Use 2 GB, which is the same as all the PVs you created earlier in this chapter.

After you fill in the fields, click the Create button to return to the Storage page. Your new PVC is listed beside the one you created earlier (see figure 7.5).

This page also confirms the capacity, access mode, and PV that your PVC has reserved. In this example, our newly created app-gui PVC has bound itself to PV01. The next step is to attach this PVC to an application as a PV.

Persistent Volume Claims

Create Storage

Name	Status	Capacity	Access Modes	Age
app-gui	✔ Bound to volume **pv01**	2 GiB	RWX (Read-Write-Many)	18 hours
app-cli	✔ Bound to volume **pv05**	2 GiB	RWX (Read-Write-Many)	18 hours

Figure 7.5   The storage-overview page after you create the PVC for app-gui using the web interface

ATTACHING STORAGE TO AN APPLICATION WITH THE WEB INTERFACE

To attach a PVC to an application, you start on the project overview page. Just as you did at the command line, you need to add the PVC you created to your application as a PV. On the command line, you made a change to the deployment config for app-cli: this caused your application to be redeployed with your PVC attached in the pod. In the web interface, you need to do the same thing.

Figure 7.6 points out an easy way to access an application's current deployment config. Click the app-gui link to open the Deployments page for app-gui.

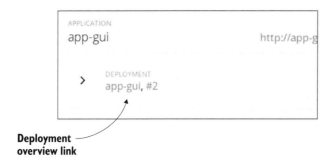

Deployment overview link

Figure 7.6   In the web interface, use the link to the deployment overview to edit your applications.

The Deployments page, a portion of which is shown in figure 7.7, lists all the deployments for the app-gui application. There's currently only the initial deployment from when you built the application. Adding the PVC as a volume to the application will trigger a new deployment for app-gui.

To add the volume, choose Actions > Add Storage to open the Add Storage wizard for app-gui. Using the wizard, you need to select the PVC that you want to use: in this case, the app-gui PVC. The only other field that's required for your mount to work is Mount Path. This will be the same as the mount path for the command-line example earlier in this chapter: you want to mount the PVC at /opt/app-root/src/uploads in your application (see figure 7.8).

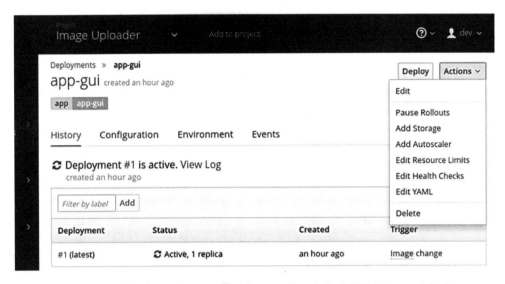

Figure 7.7 The app-gui Deployments page. There's currently only the initial deployment for the application. Adding the PVC as a PV will trigger a new deployment.

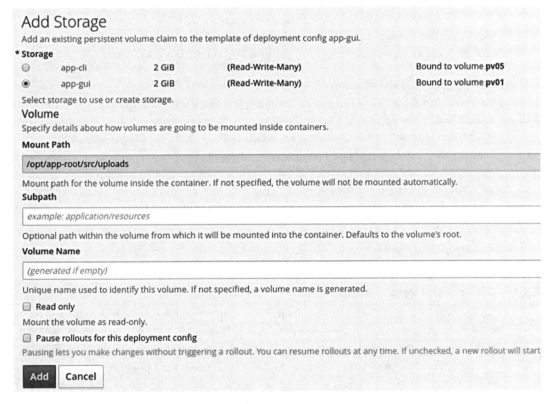

Figure 7.8 Adding a persistent volume to app-gui

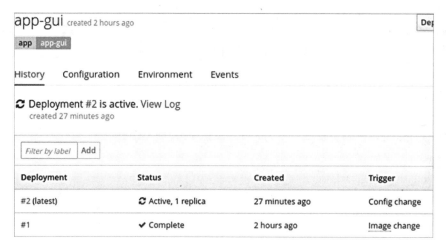

Figure 7.9   After adding a new PV, OpenShift redeploys the app-gui application to incorporate the persistent storage in the pod.

Once you've selected your storage and filled out the mount path, click the Create button to return to the Deployments page for app-gui. Figure 7.9 shows that OpenShift redeployed the application.

After a few seconds, the new version of app-gui should be functional and active, including the newly mounted persistent storage. With PVs up and active in both app-cli and app-gui, now is the time to test them and see what's happening.

7.5   *Testing applications after adding persistent storage*

First, the fun stuff. Because app-gui and app-cli are individual instances of the same Image Uploader application, they both have web pages that you can access through your browser. Each application has an active URL address that leads you to the application (see figure 7.10). For both app-gui and app-cli, browse to the web interfaces and upload a few pictures. These pictures are stored in the uploads directory in each application's pod. That means the pictures are stored on the two PVs you just configured. In my case, I uploaded pictures of container ship accidents into app-cli, and I uploaded pictures of my daughter into app-gui.

> **NOTE** To upload pictures with the Image Uploader program, use the Choose File button on the main page to select pictures from your workstation.

7.5.1   *Data doesn't get mixed up*

Notice that you don't see pictures in the wrong places after you upload them. That's because each application deployment is using its own NFS volume to store data. Each NFS volume is mounted into its application's mount namespace, as we talked about in chapter 3, so the application's data is always separated. It isn't possible for one application to inadvertently put data, or funny pictures, in the wrong place. The true test will come when you force OpenShift to create a new copy of your application's pod.

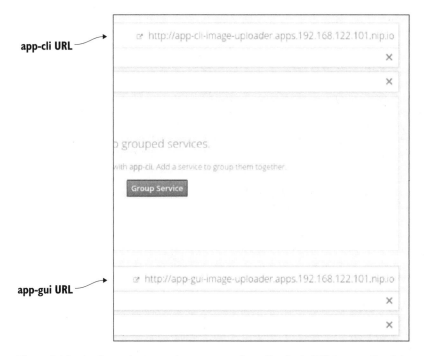

app-cli URL

app-gui URL

Figure 7.10　On the project overview page, each application's URL is an active link to the application.

7.5.2　*Forcing a pod restart*

At the beginning of the chapter, you deleted a pod and noticed that the uploaded pictures were lost when OpenShift automatically replaced the deleted pod. Go ahead and repeat the experiment, this time for both applications. Here's the process in action:

```
$ oc get pods
NAME                 READY     STATUS      RESTARTS    AGE
app-cli-1-build      0/1       Completed   0           1d
app-cli-2-1bwrd      1/1       Running     0           1d
app-gui-1-build      0/1       Completed   0           3h
app-gui-2-1kpn0      1/1       Running     0           1h

$ oc delete pod app-cli-2-1bwrd app-gui-2-1kpn0
pod "app-cli-2-1bwrd" deleted
pod "app-gui-2-1kpn0" deleted

$ oc get pods
NAME                 READY     STATUS      RESTARTS    AGE
app-cli-1-build      0/1       Completed   0           1d
app-cli-2-m2k7v      1/1       Running     0           34s
app-gui-1-build      0/1       Completed   0           3h
app-gui-2-27h64      1/1       Running     0           34s
```

After this, look at the app-gui and app-cli websites again. Are your pictures still there? Did they survive a pod deletion? Yes, they did! You've deployed persistent storage in multiple applications in OpenShift. What does that look like on the host running the containers? Let's take a look.

7.5.3   *Investigating persistent volume mounts*

Because you're using NFS server exports as the source for your PVs, it stands to reason that somewhere on the OpenShift node, those NFS volumes are mounted. You can see that this is the case by looking at the following example. SSH into the OpenShift node where the containers are running, run the `mount` command, and search for mounted volumes from the IP address of the NFS server. In my environment, the IP address of my OpenShift master server is 192.168.122.100:

```
$ mount | grep 192.168.122.100
192.168.122.100:/var/nfs-data/pv05 on /var/lib/origin/openshift.local.
➥ volumes/pods/b693b1ad-5496-11e7-a7ee-52540092ab8c/volumes/
➥ kubernetes.io~nfs/pv05 type nfs4 (rw,relatime,vers=4.0,rsize=524288,
➥ size=524288,namlen=255,hard,proto=tcp,port=0,timeo=600,retrans=2,sec=sys,
➥ clientaddr=192.168.122.101,local_lock=none,addr=192.168.122.100)
192.168.122.100:/var/nfs-data/pv01 on /var/lib/origin/openshift.local.
➥ volumes/pods/b69da9c5-5496-11e7-a7ee-52540092ab8c/volumes/
➥ kubernetes.io~nfs/pv01 type nfs4 (rw,relatime,vers=4.0,rsize=524288,
➥ wsize=524288,namlen=255,hard,proto=tcp,port=0,timeo=600,retrans=2,
➥ sec=sys, clientaddr=192.168.122.101,local_lock=none,addr=192.168.122.100)
```

You get two results, one for each pod for each application. Earlier in this chapter, you used the `oc get pv` command and confirmed that pv05 was being used by app-cli. But that doesn't explain how the NFS volume is made available in the app-cli container's mount namespace.

Chapter 3 looked at how the filesystem in a container is isolated from the rest of the application node using a mount namespace. The pv05 NFS mount isn't added to the app-cli mount namespace, though. Instead, the NFS mount is made available in the container using a technology called a *bind mount*.

A bind mount in Linux is a special type of mounted volume where part of a filesystem is mounted in a new, additional location. For app-cli, the NFS mount for pv05 is mounted using a bind mount at /opt/app-root/src/uploads in the container's mount namespace. Using a bind mount makes the content available simultaneously in two locations. A change in one location is automatically reflected in the other location (see figure 7.11).

NOTE   You can find more information about bind mounts in the mount manual pages at http://man7.org/linux/man-pages/man8/mount.8.html.

Bind mounts are used for volumes for two primary reasons. First, creating a bind mount on a Linux system is a lightweight operation in terms of CPU requirements. That means redeploying a new container to replace an old one doesn't involve remounting a remote volume. This keeps container-creation time low.

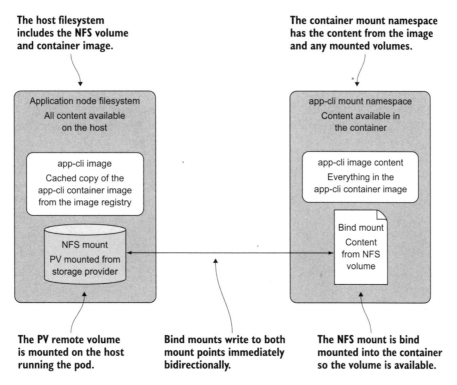

The host filesystem includes the NFS volume and container image.

The container mount namespace has the content from the image and any mounted volumes.

Application node filesystem
All content available on the host

app-cli image
Cached copy of the app-cli container image from the image registry

NFS mount
PV mounted from storage provider

app-cli mount namespace
Content available in the container

app-cli image content
Everything in the app-cli container image

Bind mount
Content from NFS volume

The PV remote volume is mounted on the host running the pod.

Bind mounts write to both mount points immediately bidirectionally.

The NFS mount is bind mounted into the container so the volume is available.

Figure 7.11 Volumes are bind mounted into the container from the host

Second, this approach separates concerns for persistent storage. Using bind mounts, the container definition doesn't have to include specific information about the remote volume. The container only needs to define the name of the volume to mount. OpenShift abstracts how to access the remote volume and make it available in containers. This separation of concerns between administration and usage of a cluster is a consistent OpenShift design feature.

The goal of this chapter was to walk you through configuring the components that make persistent storage work in OpenShift. In the following chapters, you'll use persistent storage to create more scalable and resilient applications.

7.6   *Summary*

- When an application pod is removed or dies, OpenShift automatically replaces it with a new instance of the application.
- OpenShift can use multiple network storage services, including NFS, to provide persistent storage for applications.
- When using persistent storage, applications in OpenShift can share data and provide data across upgrades, upgrades, and container replacement.
- OpenShift uses persistent volumes to represent available network storage volumes.

- Persistent volume claims are associated with a project and match criteria such as capacity needed and access mode to bind to and reserve a persistent volume.
- Persistent volume claims can be mounted into OpenShift applications as volumes, mounting the network storage into the container's filesystem in the desired location.
- OpenShift manages the persistent volume using the proper network storage protocol and uses bind mounts to present the remote volumes in application containers.

Stateful applications 8

This chapter covers

- Enabling a headless service
- Clustering applications
- Configuring sticky sessions
- Handling graceful shutdowns
- Working with stateful sets

In chapter 7, you created persistent storage for the Image Uploader pods, which allowed data to persist past the lifecycle of a single pod. When a pod failed, a new pod spun up in its place and mounted the existing persistent volume locally. Persistent storage in OpenShift allows many stateful applications to run in containers. Many other stateful applications still have requirements that are unsatisfied by persistent storage alone: for instance, many workloads distribute data through replication, which requires application-level clustering. In OpenShift, this type of data replication requires direct pod-to-pod networking without going through the service layer. It is also very common for stateful applications such as databases to have their own custom load balancing and discovery algorithms which require direct pod-to-pod access. Other common requirements for stateful applications include the ability to support sticky sessions as well as implement a predictable graceful shutdown.

147

One of the main goals of the OpenShift container platform is to be a world-class platform for stateless and stateful applications. In order to support stateful applications, a variety of tools are available to make virtually any application container-native. This chapter will walk you through the most popular tools, including headless services, sticky sessions, pod-discovery techniques, and stateful sets, just to name a few. At the end of the chapter, you'll walk through the power of the stateful set, which brings many stateful applications to life on OpenShift.

8.1 *Enabling a headless service*

A good example of application clustering in everyday life is demonstrated by Amazon's virtual shopping cart. Amazon customers browse for items and add them to a virtual shopping cart so they can potentially be purchased later. If an Amazon user is signed in to their account, their virtual shopping cart will be persisted permanently because the data is stored in a database. But for users who aren't signed in to an account, the shopping cart is temporary. The temporary cart is implemented as in-memory cache in Amazon's datacenter. By taking advantage of in-memory caching, end users get fast performance, which results in a better user experience. One downside of using in-memory caching is that if a server crashes, the data is lost. A common solution to this problem is data replication: when an application puts data in memory, that data can be replicated to many different caches, which results in fast performance and redundancy.

Before applications can replicate data among one another, they need a way to dynamically find each other. In chapter 6, this concept was covered through the use of service discovery, in which pods use an OpenShift service object. The OpenShift service object provides a stable IP and port that can be used to access one or more pods running the same workload. For most use cases, having a stable IP and port to access one or more replicated pods is all that's required. But many types of applications, such as those that replicate data, require the ability to find all the pods in a service and access each one directly on demand.

One working solution would be to use a single service object for each pod, giving the application a stable IP and port for each pod. Although this works nicely, it isn't ideal because it can generate many service objects, which can become difficult to manage. A better solution is to implement a *headless service* and discover the application pods using an application-specific discovery mechanism. A headless service is a service object that doesn't load-balance or proxy between backend pods. It's implemented by setting the `spec.clusterIP` field to `None` in the service API object.

Headless services are most often used for applications that need to access specific pods directly without going through the service proxy. Two common examples of headless services are clustered databases and applications that have client-side load-balancing logic built-in to the code. Later in this chapter, we'll explore an example of a headless service using MongoDB, a popular NoSQL database.

TIP One common traditional approach to discovery has been to use network broadcasting or multicasting, which is blocked by most public cloud providers such as Amazon Web Services (AWS) and Azure. OpenShift also blocks multicasting by default. Fortunately, OpenShift 3.6 and higher allow users to enable multicasting between pods. Because OpenShift tunnels this traffic over its software-defined network (SDN), this solution can also work on all public cloud providers. You can learn more at http://mng.bz/L33O.

8.1.1 Application clustering with WildFly

In this section, you'll deploy a classic example of application-level clustering in Open-Shift using WildFly, a popular application server for Java-based application runtimes. You'll be deploying new applications as part of this chapter, so create a new stateful-apps project as follows:

```
oc new-project stateful-apps
```

It's important to note that this new example uses *cookies* stored in your browser to track your session. Cookies are small pieces of data that servers ask your browser to hold to make your experience better. In this case, a cookie will be stored in your browser with a simple unique identifier: a randomly generated string called JSES-SIONID. When the user initially accesses the web application, the server will reply with a cookie containing the JSESSIONID field and a unique identifier as the value. Subsequent access to the application will use JSESSIONID to look up all information about the user's session, which is stored in a replication cache. It doesn't matter which pod is accessed—the user experience will be the same (see figure 8.1).

The WildFly application that you'll deploy will replicate the user data among all pods in its service. The application will track which user the request comes from by checking the JSESSIONID that's passed from the browser cookie. Because the user data will be replicated, the end user will have a consistent experience even if some pods die and new pods are accessed. Run the following command to install the Wild-Fly application template and see this in action:

```
oc create -f \
    https://raw.githubusercontent.com/OpenShiftInAction/chapter8/master/
➥ wildfly-template.yaml \
    -n stateful-apps
```

To process the template through the OpenShift console, navigate to the stateful-apps project. Click Add to Project, and enter wildfly-oia-s2i in the Service Catalog search box. Keep the default values, and click create to process the template.

The build may take up to a couple of minutes because it's pulling in a lot of dependencies. Watch for the pod to be running and ready before you proceed. When the pod is running and ready, choose Applications > Routes to see the route you just created. Click that route: you'll see the application shown in figure 8.2. If you don't see the application, go back and look at the pod logs to make sure the application is fully deployed.

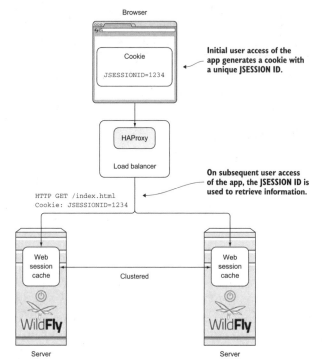

Browser

Cookie

JSESSIONID=1234

Initial user access of the
app generates a cookie with
a unique JSESSION ID.

HAProxy

Load balancer

On subsequent user access
of the app, the JSESSION ID is
used to retrieve information.

```
HTTP GET /index.html
Cookie: JSESSIONID=1234
```

Web
session
cache

Clustered

Web
session
cache

WildFly

WildFly

Server

Server

**Figure 8.1   An application
replicating cached user data**

**Figure 8.2
Home page for the
WildFly application**

NOTE Back in chapter 4, you learned that readiness probes can be used to ensure that a pod is ready to receive traffic before traffic is routed to it. The default readiness probe for the WildFly image only makes sure the application server is running as expected—it doesn't check for the application you deployed. The best practice is to create a readiness probe that's specific to each application. Because you haven't done that yet in this exercise, it's possible for traffic to be routed to the pod before the application is fully deployed.

Now that the application is deployed, let's explore application clustering with WildFly on OpenShift. To demonstrate this, you'll do the following:

1 Add data to your session by registering users on the application page.
2 Make a note of the pod name.
3 Scale the service to two replicated pods. The WildFly application will then automatically replicate your session data in memory between pods.
4 Delete the original pod.
5 Verify that your session data is still active.

8.1.2 *Querying the OpenShift API server from a pod*

Before you get started, you need to modify some permissions for the default service account in your project, which will be responsible for running the application pods. From the stateful-apps project, run the following command to add the view role to the default service account. The view role will allow the pods running in the project to query the OpenShift API server directly. In this case, the application will take advantage of the ability to query OpenShift API server to find other WildFly application pods in the project. These other instances will send pod-to-pod traffic directly to each other and use their own application-specific service-discovery and load-balancing features for communication:

```
oc policy \
    add-role-to-user \
    view \
    system:serviceaccount:$(oc project -q):default \
    -n $(oc project -q)
```

Start by registering a few users in the WildFly application page. Choose Applications > Pods, and write down your pod name. Then, click the Overview tab in the left panel and scale up to two pods by clicking the up arrow. Once the second pod starts running, the data that you generated in the first step will be sent directly from the first pod to the second pod.

The two pods discovered each other with the help of a WildFly-specific discovery mechanism designed for Kubernetes. The implementation is called *KUBE_PING*, and it's part of the JGroups project. When the second pod was started, it queried the OpenShift API for all the pods in the current project. The API server then returned a list of pods in the current project. The KUBE_PING code in the WildFly server filtered the list of pods for those with special ports labeled ping. If any of the pods in the result set returned from the API server match the filter, then the JGroups code in WildFly will attempt to join any existing clusters among the pods in the list.

> **NOTE** JGroups (www.jgroups.org) is a popular open source toolkit for reliable messaging written in Java and popular with Java application servers. WildFly uses JGroups under the covers to send messages back and forth between other application servers.

> **TIP** By default, the WildFly pods have several ports exposed. The main port that is used for direct pod-to-pod traffic is 8888. On that port is an embedded HTTP server that's used to send messages to and receive messages from other pods. If you examine the pod object, you'll notice that the port also has a matching name of ping, which is used as metadata about the port.

Take a moment to examine the result set from the pod perspective by navigating to any of the pods in the OpenShift console and clicking the Terminal tab. Then run this command to query the API server for a list of pods in the project matching the label application=wildfly-app:

```
curl -k -X GET \
  -H "Authorization: Bearer $(cat /var/run/secrets/kubernetes.io/serviceac
  ➥ count/token)" \
  https://$KUBERNETES_PORT_443_TCP_ADDR:$KUBERNETES_SERVICE_PORT_HTTPS/api
  ➥ /v1/namespaces/stateful-apps/pods?labelSelector=application%3Dwildfly-app
```

KUBE_PING also uses two environment variables that were automatically generated for you in the OpenShift template that you first used. Navigate to the Environment tab on the current page, and you'll see the OPENSHIFT_KUBE_PING_NAMESPACE and OPEN-SHIFT_KUBE_PING_LABELS variables set automatically, as shown in figure 8.3.

Figure 8.3   WildFly clustering environment variables

8.1.3 Verifying WildFly data replication

Now that two pods are successfully clustered together, delete the original pod from the OpenShift console by choosing Actions > Delete, as shown in figure 8.4. The OpenShift replication controller (RC) will notice that a pod has been deleted and will spin up a new one in its place to ensure that there are still two replicas. If clustering is working properly, the original data you entered will still be available, even though it was originally stored in memory in a pod that no longer exists. Double-check by refreshing the application in your browser. If your data is no longer there, go back and make sure you ran the `oc policy add-role-to-user` command properly from the stateful-apps project. If that doesn't resolve the issue, look at the pod logs for any noticeable errors.

Figure 8.4 Delete a WildFly application pod

8.1.4 Other use cases for direct pod access

A Java application server that needs to cluster applications is just one common use case for direct pod discovery and access. Another example is an application that has its own load-balancing or routing mechanism, such as a *sharded database.* A sharded database is one in which large datasets are stored in many small databases as opposed to one large database. Many sharded databases have intelligence built into their clients and drivers that allows for direct access to the correct shard without querying or guessing where the data resides. Sharded databases work well on OpenShift and have been implemented using MongoDB as well as Infinispan, among others.

A typical sharded-database implementation may include creating the service object as a headless service. Once a headless service object is created, DNS can be used as another service-discovery mechanism. A DNS query for a given headless service will return A records for all the pods in the service. (More information on DNS and A records is available in chapter 10.) Applications can then implement custom logic to determine which pod to access.

One popular application that uses DNS queries to determine which instances to access is *Apache Kafka*, a fast open source messaging broker. Most implementations of Apache Kafka on OpenShift and other Kubernetes-based platforms use headless services so the messaging brokers can access each other directly to send and replicate messages. The brokers find each other using DNS queries, which are made possible by implementing a headless service.

Other common use cases for direct access include more mundane IT workloads such as software agents that are used for backups and monitoring. Backup agents are often run with many traditional database workloads and implement features such as scheduled snapshots and point-in-time recovery of data. A monitoring agent often provides features such as real-time alerting and visualization of an application. Often these agents may either run locally embedded as instrumented code in the application or communicate through direct network access. For many use cases, direct network access is required because the agents may communicate with more than one application across many servers. In these scenarios, the agents require consistent, direct access to applications in order to fulfill their daily functions.

8.2   *Demonstrating sticky sessions*

In the WildFly example, data is replicated between two WildFly server instances. A cookie with a unique identifier is generated automatically by the application and stored in your browser. By using a cookie, the application can track which end user is accessing the application. This approach works well but has several drawbacks. The most obvious is that if the WildFly server didn't support application clustering or didn't have a discovery mechanism that works in OpenShift, the application would produce uneven user experiences. Without application clustering, if there were two application pods—one with user data and one without user data—then the user would see their data only 50% of the time because requests are sent in a round-robin manner between pods in a service.

One common solution to this problem is to use *sticky sessions*. In the context of OpenShift, enabling sticky sessions ensures that a user making requests into the cluster will consistently receive responses from the same pod for the duration of their session.

This added consistency helps ensure a smooth user experience and allows many applications that temporarily store data locally in the container to be run in Open-Shift. By default in OpenShift, sticky sessions are implemented using cookies for HTTP-based routes and some types of HTTPS-based routes. The OpenShift router can reuse existing cookies or create new cookies. The WildFly application you created earlier created its own cookie, so the router will use that cookie for the sticky-session implementation. If cookies are disabled or can't be used for the route, sticky sessions are implemented using a load-balancing scheme called *source* that uses the client IP address as part of its implementation.

TIP For more information on how to disable cookies, visit http://mng.bz/ OYn9. For more information on load-balancing schemes such as the source scheme, visit http://mng.bz/1wMh.

8.2.1 Toggling sticky sessions

Let's see how sticky sessions work by toggling cookies on and off using the Linux `curl` command-line tool, which can make HTTP requests to a server eight times and print the results. The WildFly application you've deployed has a couple of REST endpoints that haven't been explored yet. The first endpoint can be used to print out the pod IP and hostname. Enter the following command to print out that information from eight sequential HTTP requests to the wildfly-app route:

```
                                                      Runs the command eight
Passes the silent flag to                             times sequentially
ignore the progress bar
$ for I in $(seq 1 8); \        ◄─────┘
  do \
       curl -s \
       "$(oc get route wildfly-app -o=jsonpath='{.spec.host}')/rest/serverd
    ➥ ata/ip"; \              ◄──────────
       printf "\n"; \         ◄──────        Extracts the hostname from
  done          Adds a newline character     the route named wildfly-app
```

```
{"hostname":"wildfly-app-7-x4q1k","ip":"10.128.1.138"}
{"hostname":"wildfly-app-7-xrwsz","ip":"10.128.1.137"}
{"hostname":"wildfly-app-7-x4q1k","ip":"10.128.1.138"}
{"hostname":"wildfly-app-7-xrwsz","ip":"10.128.1.137"}
{"hostname":"wildfly-app-7-x4q1k","ip":"10.128.1.138"}
{"hostname":"wildfly-app-7-xrwsz","ip":"10.128.1.137"}
{"hostname":"wildfly-app-7-x4q1k","ip":"10.128.1.138"}
{"hostname":"wildfly-app-7-xrwsz","ip":"10.128.1.137"}
```

The output prints the hostname and IP address of each pod four times, alternating back and forth between pods in a round-robin pattern. This is as you'd expect because the `curl` command doesn't provide a cookie for the OpenShift router to track the origins of each request. Fortunately, `curl` can save cookies locally in a text file that can be used for future HTTP requests to the server. Use the following command to grab the cookie from the WildFly application and save it to a local file called cookie.txt:

```
$ curl -o /dev/null \
    --cookie-jar cookies.txt \
    $(oc get route wildfly-app \
    -o=jsonpath='{.spec.host}')/rest/serverdata/ip
```

Now that you've saved the cookie locally, send eight more requests to the wildfly-app route, using the cookie that's saved locally:

```
$ for I in $(seq 1 8); \
  do \
       curl -s \                          Sends the contents of cookies.txt
       --cookie cookies.txt \  ◄──────┘   as a cookie with the request
```

```
              "$(oc get route wildfly-app -o=jsonpath='{.spec.host}')/rest/serverd
           ➥ ata/ip"; \
              printf "\n"; \
      done
```

```
{"hostname":"wildfly-app-7-x4q1k","ip":"10.128.1.138"}
{"hostname":"wildfly-app-7-x4q1k","ip":"10.128.1.138"}
{"hostname":"wildfly-app-7-x4q1k","ip":"10.128.1.138"}
{"hostname":"wildfly-app-7-x4q1k","ip":"10.128.1.138"}
{"hostname":"wildfly-app-7-x4q1k","ip":"10.128.1.138"}
{"hostname":"wildfly-app-7-x4q1k","ip":"10.128.1.138"}
{"hostname":"wildfly-app-7-x4q1k","ip":"10.128.1.138"}
{"hostname":"wildfly-app-7-x4q1k","ip":"10.128.1.138"}
```

Sticky sessions are now working! Unlike in the previous command, the eight requests aren't sent in a round-robin pattern. Each request is sent to the same pod consistently by using a cookie.

> **TIP** Modern browsers automatically enable cookies for you, unless you've disabled this functionality.

LIMITATIONS OF USING COOKIES

One limitation of using cookies for load balancing is that they don't work for HTTPS connections that use the *passthrough* routing. In passthrough routing, there's an encrypted connection from the client—typically a browser—all the way to the application pod. In this scenario, cookies won't work, because the connection is encrypted from the client to the application; there's no way for the routing layer to view the cookie. To solve this problem, OpenShift uses the client IP address to implement sticky sessions. But this option has a couple of drawbacks.

First, many client IP addresses get translated using *Network Address Translation* (NAT) before reaching their destination. When a request is translated using NAT, it replaces the often-private IP address of the client with that of a public IP address. This frequently makes the client IP the same for all users on a particular home or business network. Imagine a scenario in which you ran three pods to run an application for everyone in your office, but everyone in your office was being routed to the same pod because the requests all appeared to show the same source IP address.

Second, OpenShift uses an internal hashing schema based on the client IP address and the number of pods to determine its load-balancing schema. When the number of replicas changes, such as when you're using autoscaling, it's possible to lose sticky sessions.

For the rest of this chapter, you won't need two instances of the WildFly application pod. So, scale back down to a single pod:

```
$ oc scale dc/wildfly-app --replicas=1
deploymentconfig "wildfly-app" scaled
```

TIP Previously, we mentioned that the WildFly application has two REST endpoints, but only one was covered. Another endpoint prints out the HTTP headers associated with the user and is available at http://wildfly-app-stateful-apps.apps.192.168.122.101.nip.io/rest/clientdata.

8.3 Shutting down applications gracefully

So far in this chapter, you've learned how to use sticky sessions to ensure that users have a consistent experience in OpenShift. You've also learned how to use custom load balancing and service discovery in OpenShift services. To demonstrate custom load balancing, you deployed an application that keeps user data in memory and replicates its data to other pods.

When looking at clustering, you entered data and then scaled up to two pods that replicated the data you entered. You then killed the original pod and verified that your data was still there.

This approach worked well but in a controlled and limited capacity. Imagine a scenario in which autoscaling was enabled and the pods were spinning up and down more quickly. How would you know the application data had been replicated before a particular pod was killed—or even which pod was killed? OpenShift has several ways to solve this issue.

8.3.1 Setting a grace period for application cleanup

The easiest and most straightforward solution is to use a *grace period* for the pod to gracefully shut down. Normally, when OpenShift deletes a pod, it sends the pod a Linux TERM signal, often abbreviated *SIGTERM*. The SIGTERM acts as a notification to the process that it needs to finish what it's doing and then exit. One caveat is that the application needs custom code to catch the signal and handle the shutdown sequence. Fortunately, many application servers have this code built in. If the container doesn't exit within a given grace period, OpenShift sends a Linux Kill signal (*SIGKILL*) that immediately terminates the application.

In this section, you'll deploy a new application to demonstrate how OpenShift grace periods work. In the same stateful-apps project that you're already in, run the following command to build and deploy the application:

```
$ oc new-app \
    -l app=graceful \
    --context-dir=dockerfile-graceful-shutdown \
    https://github.com/OpenShiftInAction/chapter8
...
--> Creating resources with label app=graceful ...
    imagestream "centos" created
    imagestream "chapter8" created
    buildconfig "chapter8" created
    deploymentconfig "chapter8" created
--> Success
    Build scheduled, use 'oc logs -f bc/chapter8' to track its progress.
    Run 'oc status' to view your app.
```


Learning more about source-to-image

Many of the applications so far in this book have used the OpenShift source-to-image (S2I) technology to build an application container image from source code. This approach extends the traditional Dockerfile approach, which uses standard Linux commands to build the container image. Both approaches are first-class citizens in OpenShift and have various advantages and disadvantages. One advantage of the Dockerfile approach is that it allows for the most extensibility and customization. S2I has a few major advantages:

- Easy-to-use.
- Customizable for most use cases.
- Removes the need to build and maintain a Dockerfile.
- Improves performance. In a Dockerfile, every command is a layer in the container image, whereas the entire S2I build processes a single layer that improves the size and speed of the container image.
- Allows platform administrators to limit how the images are built.

You can learn more about S2I at https://docs.openshift.org/latest/creating_images/s2i.html.

TIP   Many of the objects created in the examples are called chapter8 because we didn't use a template for deployment. The name is based on the Git repository when using S2I.

The application may take a minute or so to build, because it may need to pull down a new base image to build the application. Once the application is successfully built and running, delete it with a grace period of 10 seconds:

```
$ oc delete pod -l app=graceful --grace-period=10
pod "dockerfile-graceful-shutdown-demo-1-1cbv1" deleted
```

When you run delete with a grace period of 10 seconds, OpenShift sends a SIGTERM signal immediately to the pod and then forcibly kills it in 10 seconds if it hasn't exited by itself. Quickly, run the following command to see this plays out in the logs for the pod:

```
$ oc logs -f \
    $(oc get pods -l app=graceful -o=jsonpath='{.items[].metadata.name}')
pid is 1
Waiting for SIGTERM, sleeping for 5 seconds now...
Waiting for SIGTERM, sleeping for 5 seconds now...
Waiting for SIGTERM, sleeping for 5 seconds now...
...
Caught SIGTERM! Gracefully shutting down now
Gracefully shutting down for 0 seconds
Gracefully shutting down for 1 seconds
Gracefully shutting down for 2 seconds
Gracefully shutting down for 3 seconds
```

```
Gracefully shutting down for 4 seconds
Gracefully shutting down for 5 seconds
Gracefully shutting down for 6 seconds
Gracefully shutting down for 7 seconds
Gracefully shutting down for 8 seconds
Gracefully shutting down for 9 seconds
```

The process that's running is a simple bash script that waits for a SIGTERM signal and then prints a message to standard out until it's killed. In this case, the pod was given a grace period of 10 seconds, and the pod printed logs for approximately 10 seconds before it was forcibly killed. By default, the grace period is set to 30 seconds. If you have an important container that you never want to be killed, you must set the `terminationGracePeriodSeconds` field in the deployment config to -1.

> **TIP** In a container, the main process runs as process ID (PID) 1. This is important when handling Linux signals because only PID 1 receives the signal. Although most containers have a single process, many containers have multiple processes. In this scenario, the main process needs to catch the signal and notify the other process in the container. systemd can also be used as a seamless solution. For containers with multiple processes that all need to handle Linux signals, it's best to use systemd for this implementation. A CentOS base container that's available to build is available at https://hub.docker.com/r/centos/systemd.

> **TIP** You can find a full list of Linux signals at https://en.wikipedia.org/wiki/Signal_(IPC).

You no longer need the graceful app demo, so delete all the resources it created:

```
$ oc delete all -l app=graceful
buildconfig "chapter8" deleted
imagestream "centos" deleted
imagestream "chapter8" deleted
deploymentconfig "chapter8" deleted
pod "chapter8-1-1j1zx" deleted
```

8.3.2 *Using container lifecycle hooks*

Although catching basic Linux signals such as SIGTERM is a best practice, many applications aren't equipped to handle Linux signals. A nice way to externalize the logic from the application is to use a *preStop* hook and one of two *container lifecycle hooks* available in OpenShift. Container lifecycle hooks allow users to take predetermined actions during a container management lifecycle event. The two events available in OpenShift are as follows:

- `PreStop`—Executes a handler before the container is terminated. This event is blocking, meaning it must finish before the pod is terminated.
- `PostStart`—Executes a handler immediately after the container is started.

Similar to readiness probes and liveness probes, the handler can be a command (often a script) that is executed in the container, or it can be an HTTP call to an endpoint exposed by the container.

> **TIP**   Container lifecycle hooks can be used in conjunction with pod grace periods. If preStop hooks are used, they take precedence over pod deletion. SIGTERM won't be sent to the container until the preStop hook finishes executing.

Using patch to set a preStop hook

To implement a preStop hook that calls the CLI tooling to initiate a graceful shutdown, you can use the `oc patch` command. This command can be used to update object fields. Here's an example of adding a preStop hook to the wildfly-app deployment config:

```
oc patch dc wildfly-app \
    -p '{"spec": {"template": {"spec": {"containers": [{"name": "wildfly-a
    ➥ pp","lifecycle": {"preStop": {"exec": {"command":
    ➥ ["/jboss-cli.sh", "
    ➥ --connect", "command=:shutdown[timeout=10]"]}}}}]}}}}'
```

CHOOSING THE BEST GRACEFUL SHUTDOWN METHOD

Container lifecycle hooks and Linux signal handling are often used together, but in many cases users decide which method to use for their application. The main benefit of using Linux signal handling is that the application will always behave the same way, no matter where the image is run. It guarantees consistent and predictable shutdown behavior because the behavior is coded in the application. Sending SIGTERM signals on delete is fundamental not only to all Kubernetes platforms but also to the stand-alone docker engine. If the user handles the SIGTERM signal in their application, the image will behave consistently even if it's moved outside of OpenShift. Because preStop hooks need to be explicitly added to the deployment, deployment config, or template, there's no guarantee that the image will behave the same way in other environments.

Many applications, such as third-party applications, don't handle SIGTERM properly, and the end user can't easily modify the code. In this case, a preStop hook must be used. A good example is *NGINX*, a popular and lightweight HTTP server. When NGINX is sent a SIGTERM, it exits immediately. Rather than forking NGINX and adding code to handle the Linux SIGTERM signal, an easy solution is to add a preStop hook that gracefully shuts down NGINX from the command line. A general rule to follow is that if you control the code, you should code your application to handle SIGTERM. If you don't control the code, use a preStop hook if needed.

8.4   *Native API object support for stateful applications with stateful sets*

So far in this chapter, you've learned that OpenShift has many capabilities to support stateful applications:

- Implementing custom load balancing
- Implementing custom service discovery
- Obtaining DNS A records on a per-pod-basis using a headless service
- Configuring sticky sessions
- Handling a controlled startup and shutdown sequence by handling Linux signals and container lifecycle events

These let users make traditional workloads first-class citizens on OpenShift, but some applications also require even more predictable startup and shutdown sequencing as well as predictable storage and networking-identifying information. Imagine a scenario with the WildFly application in which data replication is critical to the user experience, but a massive scaling event destroys too many pods at one time while replication is happening. How will the application recover? Where will the data be replicated to?

To solve this problem, OpenShift has a special object called a *stateful set* (known as a *pet set* in older versions of OpenShift). A stateful set is a powerful tool in the OpenShift users' toolbox to facilitate many traditional workloads in a modern environment. A stateful set object is used in place of a replication controller as the underlying implementation to ensure replicas in a service, but it does so in a more controlled way.

A replication controller can't control the order of how pods are created or destroyed. Normally, if a user configures a deployment to go from one to five replicas in OpenShift, that task is passed to an RC that starts four new pods all at once. The order in which they're started and marked as ready (successfully completing a readiness probe) is completely random.

8.4.1 Deterministic sequencing of startup and shutdown order with stateful sets

A stateful set brings a deterministic sequential order to pod creation and deletion. Each pod that's created also has an ordinal index number (starting at 0) associated with it. The ordinal index indicates the startup order. For instance, if the previous WildFly application was using a stateful set with three replicas, the pods would be started and named in this order: wildfly-app-0, wildfly-app-1, and wildfly-app-2. A stateful set also ensures that each pod is running and ready (has passed the readiness probe) before the next pod is started. In the previous scenario, wildfly-app-2 wouldn't be started until wildfly-app-1 was running and ready.

The reverse is also true. An RC or replica will delete pods at random when a command is given to reduce the number of replicas. A stateful set can also be used for a controlled shutdown sequence: it starts with the pod that has the highest ordinal index (n-1 replicas) and works backward to meet the new replica requirement. A pod won't be shut down until the previous pod has been fully terminated.

This controlled shutdown sequence can be critical for many stateful applications. In the case of the WildFly application, user data is being shared between a number of pods. When the WildFly application is shut down gracefully, a data-synchronization process may occur between the remaining pods in the application cluster. This process will often be interrupted without the use of a stateful set because the pods are shut down in parallel. By using a predictable, one-at-a-time shutdown sequence, the application is less likely to lose data, which results in a better user experience.

8.4.2 *Examining a stateful set*

To see how stateful sets work, first create a new project:

```
$ oc new-project statefulset
Now using project "statefulset" on server "https://ocp-1.192.168.122.100.n
⟜ ip.io:8443".
```

Now, import the template for this chapter's stateful set example:

```
$ oc create \
 -f https://raw.githubusercontent.com/OpenShiftInAction/chapter8/master/st
 ⟜ atefulsets/mongodb-statefulset-replication-emptydir.yaml \
 -n statefulset
 template "mongodb-statefulset-replication-emptydir" created
```

**Adding the -n <namespace> tag to the end of the command
means this template is available only in the statefulset project.**

After you've installed the MongoDB template, go the statefulset project via the Open-Shift console and click Add to Project. Filter for the template you just installed by typing `statefulset` in the OpenShift service catalog, as shown in figure 8.5. Once you select the template, you can modify the parameters for the MongoDB installation. None of the parameters are required because the OpenShift template will generate random values for anything left empty. Because this template has everything you need for the example already filled in, scroll to the bottom and click Create.

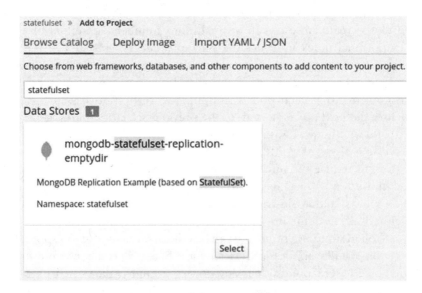

**Figure 8.5
Find the
MongoDB
stateful set
template in
the service
catalog.**

TIP The template makes reference to a *replica set*. That's the MongoDB term for replicated MongoDB instances. This template doesn't create an Open-Shift replica set object, which is similar to a replication controller.

Next, navigate to the stateful set in the OpenShift console by choosing Applications > Stateful Sets and selecting the mongodb stateful set object that was created. The details page for the stateful set object will open. Examine the two pods that the template created: as shown in figure 8.6, the bottom of the screen shows that the two pod names have an ordinal index associated with them. As mentioned earlier, that index also determines the startup and shutdown sequence.

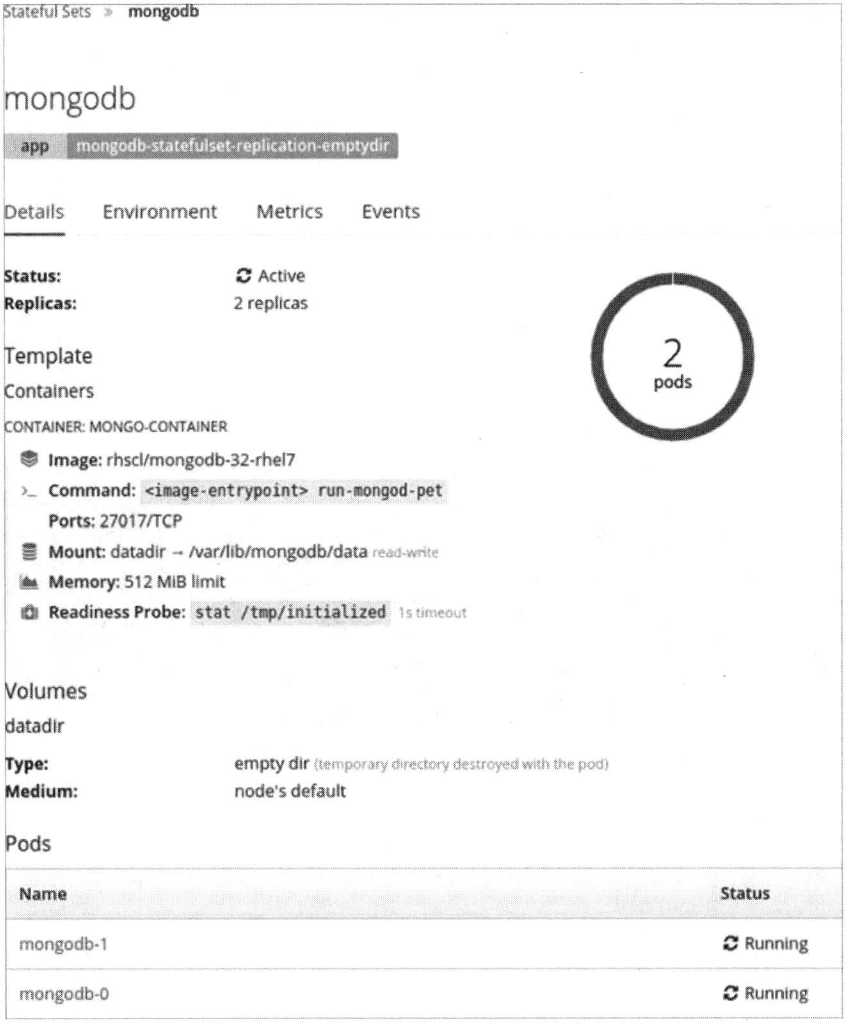

Figure 8.6   Example mongodb stateful set in the console

From the command line, modify the stateful set to spin up a third replica:

```
$ oc scale statefulsets mongodb --replicas=3
statefulset "mongodb" scaled
```

Unlike previous use of the `scale` command, this time you need to explicitly state that you're scaling a stateful set. In the OpenShift console, notice that the new pod that was created has a deterministic pod name with the ordinal index associated with it: mongodb-2.

Similar to the WildFly application, the three MongoDB pods are replicating data to each other. To check that this replication is fully functional, click any of the pods on the bottom of the mongodb stateful set Details page, and then click the Terminal tab. Any commands executed here will execute in the pod. First log in to mongodb as the admin user, as shown in figure 8.7; then check the status of the MongoDB replica set by typing `rs.status()` after a successful login.

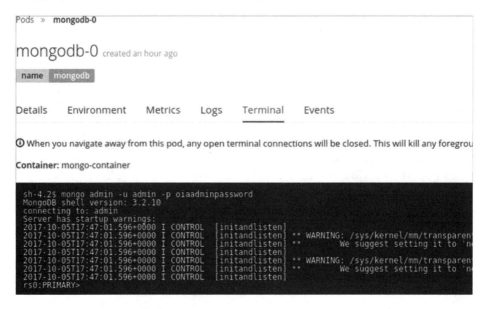

Figure 8.7 Log in as the mongo admin user.

> **TIP** The MongoDB replica set is now fully functional. You can learn more and see an architectural diagram of how this works at https://docs.mongodb.com/manual/replication.

8.4.3 *Predictable network identity*

Stateful sets also provide a consistent host-naming scheme for each pod in the set. Each predictable hostname is also associated with a predictable DNS entry. Examine the pod hostname for mongodb-0 by executing this command:

```
$ for statefulpod in $(oc get pods -l name=mongodb -o=jsonpath='{.items[*]
  ➥ .metadata.name}'); \
  do \
      oc exec $statefulpod cat /etc/hostname; \
  done
mongodb-0
mongodb-1
mongodb-2
```

The stateful set also ensures a DNS entry for each pod running in the stateful set. This can be found by executing the `dig` command using the DNS entry name for each pod. Find the IP addresses by executing the following command from one of the Open-Shift nodes. Because the command relies on the OpenShift-provided DNS, it must be run from within the OpenShift environment to work properly:

```
$ for statefulpod in $(oc get pods -l name=mongodb -o=jsonpath='{.items[*]
  ➥ .metadata.name}'); \
  do \
      dig +short $statefulpod.mongodb-internal.statefulset.svc.cluster.lo
      ➥ cal; \
  done
10.128.1.164
10.128.1.165
10.128.1.166
```

> **TIP** When you're using stateful sets, the pod hostname in DNS is listed in the format <pod name>.<service name>.<namespace>.svc.cluster.local.

Because this example also contains a headless service, there are DNS A records for the pods associated with the headless service. Ensure that the pod IPs in DNS match the previous listing by running this command from one of the OpenShift nodes:

```
$  dig +search +short mongodb-internal.statefulset.svc.cluster.local
10.128.1.164
10.128.1.165
10.128.1.166
```

8.4.4 Consistent persistent storage mappings

Pods running as part of a stateful set can also have their own persistent volume claims (PVCs) associated with each pod. But unlike a normal PVC, they remain associated with a pod and its ordinal index as long as the stateful set exists. In the previous example, you deployed an ephemeral stateful set without persistent storage.

Imagine that the previous example was using persistent storage, and the pods were writing log files that included the pod hostname. You wouldn't want the PVC to later be mapped to the volume of a different pod with a different hostname because it would be hard to make sense of those log files for debugging and auditing purposes. Stateful sets solve this problem by providing a consistent mapping through the use of a *volume claim template*, which is a template the PVC associates with each pod. If a pod dies or is rescheduled to a different node, then the PVC will be mapped only to the new pod that starts in its place with the same hostname as the old pod. Providing a separate and dedicated persistent volume claim for each pod in the stateful set is crucial for many different types of stateful applications which cannot use the typical deployment config model of sharing the same PVC across many application instances.

> **NOTE** A similar MongoDB stateful set example with persistent storage is available at http://mng.bz/LCaI.

8.4.5 *Stateful set limitations*

Under normal circumstances, pods controlled by a stateful set shouldn't need to be deleted manually. But there are a few scenarios in which a pod being controlled by a stateful set could be deleted by an outside force. For instance, if the kubelet or node is unresponsive, then the API server may remove the pod after a given amount of time and restart it somewhere else in the cluster. A pod could also exit accidentally or could be manually removed by a user. In those cases, it's likely that the ordinal index will be broken. New pods will be created with the same hostnames and DNS entries as the old pods, but the IP addresses may be different. For this reason, any application that relies on hardcoded IP addresses isn't a good fit for stateful sets. If the application can't be modified to use DNS or hostnames instead of IP addresses, you should use a single service per pod for a stable IP address.

Another limitation is that all the pods in a stateful set are replicas of each other, which of course makes sense when you want to scale. But that won't help any situation in which disparate applications need to be started in a particular order. A classic example is a Java or .NET application that throws errors if a database is unavailable. Once the database is started, then the application also needs to be restarted to refresh its connections. In that scenario, a stateful set wouldn't help the order between the two disparate services.

8.4.6 *Stateful applications without native solutions*

One of the reasons OpenShift has gained so much market adoption is that traditional IT workloads work just as well as modern stateless applications. Yet there's still work to be done. One of the biggest promises of using containers is that applications will behave the same way between environments. Containers start from well-known image binaries that contain the application and the configuration it needs to run. If a container dies, a new one is started from the previous image binary that's identical to how the previous container was started. One major problem with this model occurs for applications that are changed on the fly and store their information in a way that makes it difficult to re-create.

A good example of this issue can be seen with WordPress, an extremely popular blogging application that was designed many years before containers become popular. In a given WordPress workflow, a blogger might go to the admin portion of their website, add some text, and then save/publish it. WordPress saves all that text in a database, along with any HTML and styling. When the blogger has completed this action, the container has drifted from its original image. Container drift is normal for most applications; but in the case of WordPress, if the container crashed, the blog would be lost. Persistent storage can be used to ensure that the data is persisted. When a new WordPress pod starts, it could map to the database and would have all the blogs available.

But promoting such a snapshot of a database among various environments is a major challenge. There are many examples of using an event-driven workflow that can be triggered to export and import a database after a blogger publishes content, but it's not easy, nor is it native to the platform. Containers start from well-known immutable container images, but engineering a reverse workflow in which images are created from running container instances is more error-prone and rigid. Other examples that have worked—with some engineering—include applications that open a large number of ports, applications the rely on hardcoded IP addresses, and other legacy applications that rely on older Linux technologies.

As OpenShift continues to evolve, the ecosystem of support for OpenShift and other Kubernetes-based offerings is also evolving. OpenShift keeps adding features to support even more stateful applications, and many companies are putting significant engineering resources behind making more cloud-native applications. This will further the process of making traditional IT workloads first-class citizens on OpenShift.

8.5   *Summary*

- OpenShift supports many different types of stateful applications.
- There are many ways in OpenShift to do custom service discovery.
- Custom load balancing can be implemented with a headless service.
- The OpenShift router supports session affinity with sticky sessions.
- Pods are sent Linux SIGTERM signals before being shut down.
- You can add a configurable grace period parameter before a pod is forcibly removed with SIGKILL.
- Container lifecycle events allow for actions to be taken when containers are started and stopped.
- A stateful set object allows a consistent startup and shutdown sequence.
- Pods can obtain their own hostname and consistent PVC mapping with a stateful set.
- Applications that need hardcoded IP addresses can use a single service per pod.

Part 4

Operations and security

This part of the book focuses on cluster-wide concepts and knowledge you'll need to effectively manage an OpenShift cluster at scale. These are some of the skills required for any operations team managing OpenShift.

Chapter 9 is all about working with OpenShift's integrated role-based access control (RBAC). You'll change the authentication provider for your cluster's users and work with the system accounts built into OpenShift, along with the default roles for different user types.

Chapter 10 focuses on the software-defined network that's deployed as part of OpenShift. This is how containers communicate with each other and how service discovery works in an OpenShift cluster.

Finally, chapter 11 brings together the concepts from previous chapters and looks at OpenShift from a security perspective. We'll discuss how SELinux is used in OpenShift and how you can work with security policies to provide the most effective level of access for your applications.

Authentication
and resource access

9

This chapter covers

- Adding permissions to users by assigning roles
- Managing project resource limits and quotas
- Setting default limits and quotas for projects
- Examining how Linux enforces limits and quotas

Before we get started, let's face it: this isn't the most interesting chapter in the book. Setting up authentication sources and configuring project quotas for your applications aren't topics that will show up on the first slide of anyone's presentation. They're essential for an application platform to function correctly, however, so strap in, and let's dive into the deep, dark reaches of OpenShift.

9.1 *Proper permissions vs. the Wild West*

Application platforms like OpenShift aren't effective for multiple users without robust access and permissions management for various applications and OpenShift components. If every user had full access to all of your OpenShift cluster's resources, it would truly be the Wild West. Conversely, if it was difficult to access resources, OpenShift wouldn't be good for much, either. OpenShift has a robust authentication and access-control system that provides a good balance of self-service workflows to keep productivity up while limiting users to only what they need to get their job done.

When you first deployed OpenShift, the default configuration allowed any user-name and non-empty password field to log in. This authentication method uses the *allow-all* identity provider that comes with OpenShift.

> **TIP** In OpenShift, an *identity provider* is a plugin that defines how users can authenticate and the backend service that you want to connect to for manag-ing user information. Although the allow-all provider is good enough when you're learning to use OpenShift, when you need to enforce access rules, you'll need to change to a more secure authentication method. In the next section, you'll replace the allow-all provider with one that uses a local data-base file.

Appendix D walks you through configuring your OpenShift cluster to use an Apache htpasswd database for user access and set up a few users to use with that authentica-tion source. You'll create the following users:

- *developer*—a user with permissions typical to those given to a developer in an OpenShift cluster.
- *project-admin*—a user with permissions typical of a developer or team lead in an OpenShift cluster. They have administrative control over a single project.
- *admin*—a user with administrative control over the entire OpenShift cluster.

Please go through that now, and then continue with this chapter. After configuring OpenShift per appendix D, if you attempt to log in with your original dev user, that user can't be authenticated because it's not in your htpasswd database. But if you log in using the developer or admin user, you no longer have access to the image-uploader project. That's because the now locked-out dev user owns the image-uploader project and all the applications deployed in it.

System users and administrative access

In chapter 7, when you provisioned persistent volumes to use as storage, you used a user named system:admin. To log in as this user, you copied a file named admin.kubeconfig from the master server to your workstation.

System:admin is a member of a special class of *system users*. These users don't authenticate through the configured authentication mechanism. Instead, they authen-ticate using an SSL certificate. This certificate is what's in the admin.kubeconfig file.

On the master node, a similar user certificate is added to the default configuration for the root user. This is how you can access oc and oadm on the master node without logging in to OpenShift.

You've made your OpenShift cluster more secure by configuring it to use a more secure authentication provider. But in the process, you disabled access to the deployed applications by stopping access for the user you used to deploy your project and applications. In the next section, you'll correct this and set up more robust permissions by manipulating *user roles*.

9.2 Working with user roles

Roles are used to define permissions for all users in an OpenShift cluster. In chapter 3, you used the special system:admin user to configure physical volumes on your cluster. The system:admin is a special system account that uses SSL certificates for authentication. In this section, you'll create users with similar privileges using roles.

To work with roles, you'll use a new command-line tool named `oadm` (short for *OpenShift administration*). It's installed by default on your master server.

The default project, and working with multiple projects

The `oc` and `oadm` tools' default action is to run a command using the current working project. If you create a new project, it automatically becomes your working project. The `oc project` command changes among projects that already exist.

To specify a command to be run against a specific project, regardless of your current working project, use the `-n` parameter with the project name you want the command to run against. This is a helpful option when you're writing scripts that use `oc` and `oadm` and that act on multiple projects. It's also a good habit in general.

On your master node, the OpenShift deployment program set up the root user with the same admin-level user information that you used in chapter 3 by copying the admin .kubeconfig file to your workstation. You can see all the user information set up for the root user by running the following command as the root user on your master server:

```
oadm config view
```

This allows administrators with access to the root user on an OpenShift master server to have cluster administration access by default. It's useful, but it also means you have to make sure everyone who has root access to your master server should be able to control your OpenShift cluster. For a smaller cluster like the one you've built, this will work fine. But for a larger cluster, the people who should have root access to your servers and the people who should be able to administer OpenShift probably won't match exactly. You can distribute this administrative certificate as needed for your cluster administrator's workstations.

9.2.1 Assigning new user roles

Remember those users you created? The developer user needs permission to view and add new content to the image-uploader project. To accomplish that, first make sure you're working in the context of the image-uploader project by running the following command:

```
oc project image-uploader
```

In the project, you need to add the `edit` role to your developer user. This role gives users permission to add to a project and edit existing deployments. Adding a role to a user for a project, or even the entire OpenShift cluster, is called *binding a role* to a user. You do so by running the following command:

```
oadm policy add-role-to-user edit developer
```

To confirm that your new role is applied, log in again through the web UI or the command line as the developer user. You should now have access to the image-uploader project and the deployed applications in it.

That takes care of the developer user. Let's give your admin user a little more access. In the next section, you'll give the admin user administrator-level access to your entire OpenShift cluster.

9.2.2   *Creating administrators*

So far, your OpenShift cluster has a single project. As an OpenShift cluster grows, it typically has dozens, or even hundreds, of projects at any given time. To manage this effectively, you need users who can administer a project, or even multiple projects across the cluster.

CREATING A PROJECT ADMIN

For the image-uploader project, you'll make the project-admin user an administrator for the project. You do so much the same way you gave the developer user the ability to edit. Instead of binding the edit role to the project-admin user, however, you need to bind the admin role. This role will give the project-admin user full administrative privileges in the image-uploader project. Run the following command as root on your master server:

```
oadm policy add-role-to-user admin project-admin
```

You now have a developer who can work in the image-uploader project and a project-admin user who can administer the project. The next user role you need is one who can manage the entire OpenShift cluster.

CREATING A CLUSTER ADMIN

The cluster administrator role is important. To borrow a line from a comic book, "With great power comes great responsibility." A cluster admin can not only administer projects, but also manage all of OpenShift's internal configurations. To create a cluster admin, run the following command as root on your master node:

```
oadm policy add-cluster-role-to-user cluster-admin admin
```

This command binds the admin role to the admin user you created in the previous section. Instead of binding that role for a single project, it binds it for every project in OpenShift.

Everything you've done in this chapter until now will help you edit existing users and make sure they have the correct privileges to access what their job requires. But what happens when you add new users? In the next section, you'll configure Open-Shift to bind the edit role to new users by default when they're created.

9.2.3 *Setting default user roles*

OpenShift has three *default groups*. These groups are configured during OpenShift installation and define whether a user is authenticated. You can use these groups to target users for additional actions, but the groups themselves can't be modified:

- *system:authenticated*—Any user who has successfully authenticated through the web UI or command line, or via the API.
- *system:authenticted:oauth*—Any user who's been authenticated by OpenShift's internal oauth server. This excludes system accounts.
- *system:unauthenticated*—Users who have failed authentication or not attempted to authenticate.

In your cluster, it will be helpful to allow any authenticated user to access the image-uploader project. You can accomplish this by running the following `oadm policy` command, which binds the edit role for the image-uploader project, specified by the `-n` option, to the `system:authenticated` default group:

```
oadm policy add-role-to-group edit -n image-uploader system:authenticated
```

Any user who has successfully logged in will now be able to access the image-uploader project.

> ### When to use other default groups
> This example uses the system:authenticated group. Depending on what you need to accomplish, the other groups can be used in a similar fashion.
>
> The system:authenticated:oauth group excludes the system accounts that are used to build and deploy applications in OpenShift. We'll cover those in more depth in chapter 11. In short, this group consists of all the humans and external services accessing OpenShift
>
> System:unauthenticated can be used if you want to provide a level of anonymous access in your cluster. Its most common use, however, is to route any user currently in that group to the OpenShift login page.

To confirm that your new default user role has taken effect, add an additional user named user1 to your htpasswd database with the following command:

```
echo user1 | htpasswd --stdin /etc/origin/master/openshift.htpasswd user1
```

Log in to your cluster and confirm that your new user can see the image-uploader project by default. user1 should have the ability to work in the image-uploader project from the time of first login.

Any time you have a shared environment, you need processes in place to ensure that one user or project doesn't take up too many resources in your cluster—either accidentally or on purpose. Limit ranges and resource quotas are the processes that manage this potential problem. In OpenShift, these resource constraints are different for each deployment, depending on whether explicit resource quotas are requested.

For app-gui and app-cli, you didn't specify specific CPU or memory resources to be allocated for either deployment. These *best-effort* deployments—deployments that don't request specific resources and are assigned a best-effort quality of service (QoS)—can govern default values at the project level in OpenShift by using *limit ranges*. In the next section, we'll discuss limit ranges in more depth, and you'll create your own and apply them to the image-uploader project.

9.3   Limit ranges

For each project in OpenShift, a limit range, defined as a `LimitRange` when working with the OpenShift API, provides resource constraints for most objects that exist in a project (the documentation is at http://mng.bz/tB5m.) The objects are the types of OpenShift components that users deploy to serve applications and data. Limit ranges apply to the maximum CPU, memory, and total object count for each component. The limits for each component are outlined in table 9.1.

Table 9.1   Limit-range resource constraints

Project component	Limits
Pod	CPU and memory per pod, and total pods per project
Container	CPU and memory per container, default memory and CPU, maximum burstable ratio per container, and total containers per project
Images	Maximum image size for the internal registry
Image stream	Maximum image tag references and image references per image stream
Persistent volume claims	Minimum and maximum storage request size per PVC

Before an application is deployed or scaled up, the project limit ranges are analyzed to confirm that the request is within the limit range. If a project limit range doesn't allow the desired action, then it doesn't happen (see figure 9.1). For example, if a project's limit range defines the memory per pod as between 50 MB and 1,000 MB, a request for a new application deployment with a defined quota of 1,500 MB will fail because it's outside the pod-memory limit range for that project.

Limit ranges have the additional benefit of being able to define default compute resource values for a project. When you deployed app-gui and app-cli, you hadn't yet

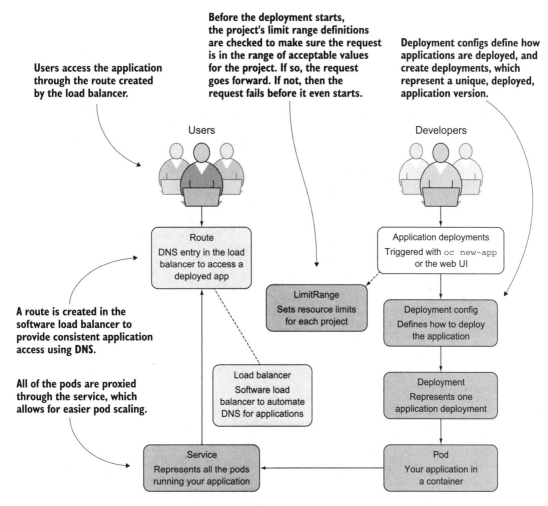

Users access the application through the route created by the load balancer.

Before the deployment starts, the project's limit range definitions are checked to make sure the request is in the range of acceptable values for the project. If so, the request goes forward. If not, then the request fails before it even starts.

Deployment configs define how applications are deployed, and create deployments, which represent a unique, deployed, application version.

Users

Developers

Route
DNS entry in the load balancer to access a deployed app

Application deployments
Triggered with `oc new-app` or the web UI

A route is created in the software load balancer to provide consistent application access using DNS.

LimitRange
Sets resource limits for each project

Deployment config
Defines how to deploy the application

Load balancer
Software load balancer to automate DNS for applications

Deployment
Represents one application deployment

All of the pods are proxied through the service, which allows for easier pod scaling.

.Service
Represents all the pods running your application

Pod
Your application in a container

Figure 9.1 Limit ranges are queried before any deployment or scaling request.

defined a limit range for the image-uploader project and didn't specify the resources for each deployment, so each application's pod was deployed with no resource constraints. In OpenShift, a deployment with no defined resource quotas is called a *best-effort* deployment. A best-effort deployment has the lowest priority in an OpenShift cluster and is the first to be killed if a system runs out of memory.

If users start accessing app-gui heavily, it can consume resources to the point that the performance of the app-cli deployment is affected. For a busy cluster with multiple users and running applications, that's a major problem. With limit ranges, you can define the default compute resources for a project that doesn't specify a quota and prevent this from happening in your cluster.

9.3.1 Defining resource limit ranges

Limit ranges define the minimum and maximum RAM and CPU an application can be allocated when it's deployed. In addition to the top and bottom of the range, you can specify default request values and limits. The difference between an application's requested value and its maximum limit is called the *burstable* range.

Millicores and mebibytes

In OpenShift, RAM is measured using the base 2 values of *kibibytes*, *mebibytes*, and *gibibytes*. For example, a mebibyte is 2^{10} bytes (1,024), whereas a megabyte is 10^3 (1,000) bytes.

To calculate millicores, when an application node is added to the OpenShift cluster, its number of CPU cores is interrogated. This value is multiplied by 1,000, and that's the number of millicores available on a given host. For example, the two VCPU virtual machines we recommend in appendix A have 2 × 1,000 millicores = 2,000 available for applications.

Millicores don't equate to the clock speed of a given CPU on a host. They're only a relative way to allocate CPU resources in an OpenShift cluster. If you have two nodes with different processor speeds, you'll notice different performance between the two nodes with the same resource allocations.

All this is a little abstract, so let's walk through a few quick examples, using as a reference the limit-range YAML template in listing 9.1:

- If you deploy an application with no requested resources, you're assigned a default request amount of 200 millicores and 100 MiB of RAM per pod. The default limit is 300 millicores and 200 MiB RAM. That means your application would be deployed with 200 millicores and 100 MiB RAM and could burst up to a maximum of 300 millicores and 200 MiB RAM if it received a spike in traffic.

- If you requested specific resources for an application deployment, you can request any CPU value between 100 millicores and 2,000 millicores (2 CPU), and RAM resources between 4 MiB and 1,000 GiB per pod. For the burstable range, your application can't exceed 10 times your defined request. This is set by `maxLimitRequestRatio` in the limit range. That means if you requested 150 millicores of CPU, the maximum your application could ever consume would be 1,500 millicores.

Let's create a limit range for the image-uploader project using the template in listing 9.1. Create a file called core-resource-limits.yaml using the contents of the template. Then, ensure that you're logged in as the proper user.

Listing 9.1   Template to create limit-range definitions for image-uploader

```
apiVersion: "v1"
kind: "LimitRange"
metadata:
  name: "core-resource-limits"          Name for the resource
                                         limits object
spec:
  limits:
    - type: "Pod"          ◁── Limit ranges for pods
      max:
        cpu: "2"
        memory: "1Gi"      ◁── Maximum memory for one pod
      min:
        cpu: "100m"
        memory: "4Mi"
    - type: "Container"    ◁── Limit ranges for containers
      max:
        cpu: "2"
        memory: "1Gi"
      min:                 ◁── Minimum CPU and memory
        cpu: "100m"            for one container
        memory: "4Mi"
      default:
        cpu: "300m"
        memory: "200Mi"
      defaultRequest:      ◁── Default requested CPU and
        cpu: "200m"            memory for one container
        memory: "100Mi"
      maxLimitRequestRatio:  ◁── Maximum burstable ratio for
        cpu: "10"               container CPU utilization
```

Annotations (left margin):
- **Maximum CPUs for one pod**
- **Minimum CPU and memory for one pod**
- **Maximum CPU and memory for one container**
- **Default maximum CPU and memory usable for one container**

To define a limit range, a user needs to have the cluster-admin role. To log in as the admin user, run the following `oc login` command:

```
oc login -u admin -p admin https://ocp-1.192.168.122.100.nip.io:8443
```

Now, execute the following `oc create` command to create the new limit range. The `-n` option can be used to specify the project you want to be affected by an `oc` command:

```
oc create -f core-resource-limits.yaml -n image-uploader
```

> **TIP**   Throughout this chapter and the rest of the book, you'll need to create YAML template files that are referenced in `oc` commands. We use relative file-name paths to keep the examples easy to read, but if you're not running `oc` from the directory where those files are created, be sure to reference the full path when you run the command.

You can use the command line to confirm that the image-uploader limit range was created and to confirm the settings you specified in the YAML template were accurately read:

```
$ oc get limitrange
NAME                     AGE
core-resource-limits     5m
$ oc describe limitrange core-resource-limits
Name:          core-resource-limits
Namespace:     image-uploader
Type           Resource   Min     Max    Default Request    Default Limit
↪ Max Limit/Request Ratio
----           --------   ---     ---    ---------------    -------------
↪ ----------------------
Pod            cpu        100m    2      -        -          -
Pod            memory     4Mi     1Gi    -        -          -
Container      cpu        100m    2      200m     300m       10
Container      memory     4Mi     1Gi    100Mi    200Mi      -
```

You also can use the web UI to confirm the limit range you just set. Choose Resources > Quotas from the image-uploader project overview page to see the limit range.

   Limit ranges act on components in a project. They also provide default resource limits for deployments that don't provide any specific values themselves. But they don't provide project-wide limits to specify a maximum resource amount. For that, you'll need to define a resource quota for image-uploader. In the next section, that's exactly what you'll do.

9.4   *Resource quotas*

Nobody likes a noisy neighbor, and OpenShift users are no different. If one project's users were able to consume more than their fair share of the resources in an OpenShift cluster, all manner of resource-availability issues would occur. For example, a resource-hungry development project could stop applications in a production-level project in the same cluster from scaling up when their traffic increased. To solve this problem, OpenShift uses project *quotas* to provide resource caps and limits at the project level.

   Whereas limit ranges provide resource minimums and maximums for individual application components, quotas provide maximum resource limits for an entire project. Quotas fall into three primary categories:

- Compute resources
- Storage resources
- Object counts

In chapter 2, we discussed pod lifecycles. Project quotas apply only to pods that aren't in a terminal (failed or succeeded) phase. Quotas apply to any pod in a pending, running, or unknown state. Before an application deployment is started or a deployed application is changed, OpenShift evaluates the project's quotas (see figure 9.2).

   TIP The full documentation for quotas in OpenShift is available at http://mng.bz/ktZj.

In the next section, you'll create a compute resource quota for the image-uploader project.

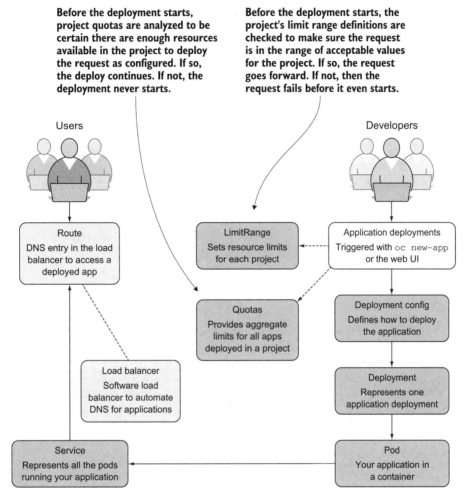

Before the deployment starts, project quotas are analyzed to be certain there are enough resources available in the project to deploy the request as configured. If so, the deploy continues. If not, the deployment never starts.

Before the deployment starts, the project's limit range definitions are checked to make sure the request is in the range of acceptable values for the project. If so, the request goes forward. If not, then the request fails before it even starts.

Users

Developers

Route
DNS entry in the load balancer to access a deployed app

LimitRange
Sets resource limits for each project

Application deployments
Triggered with `oc new-app` or the web UI

Quotas
Provides aggregate limits for all apps deployed in a project

Deployment config
Defines how to deploy the application

Load balancer
Software load balancer to automate DNS for applications

Deployment
Represents one application deployment

Service
Represents all the pods running your application

Pod
Your application in a container

Figure 9.2   Quotas are evaluated before any new resources are created in a project.

9.4.1 Creating compute quotas

Compute resource quotas apply to CPU and memory allocation. They're related to limit ranges, because they represent quotas against totals for requests and limits for all applications in a project. You can set the following six values with compute resource quotas:

- `cpu`, `requests.cpu`—Total of all CPU requests in a project, typically measured in cores or millicores. `cpu` and `requests.cpu` are synonyms and can be used interchangeably.
- `memory`, `requests.memory`—Total of all memory requests in a project, typically expressed in mebibytes or gibibytes. `memory` and `requests.memory` are synonyms and can be used interchangeably.

- `limits.cpu`—Total for all CPU limits in a project.
- `limits.memory`—Total for all memory limits in a project.

In addition to the quotas, you can also specify the *scope* the quota applies to. There are four quota scopes in OpenShift:

- `Terminating`—Pods that have a defined lifecycle. Typically, these are builder and deployment pods.
- `NotTerminating`—Pods that don't have a defined lifecycle. This scope includes application pods like app-gui and app-cli, and most other applications you'll deploy in OpenShift.
- `BestEffort`—Pods that have a best-effort QoS for CPU or memory. Best-effort deployments are those that didn't specify a request or limit when they were created.
- `NotBestEffort`—Pods that don't have a best-effort QoS for CPU or memory. The inverse of best effort, this scope is useful when you have a mixture of low-priority, transient workloads that have been deployed with best-effort QoS, and higher-priority workloads with dedicated resources.

Quotas are defined in YAML templates like all other resources in OpenShift. To create a quota for compute resources with the `NotTerminating` quota scope, create a file named compute-resources.yaml on your workstation with the content from the following listing.

Listing 9.2   Template to create CPU resource quotas

```
apiVersion: v1
kind: ResourceQuota
metadata:
  name: compute-resources
spec:
  hard:
    pods: "10"
    requests.cpu: "2"
    requests.memory: 2Gi
    limits.cpu: "3"
    limits.memory: 3Gi
  scopes:
    - NotTerminating
```

A maximum of two CPU cores can be requested.

The project can run a maximum of 10 pods.

A maximum of two gibibytes of memory can be requested.

The CPU limit is three cores total.

The project's memory limit is three gibibytes.

Scope that limits the quota to deployed application pods

To create a new quota for a project, cluster-admin level privileges are required. That means you need to be logged in as the admin user to run this command, because the developer user only has the edit role bound to it for the image-uploader project and has no privileges for the rest of the cluster. To log in as the admin user, run the following `oc login` command:

```
oc login -u admin -p admin https://ocp-1.192.168.122.100.nip.io:8443
```

Now, run the following `oc create` command to create the new CPU resource quota:

```
oc create -f compute-resources.yaml -n image-uploader
```

This command applies the compute-resources quota YAML template to the image-uploader project. To confirm that this quota was applied, run the following `oc get` command:

```
oc get resourcequota -n image-uploader
```

In the output, you should see a quota name `compute-resources`. Next, you'll create some resource quotas for image-uploader. Resource quotas provide a cap for the number of deployable resources in a project.

9.4.2 *Creating resource quotas*

Resource quotas track all resources in a project that are deployed by Kubernetes. Core components in OpenShift, like deployment configs and build configs, aren't covered by quotas; that's because these components are created on demand for each deployment and controlled by OpenShift.

The components that are managed by resource quotas are the primary resources in an OpenShift cluster that consume storage and compute resources. Keeping track of a project's resources is important when you need to plan how to grow and manage your OpenShift cluster to accommodate your applications. The following components are tracked by resource quotas:

- *Config maps*—We discussed config maps in chapter 6.
- *Persistent volume claims*—Application requests for persistent storage.
- *Resource quotas*—The total number of quotas in a project.
- *Replication controllers*—The number of RCs in a project. This is typically equal to the number of deployed applications, but you can also manually deploy applications using different workflows that could make this number change.
- *Secrets*—We discussed secrets in chapter 6.
- *Services*—The total number of services in a project.
- *Image streams*—The total number of image streams in a project.

Most of the items in this list should look familiar. We've been discussing them for several chapters now.

The following listing shows the resource quota template that you need to apply to the image-uploader project. To do this, create a file named core-object-counts.yaml on your workstation, and enter the contents of the following listing.

Listing 9.3 Template to create resource quotas

```
apiVersion: v1
kind: ResourceQuota
metadata:
  name: core-object-counts      ◁──┐ Name for the
                                    │ resource quota
```

```
spec:
  hard:                      <── Limits for resource types
    configmaps: "10"
    persistentvolumeclaims: "5"
    resourcequotas: "5"
    replicationcontrollers: "20"
    secrets: "50"
    services: "10"
    openshift.io/Image streams: "10"
```

Run the following command to apply the resource quota template to the image-uploader project. As was true for the compute quota you created, you need to be logged in to OpenShift as the admin user to run this command:

```
oc create -f core-object-counts.yaml -n image-uploader
```

Next, you can confirm that your quota was created using the command line or the web interface. At the command line, run the same oc get quota command you ran to confirm that your compute quota was applied. You should see both quotas in the command output:

```
$ oc get quota -n image-uploader          <──┐ Gets the names of
NAME                    AGE                   │ all active quotas
compute-resources       9h
core-object-counts      9h
```

To see the configuration for each quota, run oc describe resourcequota and complete the command with each quota name:

```
$ oc describe resourcequota compute-resources   <──┐ Describes the compute
Name:          compute-resources                   │ resource quota
Namespace:     image-uploader
Scopes:        NotTerminating
 * Matches all pods that do not have an active deadline.
Resource     Used    Hard
--------     ----    ----
limits.cpu     0     2
limits.memory    0     2Gi
pods           2     10        <── Pod count quota
requests.cpu     0     3
requests.memory    0     3Gi

$ oc describe quota core-object-counts        <──┐ Resource quotas, which
Name:              core-object-counts            │ are all counted correctly
Namespace:         image-uploader
Resource              Used    Hard
--------              ----    ----
configmaps               0    10
openshift.io/imagestreams    2    10
persistentvolumeclaims       1    5
replicationcontrollers       4    20
secrets                  9    50
services               2    10
```

In the web interface, you can see this information added to the quota page under Resources > Quotas, linked from the image-uploader project overview page.

Looking at the compute quota from the previous output, you can see that you've run into a problem: the app-gui and app-cli deployments aren't counting against the compute quota. The number of pods is reflected, but not the CPU or memory consumption. In the next section, we'll discuss why that is and how you can work with your newly minted quotas and limits in OpenShift.

9.5   *Working with quotas and limits*

Now that the image-uploader project has limit ranges and quotas, it's time to put them through their paces. The compute quota for app-cli and app-gui isn't being reflected yet, and your first task is to fix that.

9.5.1   *Applying quotas and limits to existing applications*

When you deployed app-gui and app-cli in chapter 2, no quotas or limits were defined for the image-uploader project. As we mentioned when you were creating limit ranges, back then your cluster was essentially the Wild West, and any deployed application could consume any amount of resources in the cluster.

If an application is created and there are no limit ranges to reference and no resources were requested (as when you deployed the metrics pod in chapter 5), the Linux kernel components that define the resource constraints for each container are created with unlimited values for the resources limits. This is what happened when you deployed app-cli and app-gui and why their CPU and memory quotas aren't reflected in OpenShift.

Now that you've applied limit ranges and quotas to image-uploader, you can have OpenShift re-create the containers for app-gui and app-cli to include these constraints. The easiest way to do this is to delete the current pods for each application. When you run the following `oc delete` command, OpenShift will automatically deploy new pods that contain the default limit ranges that you defined in the previous section:

```
$ for i in app-cli app-gui;do oc delete pod -l app=$i;done
```

This command is a `for` loop that will iterate through both app-cli and app-gui and variables. For each value, it will delete the pods in OpenShift that have the `app=VALUE` label.

Because you didn't specify specific resource values, your new app-gui and app-cli pods inherit the default request values you defined in the `core-resource-limits` limit range. Each pod was assigned 200 millicores and 100 MiB of RAM. You can see in the previous output that the consumed CPU and memory quotas for the image-uploader project are twice the default request.

TIP   It's definitely not a best practice to start using projects before you've set limits and quotas. But we had to start somewhere, and if chapter 2 was all about quotas, you'd never have gotten to chapter 3. So, for teaching purposes, we decided to begin with using OpenShift before we discussed a proper configuration.

In the next section, you'll edit the app-cli deployment config to give it more resources than the default limit.

9.5.2   *Changing quotas for deployed applications*

When you deploy a new application, you can specify limits and quotas as part of its definition. You can also edit the YAML definition for an existing deployment config directly from the command line. To edit the resource limits for your app-cli deployment, run the following `oc edit` command, which lets you edit the current YAML definition for the application:

```
oc edit dc/app-cli
```

This command attempts to open the YAML template from the OpenShift database with the default text editor on your system. To edit the resource limits, you need to find the `spec.containers.resources` section of the configuration. This section is currently empty because nothing was defined when the application was deployed:

```
spec:
    containers:
      ...
      resources: {}
      ...
```

Let's add memory and CPU requests and limits that are slightly larger than the default request values you defined in your limit range. Replace the `{}` in the `resources` section, and edit the file to look like the following listing, adding a larger quota request and limit for CPU and memory resources.

> **Listing 9.4   Editing the deployment config to increase limits and resource requests**

```
resources:
  requests:
    cpu: "750m"
    memory: "500Mi"
  limits:
    cpu: "1"
    memory: "1000Mi"
```

Saving the new configuration file will trigger a new deployment for app-cli. This new deployment will incorporate your new resource requests and limits. Once the build completes, your app-cli deployment will be available with more guaranteed resources.

You can confirm this by looking at the web interface page for the latest deployment, or from the command line by running the following `oc describe` command:

```
oc describe dc/app-cli
```

You can edit a deployment config to make complex changes to deployed applications, but it's a manual process. For new application deployments, your projects should use the default limit ranges whenever possible, to inherit default values.

While your resource requests and limit ranges are new and fresh in your mind, let's dig a little deeper and discuss how these constraints are enforced in OpenShift by the Linux kernel with *control groups* (cgroups).

9.6   Using cgroups to limit resources

Cgroups are Linux kernel components that provide per-process limits for CPU, memory, network bandwidth, and block-storage bandwidth. In an OpenShift cluster, they enforce the limits and quotas configured for applications and projects.

9.6.1   Cgroups overview

Cgroups are defined in a hierarchy in the /sys/fs/cgroup/ directory on the application node. Within this director is a directory for each type of cgroup *controller* that's available. A controller represents a specific system resource that can be controlled by cgroups (see figure 9.3).

In this section, we're focusing on the cpu and memory cgroup controllers. In the directories for the cpu and memory controllers is a directory named kubepods.slice. Cgroup *slices* are used to create subdivisions within a cgroup controller. Slices are used as logical dividers in a controller and define resource limits for groups of resources below them in the cgroup hierarchy.

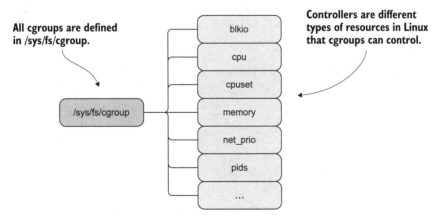

Figure 9.3   Cgroup controller hierarchy

The kubepods slice is where the configurations to enforce OpenShift requests and limits are located (figure 9.4). Within kubepods.slice are two additional slices:

- kubepods-besteffort.slice
- kubepods-burstable.slice

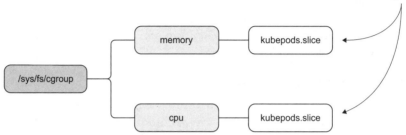

Figure 9.4   **kubepods.slice cgroup slices**

These two slices are how resource limits for best-effort and burstable QoS levels that we've discussed in this chapter are enforced. Because you defined resource requests for app-cli and app-gui, they both will be defined in kubepods-burstable.slice.

Within kubepods-besteffort.slice and kubepods-burstable.slice are multiple additional slices. There isn't an immediate identifier to tell you which slice contains the resource information for a given container, but you can get that information directly from docker on your application node.

> **NOTE**   In the following sections, you'll interact with docker to extract low-level information about the containers that OpenShift creates. Working with docker is outlined in appendix C; if you haven't already, read appendix C, and then move on to the next section.

9.6.2   *Identifying container cgroups*

To determine which cgroup slice controls the resources for your app-cli deployment, you need to get the cgroup information from docker. The cgroup slice that each container belongs to is listed in the information from docker inspect. To obtain it, use the -f parameter and specify the {{ .HostConfig.CgroupParent }} object accessor. This limits the output to only the cgroup slice information. In our example cluster, the cgroup slice for app-cli is kubepods-burstable-pod7bdf36bb_a3eb_11e7_a480 _001cc4000001.slice, as you can see here:

```
# docker inspect -f '{{ .HostConfig.CgroupParent }}' 80366fd64c36
kubepods-burstable-pod7bdf36bb_a3eb_11e7_a480_001cc4000001.slice
```

As we mentioned earlier, app-cli's cgroup is in the burstable slice. The slice defined in the app-cli `docker inspect` output is in the burstable slice. Slices don't define resource constraints for individual containers, but they can set default values for multiple containers. That's why the hierarchy of slices looks a little excessive here.

You have one more layer to go to get to the resource constraints for the app-cli container. In the lowest slice is a scope directory. Cgroup scopes are where individual process resource constraints are defined. Each scope is named after the full hash that a container's short ID is based on. In our example, app-cli's resource constraints are defined in the scope named docker-80366fd64c3630651d80076e5333475438fb6fc8 e34f4525aa94fc99a0e15750.scope. This is how cgroups are mapped to containers in OpenShift (see figure 9.5).

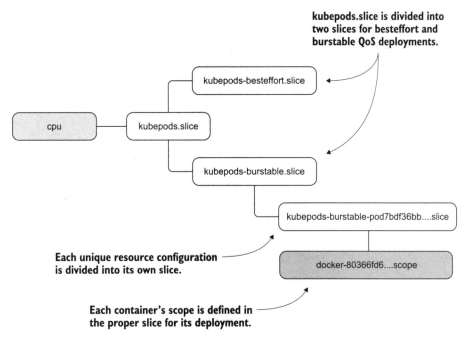

Figure 9.5 Cgroup hierarchy, down to the container-specific scope

Cgroup configurations are created on OpenShift application nodes using this process. It's a little complex; and because cgroups are listed according to the cgroup controller and not the PID they manage, troubleshooting them can be a challenge on a busy system.

When you need to see the cgroup configuration for a single container, the process is more straightforward. In the next section, we'll look at how the cgroup information from the host is mounted into each container that's created.

Viewing cgroups on the command line

This information is also available on the command line by using the `systemctl-cgls`
command to get a tree view of all the active cgroups on the application node. This
output shows every process on the system, organized by the cgroup it belongs to, so
it's pretty long. The output for the kubepods slice from `systemctl-cgls` is as follows:

```
...
|  └─kubepods.slice
|    ├─kubepods-burstable.slice
|    │  ├─kubepods-burstable-pod7bdf36bb_a3eb_11e7_a480_001cc4000001.slice
|    │  │ │?docker-
80366fd64c3630651d80076e5333475438fb6fc8e34f4525aa94fc99a0e15750.scope
|    │  │ │  ├─55965 httpd -D FOREGROUND
|    │  │ │  ├─56068 /usr/bin/cat
|    │  │ │  ├─56069 /usr/bin/cat
|    │  │ │  ├─56070 httpd -D FOREGROUND
|    │  │ │  ├─56073 httpd -D FOREGROUND
|    │  │ │  ├─56076 httpd -D FOREGROUND
|    │  │ │  ├─56091 httpd -D FOREGROUND
|    │  │ │  ├─56094 httpd -D FOREGROUND
|    │  │ │  ├─56098 httpd -D FOREGROUND
|    │  │ │  ├─56102 httpd -D FOREGROUND
|    │  │ │  ├─56105 httpd -D FOREGROUND
|    │  │ │  └─56966 httpd -D FOREGROUND
|    │  │
...
```

The `systemctl-cgls` tool displays the processes that are controlled by each cgroup
scope. But `systemctl-cgls` doesn't provide the actual resource limits associated
with a container's scope. To get that information, you need to access information
from the container.

9.6.3   *Confirming cgroup resource limits*

When docker creates a container, it mounts the cgroup scope that applies to it in the
container in the /sys/fs/cgroup directory. It truncates the slices and scope so the container appears to have only a single cgroup controller.

We're going to focus on the limits that enforce CPU and memory constraints for
the app-cli container. Let's begin with the limits for CPU consumption. To start an
interactive shell prompt in your running container, run the following command,
edited to reference your container's short ID:

```
# docker run -it 80366fd6 bash
```

This command launches the bash shell prompt in the specified container and provides you with an interactive TTY session. You'll use this session in the next section.

VERIFYING CONTAINER CPU LIMITS

As we discussed earlier in this chapter, CPU resources in OpenShift are allocated in millicores, or one-thousandths of the CPU resources available on the server. For example, if your application node has two CPUs, a total of 2,000 millicores is available for containers on the node.

The ratio expressed here is what's represented in the cpu cgroup. The actual number isn't expressed in the same units, but the ratios are always the same.

The app-cli container has a request of 750 millicores, with a limit of 1,000 millicores, or one CPU. You need the following two values from /sys/fs/cgroup/cpu to build a ratio that confirms the limit for the app-cli container:

- `cpu.cfs_quota_us`—The time, in microseconds, that the cgroup is allowed to access a CPU during the defined period. The period of time is adjustable. For example, if the `cfs_quota_us` value is `100`, the cgroup will be allowed to access the CPU for 100 microseconds during the set period. If that period is also `100`, that means the cgroup has unlimited access to a CPU on the system. If the period were set to `1000`, the process would have access to the CPU for 100 microseconds out of every 1,000.

- `cpu.cfs_period_us`—The time period, in microseconds, during which the cgroup's quota for CPU access is measured and reallocated. This can be manipulated to create different CPU quota ratios for different applications.

For app-cli, this cgroup limits the container's access to 1 CPU during 100,000 out of every 100,000 microseconds:

```
bash-4.2$ cat /sys/fs/cgroup/cpu/cpu.cfs_quota_us
100000
bash-4.2$ cat /sys/fs/cgroup/cpu/cpu.cfs_period_us
100000
```

If you convert these values to a ratio, app-cli is allocated a maximum of 1,000 millicores, or 1 CPU. That's the limit you set for app-cli. This is how CPU limits are managed for each container in an application deployment. Next, let's look at how the request values are controlled by cgroups.

> **NOTE** The limit for app-gui is 300 millicores, the default limit range for the image-uploader project. Using the same steps, you can verify that its CPU limits match the ratio of 300/1,000 millicores.

The request limit for app-cli is managed by the value in /sys/fs/cgroup/cpu/cpu.shares. This value is a ratio of CPU resources relative to all the cores on the system.

The CPU request for app-cli is 750 millicores. Because the application node has two CPUs, it should be allocated 750/2,000 of the total CPU capacity for the application node, or 37.5%. The cpu.shares ratio for app-cli should have the same ratio.

The denominator for the cgroup ratio is the total CPU shares available to kubepods .slice on the host. This value is set by multiplying the number of CPUs by 1,024. You can verify this with the `cpu.shares` value for kubepods.slice, as shown in the following example from the application node:

```
# cat /sys/fs/cgroup/cpu/kubepods.slice/cpu.shares
2048
```

To get the numerator for this ratio, run `cat /sys/fs/cgroup/cpu/cpu.shares` from inside the app-cli container:

```
$ cat /sys/fs/cgroup/cpu/cpu.shares
768
```

The app-cli container is allocated 768/2,048 CPU shares on the application node, or 37.5%. The numbers are identical. This is how OpenShift uses the Linux kernel to ensure that resource requests and limits are met for deployed containers.

Next, let's look at how cgroups enforce memory limits and requests.

VERIFYING CONTAINER MEMORY LIMITS

The memory limit for app-cli is controlled by the value in `/sys/fs/cgroup/memory/` `memory.limit_in_bytes` in the app-cli container. This value is expressed in bytes. If you convert it to mebibytes, the value you created the memory limit in, you get 1,000 MiB. This is the defined memory limit for app-cli. To view the value for the upper memory limit for app-cli, use the `cat` command to echo the file contents from inside the app-cli container:

```
bash-4.2$ cat /sys/fs/cgroup/memory/memory.limit_in_bytes
1048576000
```

Resource limits for OpenShift containers are enforced with kernel cgroups. The only exception is the memory request value. There's no cgroup to control the minimum amount of RAM available to a process; this value is primarily used to determine which node a pod is assigned to in your OpenShift cluster.

This chapter covered a lot of what's required to create and maintain a healthy OpenShift cluster. We've gone far down into the Linux kernel to confirm how container resource limits are enforced. Although limits, requests, and quotas aren't the most exciting things to work through, they're absolutely critical to make OpenShift ready to handle production workloads effectively.

Your cluster is now connected with an authentication database, and the project you've been working with has effective resource limits and quotas. In the following chapters, you'll keep building on that momentum.

9.7   *Summary*

- OpenShift can use a long list of user databases for user authentication.
- Special service accounts authenticate with SSL certificates that bypass the user database.
- OpenShift can bind roles that represent project or cluster permission sets to users and groups, to create a full role-based, access-control environment.
- Limit ranges provide minimum, maximum, and default compute resource limits for pods and containers at the project level.
- Limit ranges provide caps for the number of application components, such as services and persistent volume claims, that can be created in a single project.
- Quotas provide aggregate CPU and memory limits for projects. They have multiple scopes so different quotas can be applied to different types of project resources.
- Limits and requests are enforced in the Linux kernel by cgroups.
- Cgroups can be examined from the application node and used to troubleshoot issues when they arise.

Networking 10

This chapter covers

- Designing cluster networks
- Understanding network traffic flow in OpenShift
- Configuring Open vSwitch
- Configuring OpenShift network plugins
- Using DNS in OpenShift

The importance of the networking configuration in an OpenShift cluster can't be overstated; it's the fabric that binds your cluster together. With that perspective, OpenShift does a lot of work to make sure its networking configuration is stable, performs well, and is highly configurable. Those principles are what we'll cover in this chapter. Let's start with an overview of how the network in OpenShift is designed.

10.1 OpenShift network design

Up to this point, all your OpenShift applications have run on a single application node. It's time to fix that. Section A.8 in appendix A walks through the steps to provision a third server and add it to your OpenShift cluster as an application node. Go ahead and use that walkthrough to scale your cluster with an additional application node. When you're finished, your cluster will consist of a single master server and two application nodes.

When you initially deployed OpenShift, a private network called the *pod network* was created. Each pod in your OpenShift cluster is assigned an IP address on the pod network when it's deployed. This IP address is used to communicate with each pod across the cluster. The pod network spans all nodes in your cluster and was extended to your second application node when that was added to the cluster (see figure 10.1).

The pod network uses the 10.128.0.0/14 classless inter-domain routing (CIDR, (defined at http://mng.bz/28or) IP address block by default. Each node in the cluster is assigned a /23 CIDR IP address range from the pod network block. That means, by default, that each application node in OpenShift can accommodate a maximum of 512 pods. The IP ranges for each node are controlled by *OpenFlow*, a component in OpenShift's networking solution. OpenFlow (https://www.sdxcentral.com/sdn/definitions/what-is-openflow/) is a software-defined networking control-plane manager that OpenShift uses to route network traffic in the cluster without having to change the configuration of the host's networking stack. Open control lets OpenShift maintain the IP address ranges for each host without having to alter the application

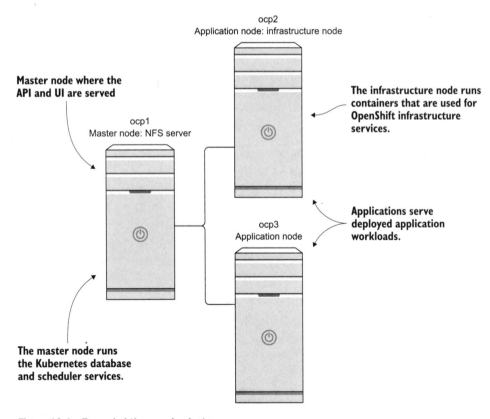

Figure 10.1 Expanded three-node cluster

node's network routing tables. To see information about the pod network, including the IP ranges allocated to each node, run the `oc get hostsubnet` command:

```
oc get hostsubnet
NAME                            HOST                            HOST IP
➥ SUBNET
ocp1.192.168.122.100.nip.io     ocp1.192.168.122.100.nip.io     192.168.122.100
➥ 10.129.0.0/23
ocp2.192.168.122.101.nip.io     ocp2.192.168.122.101.nip.io     192.168.122.101
➥ 10.128.0.0/23
ocp3.192.168.122.102.nip.io     ocp3.192.168.122.102.nip.io     192.168.122.102
➥ 10.130.0.0/23
```

All pods deployed on ocp2 have an IP address in the 10.128.0.0/23 range.

If you're already using the pod network IP address range

Your pod network IP addresses can't be used on your network by any network that OpenShift might need to communicate with. OpenShift's internal network routing follows all the rules of any network, and multiple destinations for the same IP address lead to confusion.

If you're using all or part of the 10.128.0.0/14 network range, you can change the pod network IP address range. When you configure the installation inventory file before deploying OpenShift, set the `osm_cluster_network_cidr` variable to the IP address range you want to use for the pod network. This variable and many others are documented at http://mng.bz/efu3. Be careful when you select the IP range for the pod network—once you deploy OpenShift, it's all but impossible to change it.

We already mentioned OpenFlow and that it's used to manage how IP addresses are allocated to each application node. The interfaces on the nodes that make up the pod network, and also the encrypted connections between nodes, are created and managed by Open vSwitch (OVS; www.openvswitch.org). Combined with the iptables firewall on each host, open control and OVS are referred to collectively as the *OpenShift SDN network plugin*. The term *software-defined networking* (SDN) can be used for any networking solution that uses interfaces and components that are created using software instead of physical interfaces. Next, we'll look at how OVS is used in OpenShift SDN.

TIP If you'd like more in-depth documentation for these open source projects, you can use these links for the OpenShift SDN components: OVS, http://docs.openvswitch.org/en/stable; open control, http://docs.openvswitch.org/en/latest/topics/openflow; and iptables, https://netfilter.org/documentation.

10.2 Managing the OpenShift SDN

OVS is an enterprise-grade, scalable, high-performance SDN. In OpenShift, it's the default SDN used to create the pod network in your cluster. It's installed and configured when you deploy OpenShift or add a node to an existing cluster. OVS runs as a service on each node in the cluster. You can check the status of the service by running the following `systemctl` command on any node:

```
systemctl status ovs-vswitchd
```

The `ovs-vswitchd` service is automatically enabled on all cluster nodes as part of OpenShift's deployment.

> ### Integrating OVS and Kubernetes
>
> The configuration file for OVS is located at /etc/sysconfig/openvswitch, and each node's local OVS database is located in the /etc/openswitch directory. For day-to-day operations, OVS should be transparent. Its configuration and updates are controlled by OpenShift. Using OVS provides several advantages to OpenShift.
>
> This transparent operation is possible because OpenShift uses the Kubernetes Container Network Interface (CNI; http://mng.bz/vRJa). The Kubernetes CNI provides a plugin architecture to integrate different SDN solutions to create and manage the pod network. OpenShift uses OVS as its default, but it can function with other network providers as well; these are documented at http://mng.bz/y145.

OVS is used in your OpenShift cluster as the communications backbone for all of your deployed pods. Traffic in and out of every pod is affected by OVS in the OpenShift cluster. For that reason, you need to know how it works and how to effectively use it for your needs. Let's start with the network configuration for your OpenShift application nodes.

10.2.1 Configuring application node networks

When a node is added to an OpenShift cluster, several network interfaces are created in addition to the standard `lo` loopback interface and `eth0` physical interface. For our purposes, we'll call `eth0` the physical interface even though you're using VMs for your cluster's infrastructure. That's because OpenShift creates the following additional virtual interfaces to route traffic:

- `br0`—An OVS bridge all OpenShift SDN interfaces are associated with. OVS creates this interface when the node is added to the OpenShift cluster.
- `tun0`—Attached to `br0`. Acts as the default gateway for each node. Traffic in and out of your OpenShift cluster is routed through this interface.
- `vxlan_sys_4789`—Also attached to `br0`. This virtual extensible local area network (VXLAN) is encrypted and used to route traffic to containers on other nodes in your cluster. It connects the nodes in your OpenShift cluster to create your pod network.

Additionally, each pod has a corresponding virtual Ethernet (veth) interface that's linked to the eth0 interface in the pod by the Linux kernel. Any network traffic that's sent to either interface in this relationship is automatically presented to the other. (We'll get into more detail in the next section.) All of these relationships are illustrated in figure 10.2.

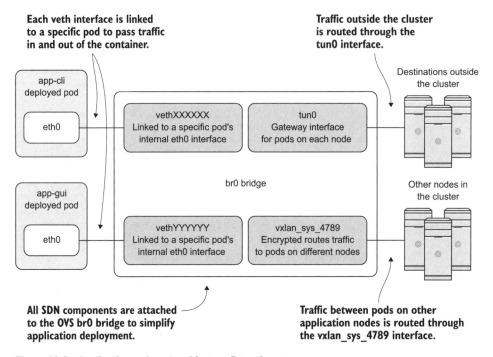

Figure 10.2 Application node networking configuration

What are Linux bridges, TUN interfaces, and VXLANs?

A Linux *bridge* is a virtual interface that's used to connect other interfaces together. If two interfaces on a host are attached to a bridge, they can communicate with each other without routes needing to be created. This helps with communication speed as well as keeping networking configurations simple on the host and in the container. For more details, see https://wiki.archlinux.org/index.php/Network_bridge.

A *VXLAN* is a protocol that acts as an *overlay* network between the nodes in your OpenShift cluster. An overlay network is a software-defined network that's deployed on top of another network. The VXLANs used in OpenShift are deployed on top of the networking configuration of the hosts.

To communicate securely between pods, the VXLAN encapsulates pod network traffic in an additional layer of network information so it can be delivered to the proper pod on the proper server by IP address. The overlay network is the pod network in your OpenShift cluster. The VXLAN interfaces on each node provide access to and from that network. You can find the full definition and specifications for a VXLAN in the RFC documentation at https://tools.ietf.org/html/rfc7348.

A *TUN interface* (short for network TUNnel) is a virtual network device that mimics the functionality of a physical interface. In the case of OpenShift, the tun0 interface acts as the default gateway on each node for the pod network. Because it's a virtual device and not a physical one, it can be used to route traffic on and off the non-routable pod network. In-depth information about TUN interfaces is available at www.kernel.org/doc/Documentation/networking/tuntap.txt.

All of these devices are controlled by OVS and form the network topology for OpenShift SDN.

You can see these interfaces on your application nodes by running the ip a command. The following sample output has been trimmed with a little command-line magic for brevity and clarity:

```
# ip a | egrep '^[0-9].*:' | awk '{ print $1 $2}'
1:lo:
2:eth0:
3:ovs-system:
6:br0:
7:docker0:
8:vxlan_sys_4789:
9:tun0:
10:veth68d047ad@if3:
11:veth875e3121@if3:
12:vethb7bbb4d5@if3:
13:vethd7768410@if3:
14:veth8f8e1db6@if3:
15:veth334d0271@if3:
```

The networking configuration for the master node is essentially the same as an application node. The master node uses the pod network to communicate with pods on the application nodes as they're deployed, deliver their applications, and are eventually deleted. In the next section, we'll look more deeply at how the interface in the container is linked to a corresponding veth interface on the application node.

10.2.2 *Linking containers to host interfaces*

In chapter 3, we talked about the network namespace and how each container contains a unique loopback and eth0 interface for network communications. From the
perspective of applications in a container, these two interfaces are the only networks
on the host. To get network traffic in and out of the container, the eth0 interface in
the container is linked in the Linux kernel to a corresponding veth interface in the
host's default network namespace.

The ability to link two interfaces is a feature of the Linux kernel. To determine
which veth interface a container is linked to, you need to log in to the application
node where the container is running. You can figure this out in just a few steps. Let's
use the app-cli application as an example.

Run the oc get pods -o wide command to confirm where the app-cli pod is
deployed:

```
$ oc get pods -o wide -n image-uploader --show-all=false
NAME                    READY      STATUS      RESTARTS    AGE        IP
 NODE
app-cli-4-vt840    1/1        Running    1          3d         10.130.0.17
 ocp3.192.168.122.102.nip.io
app-gui-2-2jwp8    1/1        Running    1          3d         10.130.0.16
 ocp3.192.168.122.102.nip.io
test-1-dzs4r       1/1        Running    3          5d         10.130.0.18
 ocp3.192.168.122.102.nip.io
```

The app-cli pod is deployed on ocp3.

Any virtual interface on a Linux system can be linked by the kernel to another virtual
or physical interface. When an interface is linked to another, the kernel makes them
essentially the same interface. If something happens to one interface, it automatically
happens to its linked interface. In an interface's iflink file—a file created and maintained by the running Linux kernel at /sys/class/net/<interface name>/iflink—is the
index number for its linked interface. To find the linked interface number for the
app-cli container, run the following oc exec command, making sure to use the pod ID
for your app-cli deployment. This command uses the cat command-line tool to echo
the contents of the app-cli container's iflink file:

```
$ oc exec app-cli-4-vt840 cat /sys/class/net/eth0/iflink
11
```

The eth0 interface in the app-cli pod is linked to interface 11 on application node
ocp3. But which veth interface is number 11? That information is available in the output from the ip a command. The link ID, also called the ifindex for each interface,
is the number at the beginning of each interface listed. For each eth0 interface in a
container, its iflink value is the ifindex value of its corresponding veth interface
(see figure 10.3).

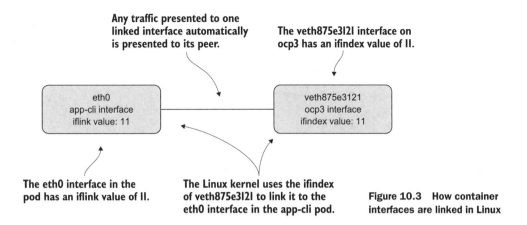

Any traffic presented to one linked interface automatically is presented to its peer.

The veth875e3l2l interface on ocp3 has an ifindex value of ll.

eth0
app-cli interface
iflink value: 11

veth875e3121
ocp3 interface
ifindex value: 11

The eth0 interface in the pod has an iflink value of ll.

The Linux kernel uses the ifindex of veth875e3l2l to link it to the eth0 interface in the app-cli pod.

Figure 10.3 How container interfaces are linked in Linux

You previously confirmed that app-cli is deployed on ocp3. To confirm that the index for the veth interface app-cli is linked to, SSH to ocp3 (this may be different on your cluster). To view only the interface with `ifindex` 11 on ocp3, run the following `ip a` command (we've trimmed the command-line output):

```
# ip a | egrep -A 3 '^11.*:'
11: veth875e3121@if3: <BROADCAST,MULTICAST,UP,LOWER_UP> mtu 1450 qdisc➡
 noqueue master ovs-system state UP
    link/ether 1e:5f:8f:29:ff:59 brd ff:ff:ff:ff:ff:ff link-netnsid 1
    inet6 fe80::1c5f:8fff:fe29:ff59/64 scope link
       valid_lft forever preferred_lft forever
```

You've now confirmed that the app-cli pod is linked by the Linux kernel to veth875e3121 on the ocp3 application node. This is how network traffic enters and exits containers in general. Next, let's confirm that veth875e3121 on ocp3 is connected to the cluster's pod network so network traffic can get in and out of the OpenShift cluster.

10.2.3 *Working with OVS*

The command-line tool to work with OVS directly is `ovs-vsctl`. To use this tool, you need to be logged in to the host you're looking for information about. In these examples, we're logged in to ocp3, where app-cli is deployed and where we've already identified the linked interface for app-cli.

We mentioned earlier in this chapter that all OpenShift SDN interfaces are attached to an OVS bridge named `br0`. We make the distinction of calling it an OVS bridge because it's a bridge interface that's created and controlled by OVS. You can also create a bridge interface with the Linux kernel. A Linux bridge is created and managed using the `brctl` command. You can confirm that the `br0` interface is being controlled by OVS by running the following `ovs-vsctl` command to list all active OVS bridges:

```
# ovs-vsctl list-br
br0
```

If you've used Linux bridges before, it can seem confusing when you know a bridge should be present but none appears when you run `brctl`, because they're being managed by OVS. Ocp3 has a single OVS bridge named `br0`, which aligns with what we discussed earlier. To list the interfaces connected to `br0`, run the following `ovs-vsctl` command:

```
# ovs-vsctl list-ifaces br0
```

The output of this command lists all interfaces connected to `br0`:

- `tun0` interface that's the default gateway for the pod network on ocp3.
- `vxlan0` interface, which is how the `vxlan_sys_4789` interface is referenced in the OVS database

Also included is a veth interface for each pod running on the node, including veth875e3121, which is the interface linked to `eth0` in the app-cli pod:

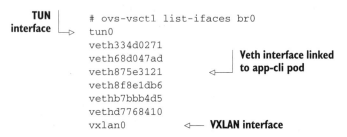

This is how OpenShift SDN functions. When a new pod is deployed, a new veth interface is created and attached to `bro`. At that point, the pod can send and receive network traffic on the pod network. It can communicate outside the cluster through `br0` and communicate to pods on other application nodes using the `vxlan_sys_4789` interface (see figure 10.4).

In the next section, you'll put OpenShift's SDN to work by digging deeper into how application traffic is routed and how applications communicate in your cluster. Let's start at the beginning, with a request for the app-cli deployment.

10.3 *Routing application requests*

When you browse to http://app-cli-image-uploader.apps.192.168.122.101.nip.io/, your request goes to ocp2 (192.168.122.101) on port 80, the default HTTP port. Log in to ocp2, and run the following `netstat` command to determine which service is listening on port 80:

```
# netstat -tpl --numeric-ports | grep 80
tcp        0      0 0.0.0.0:80              0.0.0.0:*               LISTEN
➥ 42625/haproxy
```

There's an `haproxy` service running on ocp2 as PID 42625. Let's look at this in more detail.

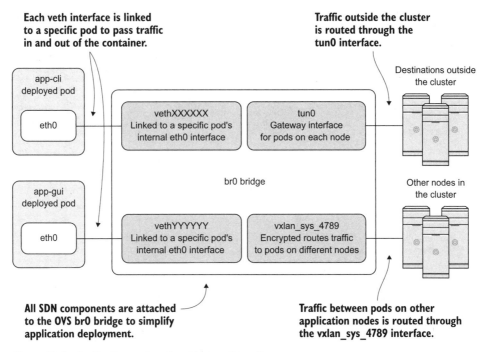

Figure 10.4 Application node networking configuration

10.3.1 *Using HAProxy to route requests*

HAProxy (www.haproxy.org) is the front door to your applications in OpenShift. HAProxy is an open source, software-defined load balancer and proxy application. In OpenShift, it takes the URL route associated with an application and proxies those requests into the proper pod to get the requested data back to the requesting user. We won't dig too deeply into all that HAProxy can do—we're focusing on how OpenShift uses HAProxy. If you'd like more information about HAProxy, you can find documentation for its different versions at www.haproxy.org/#docs.

> **TIP** Like the networking configuration, the router in OpenShift is built using a plugin architecture. The default plugin is the HAProxy plugin we're discussing in this chapter. But OpenShift also ships with a routing plugin that uses the BigIP F5 load-balancer platform (https://f5.com/products/big-ip/local-traffic-manager-ltm). You can find more information about configuring router plugins at https://docs.openshift.org/latest/install_config/router/index.html.

The router pod runs in the project named "default" in OpenShift. The router pod handles incoming user requests for your OpenShift cluster's applications and proxies them to the proper pod to be served to the user. The router pod listens directly on the host interface for the node it's deployed on and uses the pod network to proxy requests for different applications to the proper pod. The session then returns to the user from the pod's host through its TUN interface (see figure 10.5).

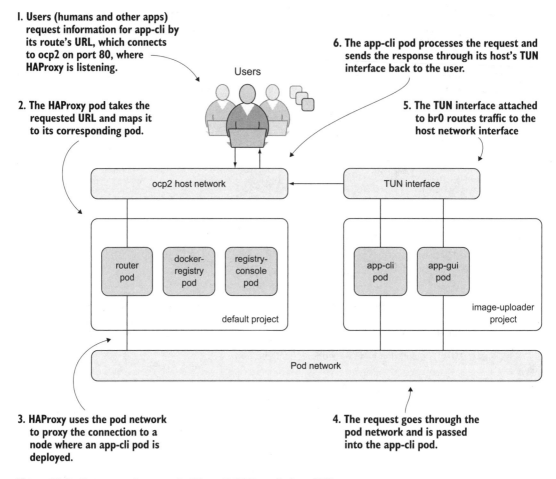

1. Users (humans and other apps) request information for app-cli by its route's URL, which connects to ocp2 on port 80, where HAProxy is listening.

6. The app-cli pod processes the request and sends the response through its host's TUN interface back to the user.

2. The HAProxy pod takes the requested URL and maps it to its corresponding pod.

5. The TUN interface attached to br0 routes traffic to the host network interface

Users

ocp2 host network

TUN interface

router pod

docker-registry pod

registry-console pod

default project

app-cli pod

app-gui pod

image-uploader project

Pod network

3. HAProxy uses the pod network to proxy the connection to a node where an app-cli pod is deployed.

4. The request goes through the pod network and is passed into the app-cli pod.

Figure 10.5   How requests are routed through HAProxy in OpenShift

Because the router listens directly on the host's interface, it's configured differently than a typical pod in OpenShift. In the next section, we'll investigate the HAProxy pod in more detail.

How HAProxy always deploys to the same node

When you deployed your OpenShift cluster, you added a label to the ocp2 node that added it to a region named `infra`:

```
- connect_to: 192.168.122.101 ... node_labels: '{''region'': ''infra''}'
```

Labels are arbitrary key-value pairs you can use in OpenShift workflows to manage applications and a host of interactions. You can add labels to the nodes in your cluster and use those labels to specify where specific pods are deployed.

> To specify a specific node or group of nodes by label, specify a `nodeSelector` value in your application's deployment config component. The default OpenShift router has a node selector that specifies the node with the matching `region=infra` label. You can see this node selector in the router's deployment config:
>
> ```
> $ oc export dc/router -n default | grep -A1 nodeSelector
>     nodeSelector:
>         region: infra
> ```
>
> Node selectors are powerful tools when you need to separate different types of applications in your OpenShift cluster. You can see a great demo at http://mng.bz/2HDH. For the HAProxy router, a node selector makes the public IP address for accessing your applications predictable. Your application's DNS routes won't have to be updated, because the router will always be deployed on the node that has the `region=infra` label associated with it. As long as that node's IP address is consistent, your routes will work reliably.

10.3.2 *Investigating the HAProxy pod*

The `lsns` tool you used in chapter 3 displays the namespaces associated with the haproxy process listening on port 80. The following `lsns` command works in our example cluster. Our example has PID 42625; be sure to change the PID to match your own cluster:

```
lsns -p 42625
```

Instead of having unique network and UTS namespaces, the router pod uses the UTS and network namespaces from the host system:

**Network namespace created by
systemd when the host was booted**

```
NS TYPE  NPROCS    PID USER        COMMAND
4026531837 user      299    1 root
⮡ /usr/lib/systemd/systemd --switched-root --system --deserialize 20
4026531838 uts       265    1 root
⮡ /usr/lib/systemd/systemd --switched-root --system
⮡ --deserialize 20
4026531956 net       265    1 root
⮡ /usr/lib/systemd/systemd --switched-root --system
⮡ --deserialize 20
4026532506 ipc        4 11699 1001        /usr/bin/pod
4026532708 mnt        3 12199 1000000000 /usr/bin/openshift-router
4026532709 pid        3 12199 1000000000 /usr/bin/openshift-router
```

**UTS namespace created by systemd
when the host was booted**

Using the host's network namespace lets HAProxy listen directly on the host's interfaces for incoming requests. Listening on the host's interface means HAProxy receives application requests directly, acting as OpenShift's front door for application traffic.

The router pod has its own mount namespace, which means the configuration files for HAProxy are isolated in the container. To enter the router pod, run the following `oc rsh` command, substituting the name of your router pod:

```
$ oc rsh router-1-qpfg3
sh-4.2$
```

Once you're in the container's namespace context, confirm that the router pod can see the host's network by running the `ip a` command. You see all the interfaces on the host.

> **TIP** The router pod is an example of a *privileged* pod. A privileged pod is able to run with additional permissions and resource access in the OpenShift cluster. We'll discuss these in more depth in chapter 11.

So far in this section, we've talked about how HAProxy uses the networking stack for the host it runs on, and how it's always deployed to the same node by using a node selector that specifies nodes with the `region=infra` label. Those features provide two primary benefits:

- Using the host networking stack lets HAProxy receive requests directly from users. Because HAProxy is the front door to OpenShift, it has to be the first thing a request encounters.
- Deploying to the same host makes it easier to manage the DNS routes used to access individual applications.

In the next section, we'll walk through how HAProxy takes the URL that's been requested and proxies the traffic into a pod servicing the correct application. We'll look at the HAProxy configuration in the pod, scale an application, and see how the HAProxy configuration changes.

10.3.3 *How HAProxy gets requests to the correct pods*

The configuration file for HAProxy is in the pod at /var/lib/haproxy/conf/haproxy.config. This configuration file is maintained by OpenShift. Any time an application is deployed, updated, or deleted, OpenShift updates this configuration and has the HAProxy process reload it. Let's see this in action.

With app-cli scaled to a single-pod replica, run the following command to search for the app-cli HAProxy configuration in the router pod:

```
                     $ grep app-cli /var/lib/haproxy/conf/haproxy.config
    app-cli pod      backend be_http:image-uploader:app-cli
    entry in the       server pod:app-cli-1-c7t85:app-cli:10.128.0.73:8080 10.128.0.73:8080
    HAProxy          ➥ cookie 10c2a5a2bcb4ba518fc9b08053a8b544 weight
configuration    ┗➙ ➥ 100 check inter 5000ms
```

We won't go too deep into how the configuration works, but you can see the pod name, IP address, and port to access app-cli.

Next, scale app-cli to two pods, either in the web UI or with the following oc command from a workstation that can log in to OpenShift:

```
$ oc scale dc/app-cli --replicas=2 -n image-uploader
```

This command takes a few seconds to complete. After it's done, rerun the search in the router pod for app-cli. Kubernetes has updated the HAProxy configuration to add an entry for the newly created app-cli pod:

Original pod entry

```
$ grep app-cli /var/lib/haproxy/conf/haproxy.config
backend be_http:image-uploader:app-cli
   server pod:app-cli-1-c7t85:app-cli:10.128.0.73:8080 10.128.0.73:8080 cookie
➥ 10c2a5a2bcb4ba518fc9b08053a8b544 weight
➥ 100 check inter 5000ms
   server pod:app-cli-1-3lqbw:app-cli:10.128.0.75:8080 10.128.0.75:8080 cookie
➥ 3208c76c647df4c7f738539068c8a368 weight
➥ 100 check inter 5000ms
```

The scaled-up pod IP address is added automatically to HAProxy configuration when the pod deploys.

HAProxy takes the request from the user, maps the requested URL to a defined route in the cluster, and proxies the request to the IP address for a pod in the service associated with that route. All this traverses the pod network created by OpenShift SDN (see figure 10.6)

This process works in concert with iptables on each host. OpenShift uses a complex, dynamic iptables configuration to make sure requests on the pod network are routed to the proper application pod. Iptables are a complex topic that we don't have space to cover here, but we wanted to mention them so you know they should be running on your cluster nodes, and they're crucial to your cluster's effective operation. For more information, visit http://mng.bz/p58R.

The method for routing requests in OpenShift works well. But it poses a problem when you're deploying applications that depend on each other to function. If a new pod is added to an application or a pod is replaced and it receives a new IP address, the change would require all applications that reference it to be updated and redeployed. This isn't a serviceable solution. Luckily, OpenShift incorporates a DNS service on the pod network. Let's examine it next.

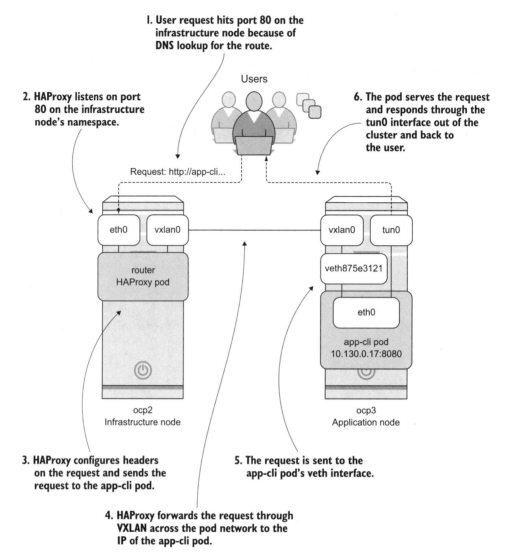

1. User request hits port 80 on the infrastructure node because of DNS lookup for the route.

Users

2. HAProxy listens on port 80 on the infrastructure node's namespace.

6. The pod serves the request and responds through the tun0 interface out of the cluster and back to the user.

Request: http://app-cli...

eth0   vxlan0   vxlan0   tun0

router HAProxy pod

veth875e3121

eth0

app-cli pod 10.130.0.17:8080

ocp2 Infrastructure node

ocp3 Application node

3. HAProxy configures headers on the request and sends the request to the app-cli pod.

5. The request is sent to the app-cli pod's veth interface.

4. HAProxy forwards the request through VXLAN across the pod network to the IP of the app-cli pod.

Figure 10.6   OpenShift SDN network interfaces

10.4   *Locating services with internal DNS*

Applications depend on each other to deliver information to users. Middleware apps depend on databases. Web presentation apps depend on middleware. In an application spanning multiple independently scalable pods, these relationships are complex to manage. To make this easier, OpenShift deploys *SkyDNS* (https://github.com/sky-netservices/skydns) when the cluster is deployed and makes it available on the pod network. SkyDNS is a DNS service that uses etcd, the primary Kubernetes database, to store DNS records. DNS records, also known as *zone files*, are configuration files where

DNS records are recorded for a domain controlled by a DNS server. In OpenShift, SkyDNS controls the zone files for several domains that exist only on the pod network:

- *cluster.local*—Top-level domain for everything in your OpenShift cluster
- *svc.cluster.local*—Domain for all services running in your cluster

Domains for each project are also created. For example, image-uploader.svc.cluster .local is used to access all the services created in the image-uploader project.

A DNS A record (http://support.dnsimple.com/articles/a-record) is created in SkyDNS for each service in OpenShift when an application is deployed. A service represents all the deployed pods for an application. To view the services for the image-uploader project, run the following oc command:

```
$ oc get services -n image-uploader
NAME       CLUSTER-IP      EXTERNAL-IP    PORT(S)     AGE
app-cli    172.30.86.81    <none>         8080/TCP    3h
app-gui    172.30.90.249   <none>         8080/TCP    3h
```

Let's examine how DNS resolution works in your OpenShift cluster.

10.4.1 DNS resolution in the pod network

When a pod is deployed, the /etc/resolv.conf file from the application node is mounted in the container in the same location. In Linux, /etc/resolv.conf configures the servers and configuration used for DNS resolution. By default, /etc/resolv.conf on the application node is configured with the IP address for the node itself. DNS requests on each application node are forwarded to SkyDNS running on the master server.

The search parameter in /etc/resolv.conf is also updated when it's mounted in the container. It's updated to include cluster.local, svc.cluster.local, and all other domains managed by SkyDNS.

Any domains defined in the search parameter in resolv.conf are used when a fully qualified domain name (FQDN) isn't used for a hostname. FQDNs are defined at https://tools.ietf.org/html/rfc4703; but because not everyone loves to read RFC documents, a good rule of thumb is that an FQDN has to be a complete address on a network. The domain server.domain.com is fully qualified, where server isn't a complete domain name. The search parameter provides one or more domains that are automatically appended to non-FQDNs to use for DNS queries.

When a request comes in from your cluster, those requests are automatically forwarded to the master server where SkyDNS handles requests. Let's test it in action in your cluster.

From an OpenShift node, you can access the services using DNS if you use its FQDN. The format is service_name.project_name.svc.cluster.local:port. The following example is run from ocp3, connecting to the app-cli service:

```
# curl app-cli.image-uploader.svc.cluster.local:8080
<html>
<head>
<title>Image Library Demo Application by </title><style>
body {
...
</body>
</html>
```

You can run the same command from within a pod without specifying the FQDN, because /etc/resolv.conf has the SkyDNS search domains added. Using `oc rsh`, you can enter the namespaces for the app-cli pod and use `curl` to download the index page from app-gui service and the default page for the router service:

```
$ oc rsh app-cli-1-31qbw        ⟵ Connects to the app-cli pod


$ curl app-gui.image-uploader:8080      ⟵ Browses the app-gui service
<html>
<head>
<title>Image Library Demo Application by </title><style>
body {
...
</body>
</html>
                                    Browses wildfly-app in
                                    the stateful-apps project
$ oc rsh app-gui-1-2zrqx        ⟵
sh-4.2$ curl wildfly-app.stateful-apps:8080
<!DOCTYPE html>
<!--
    JBoss, Home of Professional Open Source
    Copyright 2014, Red Hat, Inc. and/or its affiliates, and individual
```

Using OpenShift's implementation of SkyDNS, you can access any deployed application using the DNS record for its service. In OpenShift, application relationships remain stable, and no information about the application's pods is required. This abstraction makes it easy to add references to other services in applications' configurations when they're deployed, without having to know the actual pod-level information about them.

In the previous example, you accessed an application from one project (wildfly-app in the stateful-apps project) from an application pod in another project (the app-cli pod in the image-uploader project). You do so because the default configuration of OpenShift's pod network uses a flat network topology. Applications from one project are able to communicate with applications in all other projects.

This configuration works well when OpenShift is used by a single team. But when you need a multitenant environment to support multiple teams who don't need to view each other's applications, OpenShift handles that situation as well. In the next section, you'll change OpenShift's network configuration so it isolates the network traffic for each project.

10.5 *Configuring OpenShift SDN*

When you deploy OpenShift, the default configuration for the pod network's topology is a single flat network. Every pod in every project is able to communicate without restrictions. OpenShift SDN uses a plugin architecture that provides different network topologies in OpenShift. There are currently three OpenShift SDN plugins that can be enabled in the OpenShift configuration without making large changes to your cluster:

- *ovs-subnet*—Enabled by default. Creates a flat pod network, allowing all pods in all projects to communicate with each other (see figure 10.7).
- *ovs-multitenant*—Separates the pods by project. The applications deployed in a project can only communicate with pods deployed in the same project. You'll enable this plugin in this chapter.
- *ovs-networkpolicy*—Provides fine-grained ingress and egress rules for applications. This plugin provides a lot of configuration power, but the rules can be complex. This plugin is out of scope for this book.

The Kubernetes CNI accepts different networking plugins. OpenShift SDN is the default CNI plugin in OpenShift; it configures and manages the pod network for your cluster (see figure 10.7).

Let's review the available OpenShift SDN plugins, starting with ovs-subnet.

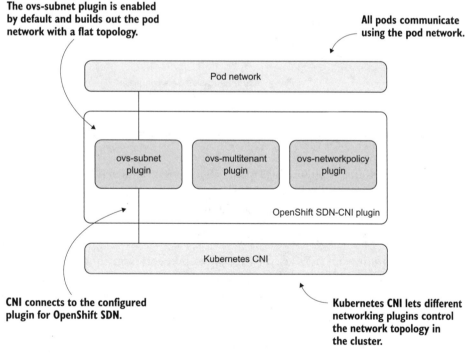

Figure 10.7 SDN plugins and overview

10.5.1 Using the ovs-subnet plugin

Earlier, you were able to communicate directly with an application from the stateful-apps project from a pod in the image-uploader project; you could do so because of how the ovs-subnet plugin configured the pod network. A flat network topology for all pods in all projects lets communication happen between any deployed applications (see figure 10.8).

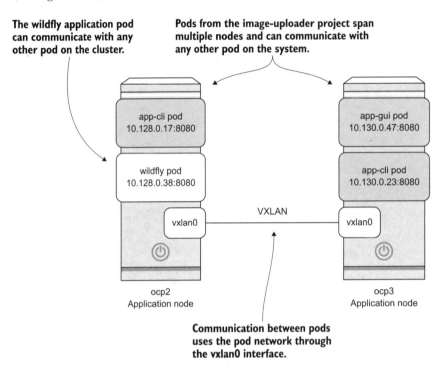

Figure 10.8 With the ovs-subnet plugin all pods can communicate with each other.

With the ovs-subnet plugin, an OpenShift cluster is deployed like a single tenant, with all resources available to one another. If you need to separate network traffic for multiple tenants, you can use the ovs-multitenant plugin.

10.5.2 Isolating traffice with the ovs-multitenant plugin

The ovs-multitenant network plugin isolates pod communications at the project level. Each pod for each application deployment can communicate only with pods and services in the same project on the pod network. For example, the app-gui and app-cli pods can communicate directly because they're both in the image-uploader project. But they're isolated from the wildfly-app application in the stateful-apps project in your cluster. This isolation relies on two primary tools in Open vSwitch:

- *VXLAN network identifier (VNID)*—A VNID acts in a fashion similar to a VLAN in a traditional network. It's a unique identifier that can be associated with an interface and used to isolate communication to interfaces with the same VNID.
- *OpenFlow*—OpenFlow (www.sdxcentral.com/sdn/definitions/what-is-openflow) is a communications protocol that can be used to map network traffic across a network infrastructure. OpenFlow is used in OpenShift to help define which interfaces can communicate and when to route traffic through the `vxlan0` and `tun0` interfaces on each node.

When the ovs-multitenant plugin is enabled, each project is assigned a VNID. The VNID for each project is maintained in the etcd database on the OpenShift master node. When a pod is created, its linked veth interface is associated with its project's VNID, and OpenFlow rules are created to make sure it can communicate only with pods in the same project.

> **NOTE** The router and registry pods in the default project are assigned VNID 0. This is a special VNID that can communicate with all other VNIDs on a system. If a pod needs to communicate with a pod on another host, the VNID is attached to each packet on the network as part of the VXLAN encapsulation process (see figure 10.9).

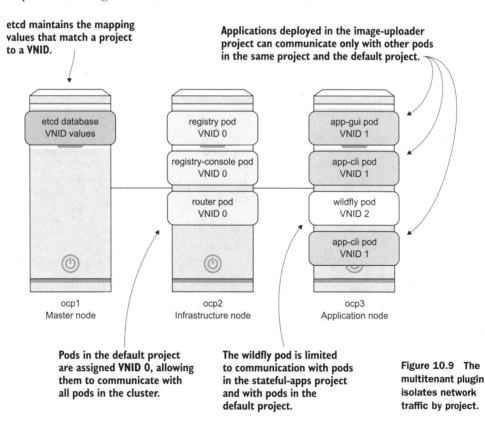

Figure 10.9 The multitenant plugin isolates network traffic by project.

With the multitenant plugin enabled, if a pod needs to communicate with a pod in another project, the request must be routed off the pod network and connect to the desired application through its external route like any other external request. This isn't always the most efficient architecture. The OpenShift SDN's ovs-networkpolicy plugin provides more fine-grained control over how applications communicate across projects.

10.5.3 *Creating advanced network designs with the ovs-networkpolicy plugin*

The ovs-networkpolicy plugin provides fine-grained access control for individual applications, regardless of the project they're in. These rules can become complex very quickly. We don't have space in this book to cover creating network policies, but if you want to learn about it, a good starting place is the documentation at http://mng.bz/LIUA.

Let's enable the ovs-multitenant plugin and make sure it isolates traffic in your cluster as we've discussed.

10.5.4 *Enabling the ovs-multitenant plugin*

To enable the ovs-multitenant plugin, you need to SSH to your master and application nodes and edit a configuration file on each. Follow these steps to edit the master configuration:

1 Open the master configuration file located at /etc/origin/master/master-config.yaml.
2 Locate the `networkPluginName` parameter in the file. The default value that enables the ovs-subnet plugin is `redhat/openshift-ovs-subnet`. Edit this line as shown next.

Listing 10.1   Editing `networkPluginName` in the master config

```
...
networkPluginName: redhat/openshift-ovs-multitenant
...
```

3 Restart the origin-master service:

```
# systemctl restart origin-master
```

Next you need to edit the application node configurations. Here are the steps:

1 On each application node, the configureation file is located at /etc/origin/node/node-config.yaml. In this file, you need to edit two lines. They're the same as the line you changed in the master configuration.

> **Listing 10.2　Editing `networkPluginName` in the application node config**

```
....
networkPluginName: redhat/openshift-ovs-multitenant 1((CO8-1))
# networkConfig struct introduced in origin 1.0.6 and OSE 3.0.2 which
# deprecates networkPluginName above. The two should match.
networkConfig:
    mtu: 1450
    networkPluginName: redhat/openshift-ovs-multitenant
...
```

Edit both lines to reference the multitenant plugin.

2　Restart the node service on each application node with the following command:

```
# systemctl restart origin-node
```

And that's it. You've changed your OpenShift cluster to use the multitenant network plugin. To make sure, let's test it.

10.5.5　*Testing the multitenant plugin*

Previously in the chapter, you logged in to the app-cli pod using `oc rsh` and downloaded web pages from other pods. Let's test this now with the ovs-multitenant plugin in place. Follow these steps:

1　Connect to the app-cli pod:

```
$ oc rsh app-cli-1-3lqbw
sh-4.2$
```

2　From the app-cli pod, use the `curl` command to download the index page for the app-gui pod using its DNS record:

```
sh-4.2$ curl app-gui:8080
<html>
<head>
...
```

Because these two applications are in the same project, you can communicate between these pods with no issues.

3　Try to access the router pod in the default project:

```
sh-4.2$ curl router.default
<html>
    <head>
...
```

Because the default project is assigned VNID 0, the app-cli pod can access it as needed.

4 Attempt to access the wildfly-app pod in the stateful-apps project:

```
sh-4.2$ curl wildfly-app.stateful-apps
```

This request eventually times out. The app-cli pod can't connect to the wildfly-app pod because they're in different projects. The multitenant plugin stops this communication from happening by design.

NOTE You can learn more about how the ovs-multitenant plugin uses VNIDs at http://mng.bz/dkj0, including information about how VNID 0 is used for the default project.

This chapter has been quite a journey through the network in your OpenShift cluster. Managing a network effectively in an application platform is a huge challenge. OpenShift uses Open vSwitch and its components to do so effectively in a dynamic cluster. All you have to do is decide how you want your pod network configured and then edit your cluster configuration files.

10.6 *Summary*

- OpenShift uses a non-routable pod network to handle traffic in the cluster.
- OpenShift SDN is a software-defined networking implementation using Open vSwitch (OVS) to create a scalable and highly configurable network for OpenShift traffic.
- Network traffic is passed in and out of containers using multiple OVS interfaces configured together on each host.
- Each container has a corresponding veth interface on the host that's linked to the container interface using the Linux kernel.
- OpenShift provides an internal DNS service to make interactions between pods easy to manage and scale.
- OpenShift SDN's default plugin provides a flat network topology that allows all pods to communicate with each other in the cluster.
- You can change networking plugins to the multitenant plugin, which effectively isolates network communications at the project level for applications.

11

Security

This chapter covers

- Learning how SELinux isolates container resources
- Understanding security contexts and application permissions
- Scanning container images for security issues
- Using security context constraints
- Analyzing OpenSCAP security scan reports

Each topic in this chapter is specific to security and to making OpenShift a secure platform for your applications. This chapter isn't a comprehensive summary of OpenShift's security features—that would take 100 pages or more and is a great idea for another OpenShift book. What we'll do in this chapter is walk through the fundamentals of OpenShift security. We want to give you examples of what we think are the most crucial concepts, and we'll do our best to point you in the right direction for the topics we don't have room to cover.

We began discussing important security concepts and making OpenShift secure not long after page 1 of this book:

- Understanding OpenShift's role in your environment: chapter 1
- Deploying applications associated with specific users: chapter 2
- Diving deep into how container processes are isolated: chapter 3
- Confirming application health and status: chapter 4
- Autoscaling applications to automate resilience: chapter 5
- Creating CI/CD pipelines so humans don't have to be involved: chapter 6
- Working with persistent storage: chapter 7
- Controlling access to pods, and handling interactions between pods: chapter 8
- Using identity providers and working with roles, limits, and quotas: chapter 9
- Creating a secure, stable network: chapter 10

We may be using a broad definition of security here, but every chapter in this book contributes to your understanding of OpenShift and how to deploy it in an automated and secure fashion. Automation and security go hand in hand, because humans aren't good at repetitive tasks. The more you can automate tasks for your applications, the more secure you can make those applications. Even though we've already covered a lot of ground regarding security, we still need to devote this entire chapter to security-specific concepts.

OpenShift has layers of security, from the Linux kernel on each application node through the routing layer that delivers applications to end users. We'll begin this discussion with the Linux kernel and work our way up through the application stack. For containers and OpenShift, security begins in the Linux kernel with *SELinux*.

11.1 Understanding SELinux core concepts

SELinux is a Linux kernel module that's used to enforce *mandatory access control* (MAC). MAC is a set of access levels that are assigned to users by the system. Only users with root-level privileges can alter them. For typical users, including the automated user accounts in OpenShift that deploy applications, the SELinux configuration specified for a deployment is an immutable fact.

MAC is in contrast to *discretionary access control* (DAC) in Linux. DAC is the system of users and file ownership/access modes that we all use every day on Linux hosts. If only DAC were in effect in your OpenShift cluster, users could allow full access to their container's resources by changing the ownership or the access mode for the container process or storage resources. One of the key security features of OpenShift is that SELinux automatically enforces MAC policies that can't be changed by unprivileged users for pods and other resources, even if they deployed the application.

We need to take a few pages to discuss some fundamental information that we'll use throughout the chapter. As with security in general, this won't be a full SELinux introduction. Entire books have been written on that topic, including an SELinux coloring book available at https://github.com/mairin/selinux-coloring-book. But the following information will help you understand how OpenShift uses SELinux to create a secure platform. We'll focus on the following SELinux concepts:

- *Labels*—SELinux labels are applied to all objects on a Linux server.
- *Contexts*—SELinux contexts apply labels to objects based on filesystem locations.
- *Policies*—SELinux policies are rules that control interactions between objects with different SELinux labels.

Let's begin by taking a more detailed look at how SELinux labels are designed.

11.1.1 *Working with SELinux labels*

SELinux *labels* are applied to all objects on your OpenShift servers as they're created. An SELinux label dictates how an object on a Linux server interacts with the SELinux kernel module. We're defining an *object* in this context as anything a user or process can create or interact with on a server, such as the following:

- Files
- Directories
- TCP ports
- Unix sockets
- Shared memory resources

Each object's SELinux label has four sections, separated by colons:

- *User*—Which SELinux user has access to the objects with that SELinux label.
- *Role*—The SELinux role that can access the objects with the matching SELinux label.
- *Type*—SELinux type for each label. This is the section where most common SELinux rules are written.
- *Multi-category security (MCS)*—Often called the *MCS bit.* Unique for each container, and what we'll spend the most time on.

Figure 11.1 shows an example of a full SELinux label for the socket interface used by Open vSwitch for communication on your OpenShift nodes at /var/run/openvswitch/db.sock. To view this label, run the following `ls` command, using the `-Z` option to include SELinux information in its output:

```
# ls -alZ /var/run/openvswitch/db.sock
srwxr-x---. root root system_u:object_r:openvswitch_var_run_t:s0➡
 /var/run/openvswitch/db.sock
```

In addition to the standard POSIX attributes of mode, owner, and group ownership, the output also includes the SELinux label for /var/run/openvswitch/db.sock.

Next, let's examine how SELinux labels are applied to files and other objects when they're created.

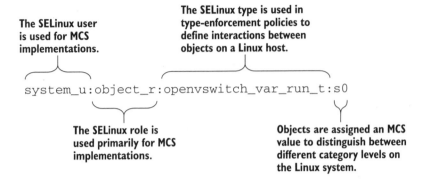

Figure 11.1   SELinux label for the Open vSwitch socket object

---

Digging deeper into SELinux

Most commands have a -z option that will include the commands' SELinux labels. Common command-line tools like ls, ps, netstat, and others accept the -z option to include SELinux information in their output.

Because objects are presented in the Linux operating system as files, their SELinux labels are stored in their filesystem extended attributes. You can view these attributes directly for the Open vSwitch socket using the following getfattr command:

```
# getfattr -d -m - /var/run/openvswitch/db.sock
getfattr: Removing leading '/' from absolute path names
# file: var/run/openvswitch/db.sock
security.selinux="system_u:object_r:openvswitch_var_run_t:s0"
```

If you're looking for full SELinux documentation, a great place to start is the Red Hat Enterprise Linux 7 SELinux Guide at http://mng.bz/G5t5.

11.1.2 *Applying labels with SELinux contexts*

Labels are applied to files using *SELinux contexts*: rules that are used to apply labels to objects on a Linux system. Contexts use regular expressions to apply labels depending on where the object exists in the filesystem.

SELinux breaks my application!

One of the worst things a sysadmin can hear is a developer telling them that SELinux "breaks" their application. In reality, their application is almost certainly creating objects on the Linux server that don't have a defined SELinux context.

If SELinux doesn't know how to apply the correct label, it doesn't know how to treat the application's objects. This often results in SELinux policy denials that lead to frantic calls and requests to disable SELinux because it's breaking an application.

To query the contexts for a system, use the `semanage` command and filter it using grep. You can use `semanage` to search for contexts that apply to any label related to any file or directory, including the Open vSwitch socket. A search for `openvswitch` in the `semanage` output shows that the context system_u:object_r:openvswitch_var _run_t:s0 is applied to any object created in the /var/run/openvswitch/ directory:

```
# semanage fcontext -l | grep openvswitch
/etc/openvswitch(/.*)?                              all files
➥ system_u:object_r:openvswitch_rw_t:s0
/var/lib/openvswitch(/.*)?                          all files
➥ system_u:object_r:openvswitch_var_lib_t:s0
/var/log/openvswitch(/.*)?                          all files
➥ system_u:object_r:openvswitch_log_t:s0
/var/run/openvswitch(/.*)?                          all files
➥ system_u:object_r:openvswitch_var_run_t:s0
/usr/lib/systemd/system/openvswitch.service         regular file
➥ system_u:object_r:openvswitch_unit_file_t:s0
/usr/bin/ovs-vsctl                                  regular file
➥ system_u:object_r:openvswitch_exec_t:s0
...
```

SELinux context to apply the correct label to the Open vSwitch socket interface

Properly applied, SELinux labels create policies that control how objects with different labels can interact with each other. Let's discuss those next.

11.1.3 Enforcing SELinux with policies

SELinux policies are complex things. They're heavily optimized and compiled so they can be interpreted quickly by the Linux kernel. Creating one or looking at the code that creates one is outside the scope of this book, but let's look at a basic example of what an SELinux policy would do. For this, we'll use an example that most people are familiar with: the Apache web server. You won't find the Apache web server on your master node—the OpenShift API and user interfaces are served by a custom web application. But Apache is common everywhere and has long-established SELinux policies that we can use as an example.

The executable file for the Apache web server is /usr/sbin/httpd. This httpd executable has an SELinux label of system_u:object_r:httpd_exec_t:s0. On CentOS and Red Hat systems, the default Apache web content directory is /var/www/html. This directory has an SELinux label of system_u:object_r:httpd_sys_content_t:s0. The default cgi-script directory for Apache is /var/www/cgi-bin, and it has an SELinux label of system_u:object_r:httpd_sys_script_exec_t:s0. There's also an http_port_t label for the following TCP port numbers:

- 80
- 81
- 443
- 488
- 8008
- 8009
- 8443
- 9000

An SELinux policy enforces the following rules using these labels for the `httpd_exec_t` object type:

- `httpd_exec_t`—Can write only to objects with an `httpd_sys_content_t` type
- `httpd_exec_t`—Can execute scripts only with the `httpd_sys_script_exec_t` type
- `httpd_exec_t`—Can read from directories with `httpd_sys_script_exec_t`, but can't write to them
- `httpd_exec_t`—Can open and bind only to ports with the `http_port_t` type

This means even if Apache is somehow compromised by a remote user, it can read content from /var/www/html and run scripts from /var/www/cgi-bin. It also can't write to /var/www/cgi-bin. All of this is enforced by the Linux kernel, regardless of the ownership or permissions of these directories and which user owns the `httpd` process (see figure 11.2).

The default type of SELinux loaded on a Linux system is the *targeted* type. The rules in the targeted SELinux type are applied only to objects that have matching contexts. Every object on a server is assigned a label based on the SELinux context it matches. If an object doesn't match a context, it's assigned an `unconfined_t` type in its SELinux label. The `unconfined_t` type has no contexts or policies associated with it. Interactions between objects that aren't covered by a policy in targeted SELinux are allowed to run with no interference.

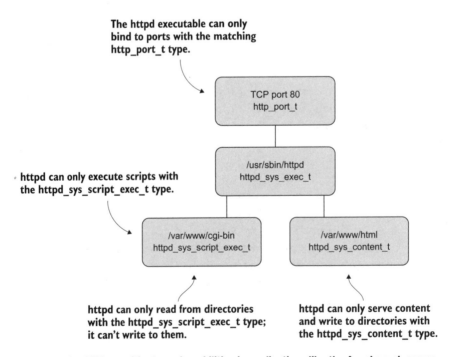

The httpd executable can only bind to ports with the matching http_port_t type.

TCP port 80
http_port_t

/usr/sbin/httpd
httpd_sys_exec_t

httpd can only execute scripts with the httpd_sys_script_exec_t type.

/var/www/cgi-bin
httpd_sys_script_exec_t

/var/www/html
httpd_sys_content_t

httpd can only read from directories with the httpd_sys_script_exec_t type; it can't write to them.

httpd can only serve content and write to directories with the httpd_sys_content_t type.

Figure 11.2   SELinux mitigates vulnerabilities in applications like the Apache web server.

For CentOS and Red Hat Enterprise Linux, the default policies use *type enforcement.* Type enforcement uses the type value from SELinux labels to enforce the interactions between objects.

Let's review what we've discussed up to this point about SELinux:

- SELinux is used to enforce MAC in your OpenShift cluster. MAC provides access controls at a deeper level than traditional user/group ownership and access mode. It also applies to objects on the operating system that aren't traditional files and directories.
- Every object on an OpenShift node is assigned an SELinux label, including a type.
- Labels are assigned according to SELinux contexts as objects are created, depending on where they exist on the filesystem.
- With labels applied, SELinux policies enforce interactions between objects. SELinux uses type-enforcement policies on your OpenShift cluster to ensure proper interactions between objects.

This SELinux configuration is standard for any CentOS or Red Hat system running with SELinux in enforcing mode. Just as in the Apache web server process we've been discussing, you know that a container is essentially a process. Each container's process is assigned an SELinux label when it's created, and that label dictates the policies that affect the container. To confirm the SELinux label that's used for containers in Open-Shift, get the container's PID from docker and use the `ps` command with the `-Z` parameter, searching for that PID with `grep`:

PID for the app-cli container

```
# docker inspect -f '{{ .State.Pid }}' 1aa4208f4b80
2534
```

```
# ps -axZ | grep 2534
system_u:system_r:svirt_lxc_net_t:s0:c7,c8 2534 ? Ss    0:01 httpd -D
FOREGROUND
```

SELinux label for the app-cli container process

SELinux in enforcing mode

OpenShift hosts operate with SELinux in *enforcing mode.* Enforcing mode means the policy engine that controls how objects can interact is fully activated. If an object attempts to do something that's against an SELinux policy present on the system, the action isn't allowed, and the attempt is logged by the kernel. To confirm that SELinux is in enforcing mode, run the following `getenforce` command:

```
# getenforce
Enforcing
```

In OpenShift, SELinux is taken care of automatically, and you don't need to worry about it. There's no reason to disable it.

> **(continued)**
> In other servers, tools like virus scanners can cause issues with SELinux. A virus scanner is designed to analyze files on a server that are created and managed by other services. That makes writing an effective SELinux policy for a virus scanner a significant challenge. Another typical issue is when applications and their data are placed in locations on the filesystem that don't match their corresponding SELinux contexts. If the Apache web server is trying to access content from /data on a server, it will be denied by SELinux because /data doesn't match any SELinux contexts associated with Apache. These sorts of issues lead to some people deciding to disable SELinux.

The user and role portions of the label aren't used for type-enforcement policies. The `svirt_lxc_net_t` type is used in SELinux policies that control which resources on the system containers can interact with. We haven't discussed the fourth part of the SELinux label: the MCS level, which isolates pods in OpenShift. Let's examine how that works next.

11.1.4   Isolating pods with MCS levels

The original purpose of the MCS bit was to implement MCS security standards (https://selinuxproject.org/page/NB_MLS) on Linux servers. These standards control data access for different security levels on the same server. For example, secret and top-secret data could exist on the same server. A top-secret-level process should be able to access secret-level data, a concept called *data dominance*; but secret processes shouldn't be able to access top-secret data, because that data has a higher MCS level. This is the security feature you can use to prevent a pod from accessing data it's not authorized to access on the host.

> **TIP** You may have noticed that the SELinux type for the app-cli container is `svirt_lxc_netsvirt_lxc_net`. SVirt (https://selinuxproject.org/page/SVirt) has been used for several years to isolate kernel-based virtual machines (KVMs) using the same MCS technology. VMs and containers aren't similar technologies, but they both use SVirt to provide security for their platforms.

OpenShift uses the MCS level for each container's process to enforce security as part of the pod's *security context*. A pod's security context is all the information that describes how it's secured on its application node. Let's look at the security context for the app-cli pod.

11.2   Investigating pod security contexts in OpenShift

Each pod's security context contains information about its security posture. You can find full documentation for the possible fields that can be defined at http://mng.bz/phit. In OpenShift, the following parameters are configured by default:

- Capabilities—Defines an application's ability to perform various tasks on the host. Capabilities can be added or dropped for each pod. We'll look at these in depth in this chapter.
- Privileged—Specifies whether the container is running with any of the host's namespaces.
- RunAsUser—UID with which to run the container's process. This can be configured, which we'll discuss later in this chapter.
- SeLinuxOptions—SELinux options for the pod. Normally, the only needed option is to set the SELinux level.

You can view the security context for a pod in the GUI by choosing Applications > Pods, selecting the pod you want information about, and then choosing Actions > Edit YAML. From the command line, the same output is available using the oc export command:

```
$ oc export pod app-cli-2-4lg8j
apiVersion: v1
kind: Pod
...
spec:
...
    securityContext:                    Security context
      capabilities:                     for the pod
        drop:
        - KILL
        - MKNOD
        - SETGID
        - SETUID
        - SYS_CHROOT
      privileged: false                 Whether the pod
      runAsUser: 1000070000             is privileged
      seLinuxOptions:
        level: s0:c8,c7                 MCS label
...
```

Pod capabilities (added or dropped) → capabilities

UID with which to run the pod → runAsUser

NOTE Looking at the output, two security contexts are defined. The one displayed here is the MCS level for the container; there's a similar security context for the pod, as well. The MCS level for the container and the pod should always be equal.

We've been discussing SELinux for a while. Let's bring the topic to a close by walking through how OpenShift uses a pod's MCS level to enhance security.

11.2.1 Examining MCS levels in OpenShift

The structure of the MCS level consists of a sensitivity level (s0) and two categories (c8 and c7), as shown in the following output from the previous command:

```
seLinuxOptions:
  level: s0:c8,c7
```

You may have noticed that the order of the categories is reversed in the `oc` output compared with the `ps` output. This makes no difference in how the Linux kernel reads and acts on the MCS level.

A detailed discussion of how different MCS levels can interact is out of scope for this book. If you're looking for that depth of information, the SELinux Guide for Red Hat Enterprise Linux at http://mng.bz/G5t5 is a great place to start. Here, we'll focus on how OpenShift uses MCS levels to isolate pods in each project.

OpenShift assumes that applications deployed in the same project will need to interact with each other. With that in mind, the pods in a project have the same MCS level. Sharing an MCS level lets applications share resources easily and simplifies the security configurations you need to make for your cluster.

Let's examine the SELinux configurations for pods in different projects. You already know the MCS level for app-cli is `s0:c8,c7`. Because app-cli and app-gui are in the same project, they should have the same MCS level. To get the MCS level for the app-gui pod, use the same `oc export` command:

```
$ oc export pod app-gui-1-cwm7t | grep -A 1 seLinuxOptions
      seLinuxOptions:
        level: s0:c8,c7      ◁— MCS level for the container
--
      seLinuxOptions:
        level: s0:c8,c7      ◁— MCS level for the pod
```

This confirms what we stated earlier: the MCS levels for app-gui and app-cli are the same because they're deployed in the same project.

Next, let's compare the same values for a pod deployed in another project. Use the wildfly-app application you deployed in chapter 8. To get the name of the deployed pod, run the following `oc get pods` command, specifying the stateful-apps project using the -n option:

```
$ oc get pods -n stateful-apps
NAME                  READY      STATUS        RESTARTS    AGE
wildfly-app-1-zsfr8   1/1        Running       0           6d
```

After you have the pod name, run the same `oc export` command, searching for seLinuxOptions and specifying the stateful-apps project using the -n option:

```
$ oc export pod wildfly-app-1-zsfr8 -n stateful-apps | grep -A 1 seLinuxOptions
      seLinuxOptions:
        level: s0:c10,c0     ◁— MCS level for the wildfly-app container
--
      seLinuxOptions:
        level: s0:c10,c0     ◁— MCS level for the wildfly-app pod
```

Each project uses a unique MCS level for deployed applications. This MCS level permits each project's applications to communicate only with resources in the same project. Let's continue looking at pod security-context components with pod capabilities.

11.2.2 *Managing pods Linux capabilities*

The capabilities listed in the app-cli security context are *Linux capabilities* that have been removed from the container process. Linux capabilities are permissions assigned to or removed from processes by the Linux kernel:

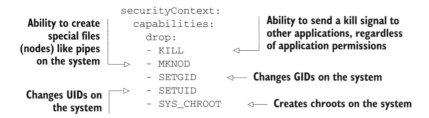

Capabilities allow a process to perform administrative tasks on the system. The root user on a Linux server can run commands with all Linux capabilities by default. That's why the root user can perform tasks like opening TCP ports below 1024, which is provided by the `CAP_NET_BIND_SERVICE` capability, and loading modules into the Linux kernel, which is provided by the `CAP_SYS_MODULE` capability.

You can add capabilities to a pod if it needs to be able to perform a specific type of task. Add them to the `capabilities.add` list in the pod's security context. (A full listing of capabilities and their functions is detailed at http://mng.bz/Qy03.) To remove default capabilities from pods, add the capabilities you want to remove to the `drop` list. This is the default action in OpenShift. The goal is to assign the fewest possible capabilities for a pod to fully function. This least-privileged model ensures that pods can't perform tasks on the system that aren't related to their application's proper function.

The default value for the `privileged` option is `False`; setting the `privileged` option to `True` is the same as giving the pod the capabilities of the root user on the system. Although doing so shouldn't be common practice, privileged pods can be useful under certain circumstances. A great example is the HAProxy pod we discussed in chapter 10. It runs as a privileged container so it can bind to port 80 on its node to handle incoming application requests. When an application needs access to host resources that can't be easily provided to the pod, running a privileged container may help. Just remember, as the comic book says, with great power comes great responsibility.

The last value in the security context that we need to look at controls the user ID that the pod is run with: the `runAsUser` parameter.

11.2.3 *Controlling the pod user ID*

In OpenShift, by default, each project deploys pods using a random UID. Just like the MCS level, the UID is common for all pods in a project, to allow easier interactions between pods when needed. The UID for each pod is listed in the security context in the `runAsUser` parameter:

```
runAsUser: 1000070000          ◁─── User ID for the app-cli pod
```

By default, OpenShift doesn't allow applications to be deployed using UID 0, which is the default UID for the system's root user. There aren't any known ways for UID 0 to break out of a container, but being UID 0 in a container means you must be incredibly careful about taking away capabilities and ensuring proper file ownership on the system. It's an ounce of prevention that can prevent the need for a pound of cure down the road.

> **TIP** Many containers available publicly on registries like Docker Hub (https://hub.docker.com) run as UID 0 by default. You can learn more about editing these images and dockerfiles, along with some best practices around OpenShift and building container images, at http://mng.bz/L4G5.

The components in a pod's or container's security context are controlled by the *security context constraint* (SCC) assigned to the pod when it's deployed. An SCC is a configuration applied to pods that outlines the security context components it will operate with. We'll discuss SCCs in more depth in the next section, when you deploy an application in your cluster that needs a more privileged security context than the default provides. This application is a container image-scanning utility that looks for security issues in container images in your OpenShift registry. Let's get started.

11.3 Scanning container images

OpenShift is only as secure as the containers it deploys. Even if your container images are built using proven, vetted base images supplied by vendors or created using your own secure workflows, you still need a process to ensure that the images you're using don't have security issues as they age in your cluster. The most straightforward solution for this challenge is to scan your container images.

Container scanning and compliance becomes its own industry

You're going to scan a single container image on demand in this chapter. In a production environment, image scanning should be an integral component in your application deployment workflows. Companies like Black Duck Software (www.blackducksoftware.com) and Twistlock (www.twistlock.com) have image-scanning and -compliance tools that integrate with OpenShift.

You must be able to trust what's running in your containers and quickly fix issues when they're found. An entire industry has sprung up in the past few years that provides container image-scanning products to help make this an everyday reality.

11.3.1 Obtaining the image-scanning application

To run this scan in OpenShift, you need a container image that includes the scanning engine. An OpenShift image scanner called Image Inspector is available at https://github.com/openshift/image-inspector. An image built using this source code is available on Docker Hub at https://hub.docker.com/r/openshift/image-inspector. We've created an OpenShift template that uses Image Inspector, making its needed inputs parameters that are easy to use in OpenShift.

Follow these steps:

1 Create a new project named image-scan using the following `oc` command:

```
oc new-project image-scan
```

2 Import the image-inspector template into the image-scan project. Creating the template in the image-scan project means it won't be visible to users who don't have access to the image-scan project.

TIP By default, all templates available in the service catalog are located in the openshift project. You can learn more about how templates work in Open-Shift at http://mng.bz/8DF6.

3 To import the template, run the following `oc` command:

```
$ oc create -f https://raw.githubusercontent.com/OpenShiftInAction/
➥ chapter11/master/image-scanner/templates/image-scanner.yaml -n image-scan
template "image-scan-template" created
```

Once it completes, the image-scanner template will be available for use in the image-scan project.

11.3.2 Deploying the image-scanning application

The image you'll scan is wildfly-app, which you deployed when you were working with stateful applications in chapter 8. The image-scan-template template has parameters defined, as shown in the following listing; these are used to specify the image that's being scanned.

Listing 11.1 Parameters in the image-scan-template template

```
parameters:
- name: APPLICATION_NAME
  displayName: Application Name
  description: The name assigned to all of the frontend objects
  ➥ defined in this template.
  value: image-inspector
  required: true
- name: IMAGE_INSPECTOR_URL
  displayName: Container Image that is doing the scans
  description: The image inspector image, defaults to CentOS, for RHEL use
  ➥ registry.access.redhat.com/openshift3/image-inspector:latest
  value: docker.io/openshift/image-inspector:latest
  required: true
- name: IMAGE_TO_SCAN_URL
  displayName: Image URL to scan with OpenSCAP
  description: The image getting scanned with OpenSCAP
  value: registry.access.redhat.com/rhel7:7.0-21
```

```
    required: true
- name: SCAN_TYPE
  displayName: Scan Type
  description: Type of scan you want image-inspect to run
  value: openscap
  required: true
- name: DOCKERCFG_SECRET
  displayName: dockercfg Secret
  description: This is the name of a pre-existing dockercfg secret with
  ➡ credentials to access the registry
  required: true
- name: SERVICE_ACCOUNT
  displayName: Service Account
  description: The Service Account to run the pod as
  value: default
  required: true
```

The default value for the IMAGE_TO_SCAN_URL parameter is registry.access.redhat
.com/rhel7:7.0-21, the publicly available Red Hat Enterprise Linux 7.0 container
image. You need to supply the full container-image URL to the image scanner
application as the IMAGE_TO_SCAN_URL value. To get the URL for the image used to
deploy widfly-app, run the following oc describe command:

```
# oc describe dc/wildfly-app -n stateful-apps | grep Image:
    Image:    docker-registry.default.svc:5000/stateful-apps/wildfly-app@sha256:
    ➡ e324ae4a9c44daf552e6d3ee3de8d949e26b5c5bfd933144f5555b9ed0bf3c84
```

OpenShift doesn't use image tags to specify an image to use when deploying an application, because tags can be changed on images in a registry. Container image tags are
mutable objects. Instead, OpenShift uses an immutable SHA256 digest to identify the
exact image to deploy a specific version of your application. This is another security
safeguard that's used in OpenShift by default. You can cryptographically prove that
the image in your registry is the image you're using to deploy applications on your
host. Pulling images by digest is defined and explained in more depth in the docker
engine documentation at http://mng.bz/81H4.

   To download a copy of this image to scan, the image-scanning application needs to
be able to download images from the OpenShift image registry. Permission to download images from the registry is controlled using a secret, similar to those you created
in chapter 6. The dockercfg secret is the JSON data used to log in to a docker registry
(http://mng.bz/O0sm) encoded as a base-64 string. It's one of several secrets created
and used by OpenShift:

Docker configuration secrets

```
# oc get secrets
NAME                      TYPE                                          DATA  AGE
builder-dockercfg-24q2h   kubernetes.io/dockercfg                       1     39d
builder-token-dslpv       kubernetes.io/service-account-token           4     39d
builder-token-rdv3n       kubernetes.io/service-account-token           4     39d
default-dockercfg-dvklh   kubernetes.io/dockercfg                       1     39d    ◁───┘
default-token-b8dq2       kubernetes.io/service-account-token           4     39d
```

```
default-token-g9b4p        kubernetes.io/service-account-token  4      39d
deployer-dockercfg-
    w8jg2 kubernetes.io/dockercfg               1      39d    1((CO8-2))
deployer-token-b761w       kubernetes.io/service-account-token  4      39d
deployer-token-zphcs       kubernetes.io/service-account-token  4      39d
```

To deploy the Image Inspector application and have it scan the wildfly-app image, use the following oc new-app command. Supply the wildfly-app URL, and parse the secret output to supply the name of the dockercfg secret as parameters:

```
$ oc new-app --template=image-scan/image-scan-template \
> -p DOCKERCFG_SECRET=$(oc get secrets -o jsonpath='{
➥ .items[*].metadata.name}' | xargs -n1 | grep 'default-dockercfg*') \
> -p IMAGE_TO_SCAN_URL=docker-registry.default.svc:5000/stateful-apps/
➥ wildfly-app@sha256:
➥ e324ae4a9c44daf552e6d3ee3de8d949e26b5c5bfd933144f5555b9ed0bf3c84
...
--> Creating resources ...
    deploymentconfig "image-inspector" created
--> Success
    Run 'oc status' to view your app.
```

We'll use the data generated by this new image-scanner application to examine the scan results for the WildFly image.

11.3.3 Viewing events on the command line

Running oc new-app deploys a deployment config. The deployment config downloads the container image for wildfly-app so it can be scanned for vulnerabilities. But something isn't right: if you wait for a few minutes, the deployment pod is running, but the application pod never gets created. To figure out what's happening, let's examine the events recorded by OpenShift for the image-scan project, including the error deploying the Image Inspector application:

```
$ oc get events -n image-scan
...
39s        3m          16           image-inspector-1
➥ ReplicationController                               Warning
➥ FailedCreate          replication-controller
➥ Error creating: pods "image-inspector-1-" is forbidden: unable to validate
➥ against any security context constraint: [spec.volumes[1]:
➥ Invalid value: "hostPath": hostPath volumes are not allowed to be used
➥ provider restricted: .spec.containers[0].securityContext.privileged:
➥ Invalid value: true: Privileged containers  are not allowed]        ◁─┐
```

The image-inspector deployment isn't allowed to deploy with its default security context.

The security context for each pod is configured based on the security context constraint (SCC) assigned to the pod when it's created. The default SCC for an application is the *restricted* SCC. The restricted SCC creates a security context that matches what you saw earlier in this chapter for the app-cli deployment:

- Limited Linux capabilities
- Privileged mode disabled
- Pod run using a specific UID
- Pod created with a specific MCS level

The error listed in the events tells you that the image-inspector pod is attempting to define the security context with privileged mode enabled, and the restricted security context prevents that configuration from deploying. To run the Image Inspector application, you need to change the SCC used to deploy the pod.

11.3.4   Changing SCCs for an application deployment

OpenShift is configured with several SCCs that provide different levels of access for pods, including the default restricted SCC. The `privileged` SCC lets a pod deploy as any UID, with all Linux capabilities, with any MCS level, and with privileged mode enabled:

Privileged SCC

```
$ oc get scc
NAME              PRIV      CAPS      SELINUX      RUNASUSER       FSGROUP
➥ SUPGROUP     PRIORITY  READONLYROOTFS  VOLUMES
...
privileged        true      [*]      RunAsAny     RunAsAny        RunAsAny
➥ RunAsAny     <none>    false         [*]
restricted        false     []       MustRunAs    MustRunAsRange
➥ MustRunAs    RunAsAny  <none>    false            [configMap
➥ downwardAPI emptyDir persistentVolumeClaim projected secret]        ◁────  Restricted
                                                                              SCC
```

The `privileged` SCC fulfills the image-inspector pod's request for privileged mode to be enabled. To change the SCC for the image-inspector pod, you need to change the default SCC for the *service account* that's used to run pods in the image-scan project.

A service account is used in OpenShift when one component is interacting with another as part of a workflow. When a project is created in OpenShift, the following three service accounts are created by default:

- *Builder*—Used by build pods. It has the system:image-builder role bound to it, and it can create images and push them to a registry.
- *Deployer*—Used to deploy applications. It's bound to the system:deployer role, allowing it to view and modify replication controllers and pods.
- *Default*—Used to run all pods unless a different service account is specified.

TIP You can create additional service accounts to fit your specific needs. The process and more details are documented at http://mng.bz/8M4n.

To view the service accounts for a project, you can run the following `oc get` command:

```
$ oc get serviceaccount -n image-scan
NAME       SECRETS   AGE
builder    2         5d
default    2         5d
deployer   2         5d
```

Default service account ← (refers to the `default` line)

To deploy Image Inspector, you need to add the `privileged` SCC to the default service account for the image-scan project. To do that, run the following `oc adm` command:

```
$ oc adm policy add-scc-to-user privileged -z default -n image-scan
=======
$ oc import-image registry.access.redhat.com/rhel7:7.0-21 --confirm
The import completed successfully.

Name:           rhel7
Namespace:        image-scan
Created:        Less than a second ago
Labels:           <none>
Annotations:
➡ openshift.io/image.dockerRepositoryCheck=2017-12-10T04:37:14Z
Docker Pull Spec:   docker-registry.default.svc:5000/image-scan/rhel7
Image Lookup:       local=false
Unique Images:      1
Tags:           1

7.0-21
  tagged from registry.access.redhat.com/rhel7:7.0-21

  * registry.access.redhat.com/rhel7@sha256:
➡ 141c69dc6ae89c73339b6ddd68b6ec6eeeb75ad7b4d68bcb7c25e8d05d9f5e60
    Less than a second ago

Image Name:   rhel7:7.0-21
Docker Image:   registry.access.redhat.com/rhel7@sha256:
➡ 141c69dc6ae89c73339b6ddd68b6ec6eeeb75ad7b4d68bcb7c25e8d05d9f5e60
Name:         sha256:➡
 141c69dc6ae89c73339b6ddd68b6ec6eeeb75ad7b4d68bcb7c25e8d05d9f5e60
Created:      Less than a second ago
Image Size:   50.37 MB
Image Created:   3 years ago
Author:         <none>
Arch:         amd64
```

With this change made, you're ready to deploy the Image Inspector application using the `privileged` SCC. Before you do that, however, you need to remove the previous, failed deployment using the following `oc delete` command:

```
# oc delete dc/image-inspector
deploymentconfig "image-inspector" deleted
```

After the previous deployment is deleted, rerun the `oc new-app` command to deploy Image Inspector:

```
$ oc new-app --template=image-scan/image-scan-template \
> -p DOCKERCFG_SECRET=$(oc get secrets -o jsonpath='{
➥ .items[*].metadata.name}' | xargs -n1 | grep 'default-dockercfg*') \
> -p IMAGE_TO_SCAN_URL=docker-registry.default.svc:5000/stateful-apps/
➥ wildfly-app@sha256:
➥ e324ae4a9c44daf552e6d3ee3de8d949e26b5c5bfd933144f5555b9ed0bf3c84
```

Downloading the image and the security scanner content into the build pod will take a minute or two, depending on your internet connection speed. During this time, your pod will be in `ContainerCreating` status:

```
# oc get pods
NAME                          READY     STATUS             RESTARTS   AGE
image-inspector-1-deploy      1/1       Running            0          16s
image-inspector-1-xmlkb       0/1       ContainerCreating  0          13s
```

After the content downloads, the image-inspector pod will be in a `Running` state, like any other pod you've worked with so far. At this point, the pod has run its scan on the container image, and the results are ready for you to view and act on.

11.3.5 *Viewing security scan results*

The image scanner in the pod uses OpenSCAP (www.open-scap.org) to scan and generate a report on the wildfly-app container image.

> **WARNING** This scanning methods relies on the RPM metadata in Red Hat base images to run properly. This scanning method may not work on images that use a different Linux distribution, including CentOS.

This report is stored in the pod at /tmp/image-results/results.html. To transfer this HTML report to your local workstation, use the following `oc rsync` command:

```
oc rsync image-inspector-1-xmlkb:/tmp/image-content/results.html .
```

Open the scan results with your web browser, and you'll see a full report of how close to compliance your wildfly-app container image is, and any errata regarding things it may be missing. Figure 11.3 shows that our results were close but had three high-level security issues.

You don't want to deploy applications when their images have potentially dangerous security issues. In the next section, you'll add an annotation to the wildfly-app image to prevent it from being run.

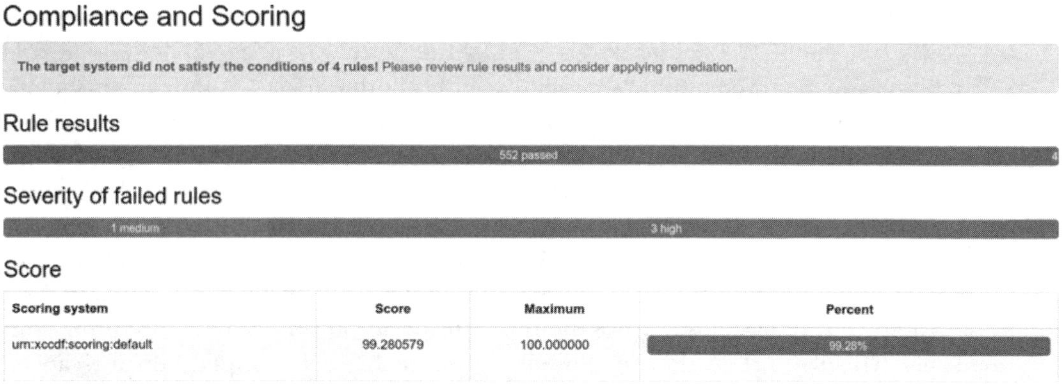

Compliance and Scoring

> The target system did not satisfy the conditions of 4 rules! Please review rule results and consider applying remediation.

Rule results

552 passed | 4

Severity of failed rules

1 medium | 3 high

Score

Scoring system	Score	Maximum	Percent
urn:xccdf:scoring:default	99.280579	100.000000	99.28%

Figure 11.3   Image scan results and scoring from the image-inspector application

11.4 *Annotating images with security information*

OpenShift is configured with *image policies* that control which images are allowed to run on your cluster. The full documentation for image policies is available at http://mng.bz/o1Po. Annotations in the image metadata enforce image policies; you can add these annotations manually. The `deny-execution` policy prevents an image from running on the cluster under any conditions. To apply this policy to the wildfly-app image, run the following `oc annotate` command:

```
oc annotate image sha256:e324ae4a... images.openshift.io/deny-execution=true
image "sha256:e324ae4a9c44daf552e6d3ee3de8d949e26b5c5bfd933144f5555b9ed0bf3c84"
➥ annotated
```

Image policies don't affect running pods, but they prevent an image with the `deny-execution` annotation from being used for deployments. To see this in action, delete the active pod for your wildfly-app deployment using the `oc delete pod` command on the active pod for wildfly-app. Normally, the replication controller for the wildfly-app deployment would automatically deploy a new version of the pod based on the correct base image. But no new pod is deployed. Looking at the events for the stateful-apps project, you can see that the image policies in OpenShift are reading the annotation you added to the image and preventing a new pod from being deployed:

```
$ oc events -n stateful-apps
...
16s        24s         14          wildfly-app-1          ReplicationController
➥ Warning    FailedCreate        replication-controller
➥ Error creating: Pod "" is invalid: spec.containers[0].image: Forbidden:
➥ this image is prohibited by policy
```

This process manually scans a container image and adds an annotation to it if security issues are found. The annotation is read by the OpenShift image-policy engine and prevents any new pods from being deployed using that image. Automated solutions like Black Duck and Twistlock handle this dynamically, including annotations about the security findings and information about the scan. These annotations can be used for security reporting and to ensure that the most secure applications are deployed in OpenShift at all times.

You started this chapter with SELinux and worked your way up to the security contexts that define how pods are assigned security permissions in OpenShift. You used the `privileged` SCC to give the Image Inspector image scanner the permissions it needed to run. You then deployed the Image Inspector application to scan an existing container image and generate a report on any security findings. Finally, you used image policies to prevent the scanned image from being deployed because you found security issues in its scan results. That sounds like a good place to end this security chapter.

As we said at the start of the chapter, this isn't a comprehensive list or a complete security workflow. Our goal has been to introduce you to what we think are the most important security concepts in OpenShift and give you enough information to begin to use and customize them as you gain experience using OpenShift.

11.5   Summary

- SELinux provides MAC security that's enforced by the Linux kernel and is immutable unless a user has root-level access to the system.
- SELinux labels, contexts, and policies all work together to control the resources available to pods in OpenShift.
- Each pod is assigned a security context that includes information about its capabilities on the host, its UID, whether the pod is privileged, and its SELinux MCS level.
- SCCs can be added for system users who build, deploy, or run pods, to give the pod different levels of access to the system during its lifecycle.
- Image policies use annotations applied to an image to prevent pods from being deployed using that image.
- Scanning container image content is a vital component of any workflow that includes OpenShift.

This also seems like a good place to wrap up *OpenShift in Action*. As was the case for this chapter, we never intended this book to be a comprehensive OpenShift manual. To be honest, OpenShift and its components are growing and changing too quickly for a truly comprehensive manual to ever be put in print. Our goal has been to focus on the fundamental knowledge that will help you implement OpenShift, even as newer versions are released and the technology evolves. We hope we've done that.

We also hope you have a fully functional cluster up and running that you can use for your ongoing learning around containers and OpenShift. We'll continue to update the code and helper applications at www.manning.com/books/openshift-in-action and https://github.com/OpenShiftInAction. We'll also continue to be active in the Manning book forum at https://forums.manning.com/forums/openshift-in-action. If you have questions or ideas for improvement, or just want to say hi, you can find us at either of those locations online. Thank you—and we hope you've enjoyed *OpenShift In Action.*

appendix A
Installing and configuring OpenShift

The purpose of this appendix is to help you get a multiple-node OpenShift cluster up and running. OpenShift runs on CentOS 7 or Red Hat Enterprise Linux 7 systems. It can run on physical servers, virtual machines (VMs), or VMs in a public cloud like Amazon Web Services (AWS) EC2. This installation should take approximately an hour, depending on your internet connection speed.

A.1 Prerequisites

This section covers what you'll need to have access to or control of to build out your OpenShift cluster.

Multiple OpenShift deployment options

Minishift (https://github.com/Minishift/minishift) is a single-node installation of OpenShift that can be stood up in a few minutes on just about any OS as a VM. As a development platform, it's a very useful tool.

We recommend going through the process of installing a full OpenShift cluster. You can run most of the examples in this book on Minishift. But you're going to run into trouble when you start working with persistent storage, metrics, complex application deployments, and networking.

We love Minishift and use it daily, but the focus of this book is to work with you to deploy an OpenShift cluster that can be the prototype for a larger cluster that's ready to do meaningful work. Minishift has a different goal in mind.

In addition to OpenShift in your datacenter, or even your laptop, hosted versions of OpenShift are available. Red Hat has a hosted version of OpenShift available at www.openshift.com that has a free usage tier. There's also an interactive learning portal at https://learn.openshift.com with guided scenarios that give you access to a single-node installation of OpenShift.

A.1.1 *Available systems or creating virtual machines*

This appendix starts during the OS installation process. The primary assumption we're making is that you have a place to house two servers. These servers can be physical or VMs.

A.1.2 *Administrator or root access*

For many of the examples, you'll use the oc command-line client to control your OpenShift cluster. This appendix will cover its installation.

oc is run from your laptop or workstation. To install oc, you need administrator access if you're using a Windows computer, or root access if you're using Linux or macOS. It's a robust application; full documentation is available on GitHub at http://mng.bz/2s9U.

A.1.3 *Internet access*

For the configuration described here and many of the examples in the book, your OpenShift cluster must be able to access the internet to download software updates and example files.

A.1.4 *Access to the servers*

You'll need several types of access to these systems to install the OS and perform the examples throughout the book.

CONSOLE ACCESS

For either a physical or virtual system, you'll need some sort of console access to install the OS. This could be direct console access on a physical system or some sort of remote console solution like *VNC* (www.realvnc.com/en/connect/download/vnc) for physical or virtual systems.

SSH ACCESS

To install OpenShift and perform some of the examples, you'll need to have *SSH* access to all the systems you create. SSH is a widely used remote access protocol that's used to manage systems over a network connection. The default SSH port is TCP port 22.

On Linux and macOS, there's a built-in command-line SSH client that you can use to access your systems once the OS installation is complete. For Windows, you can use an SSH client application like PuTTY (www.putty.org).

HTTPS ACCESS

OpenShift's default configuration uses TCP port 8443 to access its web interface as well as its API. You'll need to be able to browse to your master server on this port.

A.1.5 *Communication between servers*

To ensure that your OpenShift cluster can communicate properly, several TCP and UDP ports need to be open on the master and nodes. You can find more details at http://mng.bz/gjy1, but we usually pare this down to a simpler configuration for the sort of lab installation that you'll be creating. If you're building this cluster on an isolated network such as your laptop, you can leave all connectivity between your cluster servers open.

If your cluster will have any sort of inbound connectivity from the internet, table A.1 provides a list of ports to keep open for communication among the cluster members.

Table A.1   Ports to keep open between hosts

Port number	Network protocol	Reason
22	TCP	SSH access
1936	TCP	OpenShift router statistics
8053	TCP and UDP	Internal DNS management
4789	UDP	Software-defined networking communication
443	TCP	SSL communications
8443	TCP	Web and API services
10250	TCP	Kubernetes communication
9200	TCP	Aggregated logging collection
9300	TCP	Aggregated logging collection

A.1.6   *DNS resolution*

In OpenShift, the hostnames for all nodes must have a DNS record. This allows encrypted traffic between nodes to work properly.

You need to configure a wildcard DNS record (https://tools.ietf.org/html/rfc4592) that points to your OpenShift cluster to access the applications you deploy. If you have a DNS server that you can control, you can go that route. But as long as you have internet access, you can use the nip.io domain.

> **NOTE** If you have experience with Linux, you may be asking yourself, "Why can't I just use the /etc/hosts file in my OpenShift cluster?" The answer is that you could use /etc/hosts, but only for your server hostnames. OpenShift also can use a *wildcard DNS* domain for all the applications it deploys. This has some helpful advantages that we'll discuss later, and it's how you'll configure this cluster.

UNDERSTANDING THE NIP.IO DOMAIN

The *nip.io domain* (http://nip.io/) is a wonderful little service. Instead of having to configure and manage a DNS server, if you have access to the internet, you can create hostnames and DNS records that resolve to any IP address you choose. It works by taking any DNS record that ends with any IP address and .nip.io and returning that IP address.

Here are some examples of DNS lookups of records using the nip.io domain:

```
dig +short anything.192.168.12.150.nip.io
192.168.12.150
dig +short anything-else.192.168.65.200.nip.io
192.168.65.200
```

The only requirement is that your servers all be able to access a public DNS server.

DECIDING ON HOSTNAMES

The hostnames that we used in our cluster and will use in the examples are outlined in table A.2. We're using the nip.io domain, so the corresponding IP address is important as well. You'll configure the IP address on your servers later in this appendix.

Table A.2   Hostnames and IP addresses for our OpenShift example cluster

Hostname	IP address	OpenShift role
ocp-1.192.168.122.100.nip.io	192.168.122.100	Master
ocp-2.192.168.122.101.nip.io	192.168.122.101	Node

A.1.7   Networking information

The servers in your OpenShift cluster will have static IP addresses to ensure that the DNS and hostnames that you configure work consistently. If you didn't use static IP addresses, you'd need to be able to manage a DHCP server in your environment.

To configure a static IP address in the CentOS installer, you'll need to know some information about the network your systems will be connected to (see table A.3). You'll use this information when you configure your server's network interface.

Table A.3   Networking information needed for server installation

Network parameter	Description	Example values
Network mask (netmask)	Network mask for your network	24
Gateway	Default gateway for your network	192.168.122.1
DNS servers	DNS server(s) your systems will use	8.8.8.8

NOTE The DNS server we're using is 8.8.8.8, which is one of Google's public DNS servers. You can use any DNS server you wish, but in order to work, it must resolve public DNS queries for the nip.io domain.

Next, we'll walk through the resource requirements for the nodes.

A.2 Machine resource requirements

OpenShift Origin's official hardware requirements are published at http://mng.bz/gjy1. These are based on the premise of running a large, production-ready cluster. You're welcome to follow these guidelines, if you have those resources available. But we tested the examples in this book with smaller virtual systems, as outlined in table A.4.

Table A.4 Resources used for our example cluster

Server type	CPU/vCPU	RAM	Storage
Master	2	8 GB	2 disks: 10 GB for OS, 20 GB for persistent storage
Node	2	8 GB	2 disks: 10 GB for OS, 20 GB for container storage

You can always create systems with more resources. These are just values we tested with, and we confirmed that they work.

These server values allow you to have a fully operational OpenShift cluster in VMs on a smaller, portable laptop. This configuration won't let you run as many applications in OpenShift, but for the examples we'll go through in this book, these systems should get the job done.

There are a few nondefault configurations you need to use when you're configuring your OpenShift cluster. Let's go through those next.

A.3 Installing CentOS 7

CentOS 7 has a graphical installer you can use if you're installing it using an installation DVD image. In addition, cloud images are available at www.centos.org/download for multiple platforms like VMWare, OpenStack, and Amazon. We'll go through the installation ISO method using the standard installation DVD image, because it can be used on any platform, including bare-metal systems.

You should be able to use this guide to provision both servers and install OpenShift. If you have another process or tool you use to provision servers, it should work as well. This approach isn't exclusive, by any means. The goal of this section is to demonstrate the most universal installation method.

A.3.1 Launching the installer

When you boot your system using the installation DVD, you'll see the screen shown in figure A.1. You can press Enter, or the process will start automatically after 60 seconds.

The installer boots into the installation process. There's a media check that takes a minute or so, which confirms that the DVD image is fully functional and there were no errors during the download.

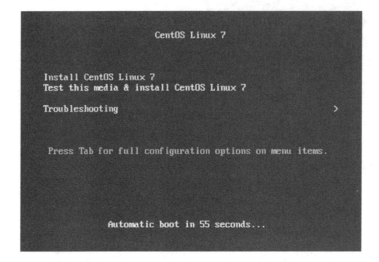

Figure A.1   The CentOS installation startup

Next, you arrive at the home screen of the graphical installer, shown in figure A.2. The graphics are buttons for various installation options. For example, if you need to adjust the time zone, you can change it on the Date & Time screen.

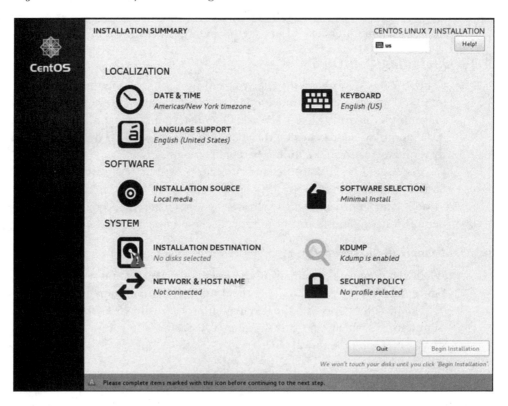

Figure A.2   The CentOS installation main screen opens immediately after the installer launches.

The first customization that must happen to install OpenShift is selecting the disk configuration for your server.

A.3.2 Configuring the disk setup

This step is the same for master and node servers. In section A.2, we noted that the OpenShift nodes need two disks. The first disk in these systems will be for the OS. The second disk won't be provisioned by CentOS: you'll take care of it on the node in a subsequent step so you can use it for container image storage. On the master, this disk will be used in appendix B to set up an NFS server.

From the Installation Destination on the main screen, click the smaller first disk, and be sure to leave the second disk unselected (see figure A.3). Then, click Done to return to the installer main screen.

The next step in getting CentOS configured properly is to set up networking for both nodes.

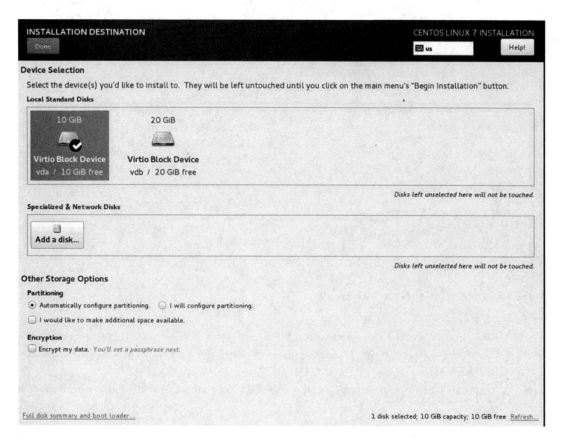

Figure A.3 The CentOS disk setup screen

A.3.3   Setting up networking

The networking configuration process is the same for the master and node servers. On the main screen, click Network & Host Name to access the networking configuration. You'll go through several screens, beginning by setting the hostname and enabling networking.

HOSTNAME RESOLUTION

The Host Name field is in the lower-left corner of the Network & Host Name screen (see figure A.4). Your server hostnames need to be resolvable on your network. Earlier, we mentioned the nip.io domain and how you can use it to resolve anything you need to any IP address you want—and you can use this service for your server hostnames. To set a hostname for your server, fill in the Host Name field, and click Apply. The current hostname appears at lower right after you apply the new hostname.

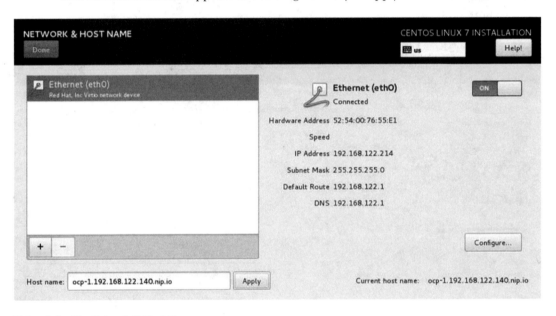

Figure A.4   The Network & Host Name screen

Also on this screen, you need to enable the server's network. By default, the network interface isn't turned on. To turn it on, click the slider button at upper right, as shown in figure A.4.

Next, you need to configure the interface on your server after the installation is complete.

A.3.4   Setting the permanent configurations on the servers

This step is the same on both the Master and the Node servers. To start, click Configure on the Network & Host Name screen to open the screen shown in figure A.5.

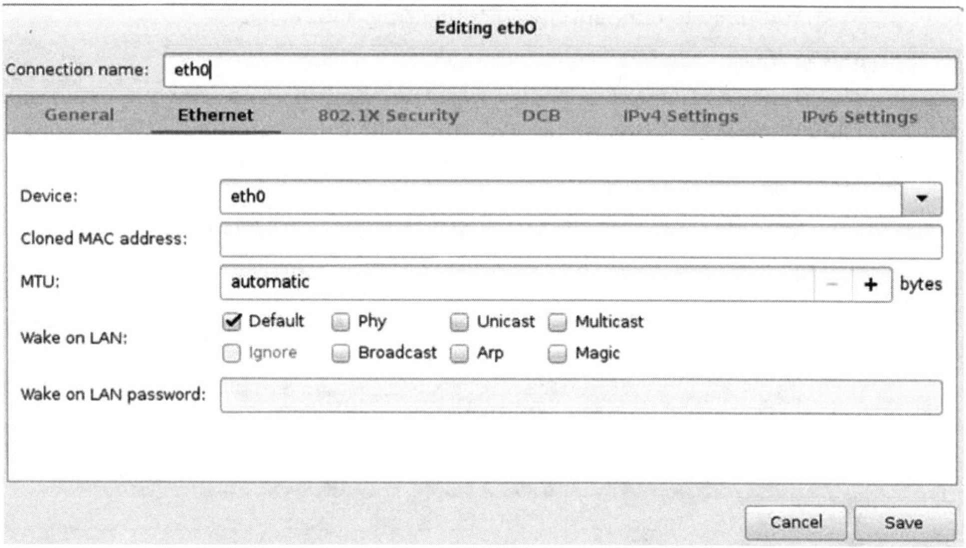

Figure A.5 The initial network configuration screen

Don't make any changes—this is a tab-oriented screen. The first tab you need to configure is the General tab.

THE GENERAL CONFIGURATION TAB

On the General tab, select the Automatically Connect to This Network When It Is Available check box, as shown in figure A.6. This will make sure the interface is brought up when the server is booted.

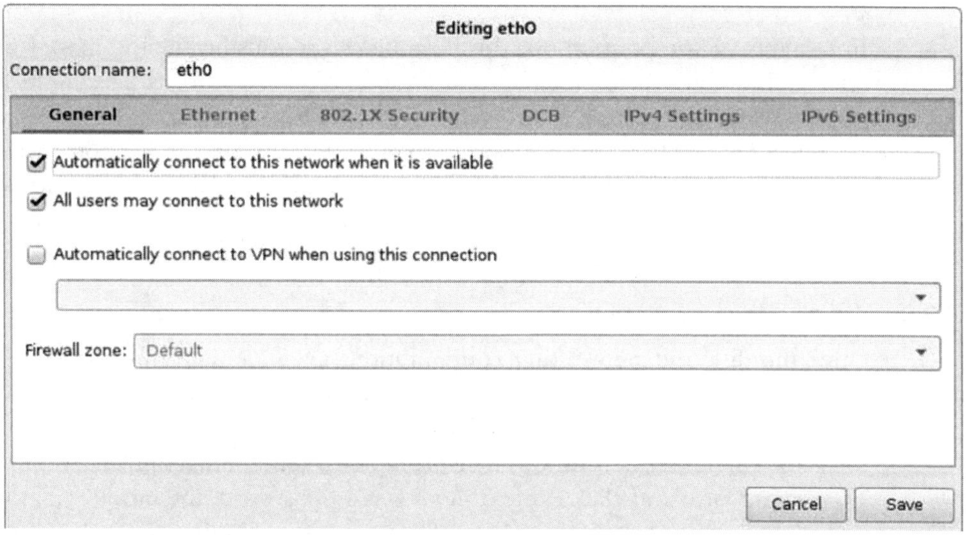

Figure A.6 Network configuration General tab configuration

Next, you need to configure the IPv4 Settings tab.

IPv4 SETTINGS

This is the last network configuration you need to make on your OpenShift servers. These systems will use a static IP address to ensure that the hostnames always resolve properly; you'll configure the static IP address on the screen shown in figure A.7.

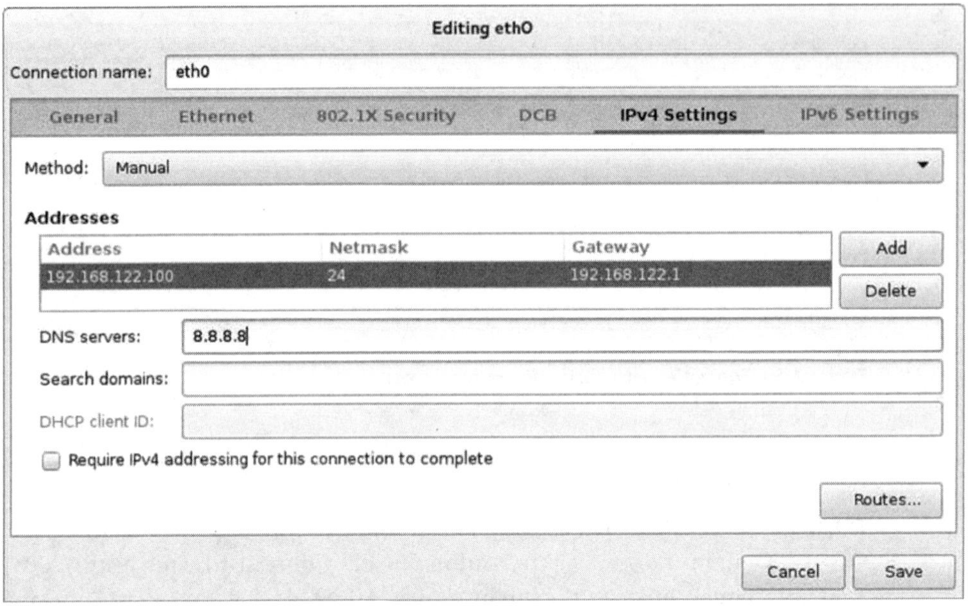

Figure A.7 Network IPv4 Settings screen configuration

In section A.1, we pointed out the hostnames we're using for the master and node servers. These are the hostnames and IP addresses we use for the examples throughout the book.

Select Manual from the Method drop-down list; this option lets you enter static IP addresses for your servers. To fill in the values, use the networking information you gathered in section A.1.5, including the IP address, netmask, and default gateway addresses. Then, click Save to return to the main installation screen.

A.3.5 *Starting the installation*

Once the disk and networking configurations are complete, the Begin Installation button becomes available on the main screen. Click it, and you're on your way.

You'll be prompted to set a password for your root user. Click the Root Password button shown in figure A.8, and you'll be prompted to enter and confirm a root password. Type a password, and click Done. If it's a weaker password, the installer may warn you and force you to either change it or click Done again to confirm that's the password you want to use. For the examples, you won't have to create any additional users.

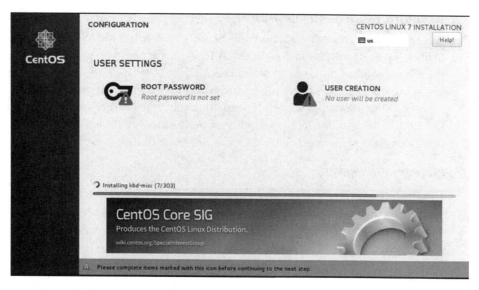

Figure A.8   The CentOS User Settings screen

Now you can sit back and wait for the installer to finish doing its job.

A.3.6   *Wrapping up and rebooting*

When the installer signals that it's finished, it will prompt you to reboot the server, as shown in figure A.9. Click Reboot to restart your server so that it can confirm everything was laid down correctly.

You're now ready to connect to your server, configure it, and install OpenShift.

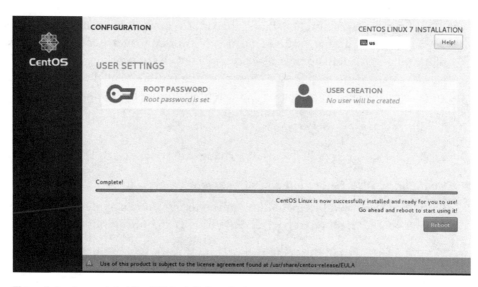

Figure A.9   A completed CentOS installation that's ready to be rebooted

A.4   Preparing to install OpenShift

All the commands in this section will be executed using an SSH connection to the proper server. If you have console access for your systems, you can use that to execute these commands. But in our experience, using an SSH client makes it possible to copy and paste text. This simple feature can save a lot of time when provisioning a system.

OpenShift has a few dependencies that you need to get out of the way before launching the installer. Just as when you built out your master and node OSs, we'll point out if the steps are different for the master and node servers here.

A.4.1   Software prerequisites

You need to install a few software packages. The software that's specific to OpenShift comes from a specialized CentOS repository, which you must install and configure on all servers.

CONFIGURING THE OPENSHIFT REPOSITORIES ON ALL SERVERS

The first step is to install the Extra Packages for Enterprise Linux (EPEL) and Open-Shift Origin repository RPMs. These configure your systems to access those software repos to pull down the needed files. To do so, run the following yum command:

```
# yum -y install epel-release centos-release-openshift-origin36
```

Once that command completes, several software packages will be common to both master and node servers; they come from the two newly enabled repositories. You can install these packages with the following command:

```
# yum -y install origin origin-clients vim-enhanced atomic-openshift-utils
➥ NetworkManager python-rhsm-certificates
```

With those packages installed, there's one more command to run on both systems: you need to enable and start *NetworkManager*. NetworkManager is a tool on Linux servers that configures and maintains all aspects of a server's networking stack. OpenShift uses NetworkManager to manage the network configurations of all the servers in the cluster. You can enable and start NetworkManager by running the following command:

```
# systemctl enable NetworkManager --now
```

In the next section, you'll make a few changes to your server's DNS configurations.

A.4.2   Configuring DNS resolution on both servers

Because DNS is used by OpenShift for everything from encrypted traffic to communication between deployed services, configuring DNS on your nodes is essential.

> **NOTE** The steps in this section apply only if you're using nip.io for your host-names. If your server's hostnames are all on the same domain, this step isn't required.

CONFIGURING /ETC/RESOLV.CONF

If you're using the nip.io domain for your server hostnames, you need to make an additional configuration to NetworkManager. In Linux, specifically CentOS 7, NetworkManager is the utility that manages the configuration for all the networking components on a server.

One of the components that NetworkManager controls is DNS resolution. In Linux, the configuration file that sets up how a server resolves DNS requests is /etc/resolv.conf.

The first line in resolv.conf lets you know that this file was created by NetworkManager. The `nameserver` parameter is the DNS server that your server will connect to for DNS queries. You can have up to three nameserver parameters listed in resolv.conf.

A deeper look at wildcard subdomains and OpenShift

The application domain you use needs to point to your node server. This is because OpenShift uses HAProxy to route traffic properly between your DNS entry and the proper containers in OpenShift. HAProxy is a popular, open source, software-based load balancer. In OpenShift, it runs in a container on a specific host in your cluster. For this installation, it will run on the single application node.

For your cluster, the domain name you specify could be your application node's hostname. But for larger clusters, you can specify which node or nodes run your HAProxy container. It's a good practice to get used to specifying a domain here; we'll use it for examples in the book.

In DNS, a *wildcard domain* means any host for this domain will automatically point to the same IP address. Let's look at a couple of examples. First, here's an actual wildcard domain that we set up on a sample domain:

```
$ dig +short *.apps.jeduncan.com
12.207.21.2
```

You can look up any other record ending in .apps.jeduncan.com, and it will return the same record:

```
$ dig +short app1.apps.jeduncan.com
12.207.21.2
$ dig +short someother.apps.jeduncan.com
12.207.21.2
```

OpenShift uses this same principle. Each application is given a domain that's a member of the wildcard domain that's configured. That way, all the DNS entries for your applications work without any additional configuration.

The other parameter that's included by default in resolv.conf is `search`. This value defaults to the domain name for your server's hostname. The `search` value is used for any DNS queries that aren't *fully qualified domain names* (FQDN). FQDNs are DNS records that are complete—that means they have a hostname, domain name, and top-level domain. For example, server.example.com is an FQDN, and server isn't.

Here's how resolv.conf looks immediately after installation:

```
# Generated by NetworkManager
search 192.168.122.100.nip.io      ◁—— search parameter
nameserver 8.8.8.8                 ◁—┐
                                     └ Listed nameserver
```

Using the nip.io domain, each octet in the IP address is separated by a period. That means each number in the IP address is a level in the domain, with nip.io being the top-level domain. Because of some configurations OpenShift adds to each container, this can cause confusion when pulling down container images from the OpenShift integrated registry. You must edit the search parameter to have only the nip.io top-level domain, as shown in the next listing.

Listing A.1   Edited resolv.conf

```
# Generated by NetworkManager
search nip.io                 ◁—— Edited search parameter
nameserver 8.8.8.8       ◁—┐
                           └ Listed nameserver
```

This configuration will work fine until you reboot your servers. That's because NetworkManager controls /etc/resolv.conf, and it will add the search parameter back when the service is restarted after a reboot. To stop this from happening, you need to configure NetworkManager to not make any further changes to /etc/resolv.conf.

CONFIGURING NETWORKMANAGER

To configure NetworkManager, you need to edit its default configuration file. On CentOS 7, the NetworkManager configuration file is located at /etc/NetworkManager/NetworkManager.conf. The default configuration shown in the following listing is an example of a standard Python configuration file. It has two sections, defined by the lines encased in square brackets: [main] and [logging].

Listing A.2   Example of the default /etc/NetworkManager/NetworkManager.conf

```
# Configuration file for NetworkManager.
#
# See "man 5 NetworkManager.conf" for details.
#
# The directory /etc/NetworkManager/conf.d/
    can contain additional configuration
# snippets. Those snippets override the settings from this main file.
#
# The files within conf.d/ directory are read in asciibetical order.
#
# If two files define the same key, the one that is read afterwards will
➥ overwrite
# the previous one.

[main]
```

```
plugins=ifcfg-rh

[logging]
#level=DEBUG
#domains=ALL
```

You need to add a line to the [main] section of this configuration file, to tell Network-Manager not to make changes to /etc/resolv.conf. Add the line dns=none as shown here:

```
[main]
plugins=ifcfg-rh
dns=none
```

After you restart NetworkManager, the change you made to /etc/resolv.conf will persist across server reboots. To restart the NetworkManager, run the following systemctl command:

```
systemctl restart NetworkManager
```

This should only take a second or so. Once it completes, confirm that Network-Manager is running using systemctl status:

```
systemctl status NetworkManager
? NetworkManager.service - Network Manager
 Loaded: loaded (/usr/lib/systemd/system/NetworkManager.service; enabled;
➥ vendor preset: enabled)
   Active: active (running) Because Sat 2017-05-13 17:05:12 EDT; 6s ago
. . .
```

The final confirmation is to check /etc/resolv.conf and make sure the search parameter hasn't been added back to the file by the freshly restarted NetworkManager service. If there's no search parameter, then everything is as it should be, and you're ready to move forward.

Now you're ready to set up software that's specific to the master and node servers. You'll start with the master server in the next section.

A.4.3 *Installing software on the master server*

Several packages need to be installed only on the master server. This primarily has to do with installing *Ansible* and ensuring that it's the correct version. Ansible (www.ansible.com) is an open source automation and deployment tool. The installation process for OpenShift is written using Ansible. One of the key features of Ansible is that it uses *YAML*, a human-readable data-transport language, to describe all the work it does.

To install OpenShift, you'll create a configuration file written in YAML. This file will be read by the Ansible engine to deploy OpenShift exactly as you want. You'll be creating a relatively simple configuration file; for more advanced installations, the full set of options is documented at http://mng.bz/CD7l.

The OpenShift installer is written and tested against a specific version of Ansible. That means you'll need to make sure that's the version of Ansible that's installed on your master. You only need to worry about Ansible on the master server, because there's no agent on the node. Ansible doesn't use an agent on the systems it's controlling; instead, it uses SSH as a transport mechanism and to execute remote commands. Start this process by running the following yum command:

```
yum -y install httpd-tools gcc python-devel python-pip
```

The python-pip package installs the Python application package manager named pip. It's used to install applications written in Python and available on the Python Package Index (www.pypi.org). With pip installed, you can use it to install Ansible and ensure that you install version 2.2.2.0, which is tested with OpenShift 3.6:

```
# pip -v install ansible==2.2.2.0
```

After Ansible is installed, you'll need to set up SSH keys from your master server to the node, and to the master as well. That's what you'll do next.

SETTING UP SSH ACCESS FROM THE MASTER SERVER

To get the OpenShift installer to function correctly, you need to create an SSH key pair on your master server and distribute the public key to your node. To create a new SSH key pair on your master server, you can use the ssh-keygen command as in this example:

```
ssh-keygen -f /root/.ssh/id_rsa -t rsa -N ''
```

This command creates an SSH key pair in the root user's home directory, /root, in the .ssh subfolder. In Linux, this is the default location for a user's SSH keys.

Next, run the following ssh-copy-id command to distribute your newly created SSH public key to your OpenShift node (if you used a different IP addresses for your master and node, adjust the command accordingly):

```
for i in 192.168.122.100 192.168.122.101;do ssh-copy-id root@$i;done
```

You'll be prompted for the root password for your OpenShift master and node. Once you confirm each password, this command will add the public key from your SSH key pair to the authorized_keys file in /root/.ssh on the OpenShift node.

This will allow the OpenShift installer to connect to the master and node to perform the installation steps. It may seem a little odd to specify the IP address of the master when you'll be running the installer from that server. This is because the OpenShift installer is designed so that it can be run from outside your OpenShift cluster if desired. For your first lab, and because we aren't 100% sure what type of computer you're using daily, it's easier to satisfy the dependencies for the installer on the master node.

This should meet all the dependencies to run the OpenShift installer on the master server. Next, you'll configure your application node.

INSTALLING SOFTWARE ON THE APPLICATION-NODE SERVER

The software requirements for the nodes are a little different. The biggest difference is that this is where docker will be installed. The libcgroup-tools package provides utilities that you'll use to inspect how applications are isolated using kernel control groups in chapter 9. To install these packages, run the following yum command:

```
# yum -y install docker libcgroup-tools
```

Once this is complete, you're ready to configure your container engine's storage on your OpenShift nodes.

A.4.4 Configuring container storage for application nodes

An application called docker-storage-setup is packaged with docker. It configures the desired storage for docker to use when it creates containers for OpenShift.

> **NOTE** The examples in this book use a *logical volume management* (LVM) configuration. This setup creates an LVM volume for each container on demand. These are small initially but can grow to the maximum size configured in OpenShift for your containers.

You can find additional details about the storage setup in the OpenShift documentation at http://mng.bz/hR82.

The first step in this process is to create a configuration file for docker-storage-setup on your OpenShift node, as shown in the next listing. The disk you specify in /etc/sysconfig/docker-storage-setup is the second disk you created for your VM. Depending on your choice of platform for your servers, the OS's name for this disk (/dev/vdb in our example) may vary, but the operation won't.

Listing A.3   Creating the docker-storage-setup configuration file

```
cat <<EOF > /etc/sysconfig/docker-storage-setup
DEVS=/dev/vdb            ◁──────┐
VG=docker-vg                     │ /dev/vdb is the 20 GB volume
EOF                              │ you added to your nodes.
```

Confirming your storage disk name

If you're unsure about the name of the disk to use for your container storage, the lsblk command gives you a list of all disks on your server. The output is in an easy-to-understand tree diagram, as in the following example:

```
                                                  Disk where CentOS
                                                    was installed
# lsblk
NAME                  MAJ:MIN  RM   SIZE  RO  TYPE  MOUNTPOINT
vda                   253:0     0    8G    0  disk         ◁──────┐
??vda1                253:1     0    8G    0  part  /
vdb                   253:16    0   20G    0  disk   ◁────┐

                      Disk to use for container storage
```

Your second disk will have no partitions, because it hasn't been formatted yet.

After you've created this file, you're ready to run the storage-setup utility. This command should run in a couple of seconds, and the output should look like this:

```
docker-storage-setup

Checking that no-one is using this disk right now ...
OK

Disk /dev/vdb: 41610 cylinders, 16 heads, 63 sectors/track
...
  Rounding up size to full physical extent 24.00 MiB
  Logical volume "docker-pool" created.
  Logical volume docker-vg/docker-pool changed.
```

A.4.5   *Enabling and starting docker on your OpenShift nodes*

With your container storage configured, it's time to start up the docker service on your OpenShift node. This is the container runtime that will start and stop containers in the OpenShift workflows. It needs to be enabled and running prior to installing OpenShift.

To enable docker to start at boot time, and to start the service initially, run the following `systemctl` command:

```
systemctl enable docker.service --now
```

Like NetworkManager, you can confirm that docker started correctly by running `systemctl status docker`:

```
[root@ocp2 ~]# systemctl status docker
? docker.service - Docker Application Container Engine
   Loaded: loaded (/usr/lib/systemd/system/docker.service; enabled;
▸ vendor preset: disabled)
  Drop-In: /etc/systemd/system/docker.service.d
           ??custom.conf
   Active: active (running) since Fri 2017-11-10 18:45:12 UTC;          ◁──   The active (running) status
▸ 12 secs ago                                                                 confirms the docker service
     Docs: http://docs.docker.com                                             is up and functioning.
 Main PID: 2352 (dockerd-current)
   Memory: 121.4M
   CGroup: /system.slice/docker.service
...
```

The next step is to modify SELinux to allow OpenShift to connect to NFS as a persistent storage source.

A.4.6   *Configuring SELinux on your OpenShift nodes*

Throughout this book, OpenShift applications will need NFS volumes to act as persistent storage. To be able to do this successfully, you have to tell SELinux on your nodes to allow containers to use NFS. You do so using the `setsebool` command-line utility:

```
# setsebool -P virt_use_nfs 1
# setsebool -P virt_sandbox_use_nfs 1
```

A.5 Installing OpenShift

OpenShift is installed using an Ansible *playbook*: a collection of tasks and configuration parameters needed to perform a task. To execute an Ansible playbook, three things must be present on your server:

- *Ansible engine*—Executes the playbook code. You installed the Ansible engine earlier in this appendix.
- *Playbook*—The code that's executed. When you installed the OpenShift packages, the deployment playbooks were included.
- *Inventory*—The list of hosts against which to run a playbook. Inventories can be divided into groups and contain any variables needed for the hosts in the inventory for the playbook to run.

To deploy OpenShift, you need to configure an Ansible inventory file for your cluster. That's what you'll do next.

A.5.1 Creating the OpenShift inventory

The Ansible inventory for OpenShift contains information about your two hosts and specifies which roles each node will have in your cluster. If you're using the IP addresses and hostnames we're using in this appendix, you can download a prepared inventory to your master node from the *OpenShift in Action* organization on GitHub:

```
# curl -o /root/hosts
➥ https://raw.githubusercontent.com/OpenShiftInAction/AppendixA/master/hosts
```

For those of you who need to customize your installation, let's go through the inventory components and how they're designed.

Ansible inventories are divided into groups. Each group consists of hosts that are defined by either hostname or IP address. In an inventory, a group can also be defined by listing child groups that belong to it using the `:children` syntax. In the following example, the group `master_group` is made up of the hosts in `group1` and `group2`. You'll use this capability in your OpenShift inventory:

```
[master_group:children]          ◁──────┐ master_group, defined
group1                                   │ by the child groups of
group2                                   │ group1 and group2

[group1]         ◁── group1 hosts
host1
host2

[group2]         ◁── group2 hosts
host3
host4

[group3]                    ◁──────┐ group3 hosts, which aren't
host5                              │ part of master_group
host6
```

Another capability of Ansible inventories that you'll use in your OpenShift inventory is defining variables for hosts and host groups. You can define variables for an entire group using a group heading and the `:vars` syntax. To define a variable for a single host, add it to the same line you use to define the host in a group:

```
[group1]
host1 var2=False var3=42          var2 and var3 are
host1 foo=bar                     defined only for host1.

                        var1 will be defined and
[group1:vars]           available for all hosts in group1.
var1=True
```

Your initial OpenShift inventory uses several groups and lots of variables:

- `OSEv3`—The group that represents your entire cluster. It's made up of the child groups `nodes`, `masters`, `nfs`, and `etcd`.
- `nodes`—All groups in your cluster, including all masters and all application nodes.
- `masters`—The nodes in your cluster that will be designated as masters.
- `nfs`—Nodes used to provide NFS shared storage for several services on the master nodes. This is required if you have multiple master servers. We aren't taking advantage of multiple masters in this initial cluster, but the group is still required for deploying OpenShift.
- `etcd`—The nodes where etcd will be deployed. etcd is the database for Kubernetes and OpenShift. Your cluster will use the master server to house the etcd database. For larger clusters, etcd can be separated into its own cluster nodes.

For the `nodes` and `masters` groups, you'll disable a few of the system checks the deployment playbook runs prior to deployment. These checks verify the amount of free space and memory available on the system; for an initial cluster, you can use smaller values than the recommendations verified by these checks. (You can learn more about these checks at http://mng.bz/r0dI.) To disable the checks, you set variables for each of these groups:

```
                                    Disables storage and memory
                                    checks for the nodes group
[nodes:vars]
openshift_disable_check=disk_availability,memory_availability,docker_storage

[masters:vars]
openshift_disable_check=disk_availability,memory_availability,docker_storage

Disables storage and memory
checks for the masters group
```

Your deployment inventory will also set variables for most of the hosts. The `ansible _connection` variable is specific to Ansible, telling the Ansible engine to connect to the host from the local system where the playbook is running. Additional Ansible variables are discussed at http://mng.bz/g3g0.

NOTE The IP addresses and hostnames used in this inventory are specific to the example cluster. If your IP addresses and hostnames are different, you'll need to change them in the inventory to successfully deploy OpenShift.

The rest of the variables are specific to the OpenShift playbook, and documented in the following listing, which is a full example of the OpenShift inventory.

Listing A.4 OpenShift inventory file

```
[OSEv3:children]                    ←┐  OSEv3 group, made up of
nodes                                └  all groups in the inventory
nfs
masters
etcd                          ┌ Cluster-wide variables applied
                              └ to all nodes in the OSEv3 group
[OSEv3:vars]                  ←┘
openshift_master_cluster_public_hostname=None
openshift_master_default_subdomain=apps.192.168.122.101.nip.io
ansible_ssh_user=root
openshift_master_cluster_hostname=None
openshift_override_hostname_check=true
deployment_type=origin
                             ┌ Variables for the nodes group
[nodes:vars]              ←──┘
openshift_disable_check=disk_availability,memory_availability,docker_storage

[masters:vars]
openshift_disable_check=disk_availability,memory_availability,docker_storage

[nodes]
192.168.122.100  openshift_public_ip=192.168.122.100
➡ openshift_ip=192.168.122.100
➡ openshift_public_hostname=ocp1.192.168.122.100.nip.io      Host entry for ocp1,
➡ openshift_hostname=ocp1.192.168.122.100.nip.io            using its IP address;
➡ connect_to=192.168.122.100 openshift_schedulable=False    includes host-specific
➡ ansible_connection=local                           ←──┐   variables
192.168.122.101  openshift_public_ip=192.168.122.101
➡ openshift_ip=192.168.122.101
➡ openshift_public_hostname=ocp2.192.168.122.101.nip.io
➡ openshift_hostname=ocp2.192.168.122.101.nip.io
➡ connect_to=192.168.122.101 openshift_node_labels="{'region': 'infra'}"
➡ openshift_schedulable=True
                              ┌ nfs group
[nfs]                      ←──┘
192.168.122.100 connect_to=192.168.122.100 ansible_connection=local
                              ┌ masters group
[masters]                  ←──┘
192.168.122.100  openshift_public_ip=192.168.122.100
➡ openshift_ip=192.168.122.100
➡ openshift_public_hostname=ocp1.192.168.122.100.nip.io
➡ openshift_hostname=ocp1.192.168.122.100.nip.io
➡ connect_to=192.168.122.100 ansible_connection=local

[etcd]          ←── etcd group
```

```
192.168.122.100  openshift_public_ip=192.168.122.100
➥ openshift_ip=192.168.122.100
➥ openshift_public_hostname=ocp1.192.168.122.100.nip.io
➥ openshift_hostname=ocp1.192.168.122.100.nip.io
➥ connect_to=192.168.122.100 ansible_connection=local
```

> **NOTE** The ocp1 node has a variable named openshift_node_labels. Node labels are arbitrary values you can apply to nodes on your cluster. The label applied during deployment, region = infra, tells OpenShift the correct node to deploy the container that runs the router to handle internet requests. You'll work with node labels in chapter 10.

After making any inventory edits required to match your environment, save your inventory on your master node as /root/hosts. The next step is to start your Open-Shift deployment.

A.5.2 Running the deployment playbook

It's time to deploy your OpenShift cluster. Ansible uses SSH to log in to each node and perform the tasks to deploy OpenShift, so this command needs to be executed as the root user on the master, which has SSH access keys on each node. To run the proper Ansible playbook, run the ansible-playbook command, specifying the inventory file and the deploy playbook installed at /usr/share/ansible/openshift-ansible/play-books/byo/config.yml:

```
# ansible-playbook -i /root/hosts \
/usr/share/ansible/openshift-ansible/playbooks/byo/config.yml
```

This launches the deployment process. Depending on your internet connection speed, the deployment could take 30-45 minutes. If everything is successful, you should see output indicating that the playbook completed. If you see a red Ansible error on the command line, it should give you an indication of what to look at.

> **My deployment failed. Help!**
>
> OpenShift is a complex application, so we can't point you to a single link of trouble-shooting tips if you run into issues with your deployment. Copying the most important parts of the error and searching for those terms on the internet is always a good starting point. Also, please feel free to contact us on the Manning forum for *OpenShift in Action* at https://forums.manning.com/forums/openshift-in-action. We'll do our best to help you get up and running!

A.6   Installation complete

Once the installation is complete, you should be able to browse to the hostname of your master server on port 8443 with HTTPS. In our example, the URL is https://ocp1.192.168.122.100.nip.io:8443 (see figure A.10). Before the page loads, you'll

Figure A.10   The OpenShift login page after a successful installation

probably get a warning about the site being insecure because the SSL certificate hasn't been properly signed. Don't worry about this—OpenShift created its own SSL certificates as part of the installation process. In our configuration, because the cluster is deployed with VMs on a laptop, the cluster is available only from the laptop the VM nodes are installed on.

If your OpenShift server looks like figure A.10, you've successfully installed OpenShift! You're ready to go through the examples beginning in chapter 2.

Many of the examples you'll go through involve using the OpenShift oc command-line tool. The next section will help you get oc installed and ready to use on Windows, macOS, or Linux.

> **TIP**   OpenShift has a robust diagnostics toolset integrated into the oc command-line tool. Documentation for running diagnostics and checks on your OpenShift cluster is available at http://mng.bz/Zo4P.

A.7   *Installing the oc OpenShift command-line utility*

The oc application has ready-to-use binaries for Linux, Windows, and macOS. They're available on the Releases GitHub page for OpenShift Origin at https://github.com/openshift/origin/releases. We're using the latest release for oc; you can find it by browsing directly to https://github.com/openshift/origin/releases/latest.

> **NOTE**   Because OpenShift Origin is a fast-moving project, there are usually one or more pre-release versions of software available for download. These versions are a little too new and untested to ensure that you have a good experience with OpenShift.

The downloadable files are listed in the Downloads section for each software release. For each OS, there's a corresponding openshift-origin-client-tools archive that you can download. These are the files you'll be using to install oc.

A.7.1   Installing oc on Windows

To install oc on Windows, download the windows Zip archive from the Downloads section of the Latest Release page. After unzipping the archive, move the oc binary in it into a directory in your Windows PATH.

You can see the directories that are in PATH on your Windows system from the Windows command line by running the following command:

```
C:\> path
```

A.7.2   Installing oc on macOS

For macOS, the binary can also be downloaded from the Releases page on GitHub. The downloaded file is a Zip binary. Extract the downloaded oc binary file, and then copy it to a directory in your PATH. To see all the directories in your PATH, you can use the Terminal application to print out the variable using the following command:

```
echo $PATH
```

With oc in your PATH, you can execute the command from the Terminal application by typing oc.

A.7.3   Installing oc on Linux

There are 32- and 64-bit versions of the oc client available for download. If you're unsure of the type of Linux you have installed on your system, you can confirm whether you have a 32- or 64-bit system by running the following uname command:

```
uname -i
```

The output should contain either x86_64 for 64-bit systems or i686 for 32-bit installations. Be sure to download the appropriate openshift-origin-client-tools archive for your Linux architecture—they aren't cross-compatible. To download the Linux archive, run the following curl command:

```
curl -L https://github.com/openshift/origin/releases/download/v3.6.0/
➥ openshift-origin-client-tools-v3.6.0-c4dd4cf-linux-64bit.tar.gz
```

After you download the archive you plan to use, extract the archive using the tar utility:

```
tar -xzf /tmp/openshift-origin-client-tools.tar.gz
```

After you extract the archive, move the `oc` file that was in it into a directory that's listed in the `PATH` variable on your system. If you aren't sure about the directories in your `PATH`, you can confirm them by echoing the variable out to your command line:

```
$ echo $PATH
/usr/lib64/qt-3.3/bin:/usr/local/bin:/usr/local/sbin:/usr/bin:/usr/sbin:/home/
➥ jduncan/.local/bin:/home/jduncan/bin
```

> **NOTE** The OpenShift Origin documentation website has a section dedicated to getting `oc` up and running. It's available at http://mng.bz/iM9L if you'd like to take a look.

A.7.4 Confirming that oc is installed and functioning correctly

Now that you've installed `oc` on your favorite OS, you need to confirm that it's functional. You can do this by asking `oc` for its version information on the command line. Your output should look like the following example. For Linux, use your favorite terminal emulator. macOS uses the Terminal application, and Windows has the command prompt. This example is from a Linux workstation:

```
$ oc version
oc v1.3.1
kubernetes v1.3.0+52492b4
features: Basic-Auth GSSAPI Kerberos SPNEGO
error: You must be logged in to the server (the server has asked for the
➥ client to provide credentials)
```

If this executes cleanly, your system should be ready to connect to OpenShift and get work done once you have OpenShift installed and configured. You can add additional nodes to an existing OpenShift cluster using the next section as a guide.

A.8 Adding an OpenShift node

Scaling your OpenShift cluster is essential as you deploy more application workloads. This section walks you through the steps required to add a second application node to your cluster. First, you need to provision a new server and install the prerequisites.

A.8.1 Preparing the new application node

OpenShift manages the resources available on a node and allocates resources to it accordingly. Your second application node's resources don't have to match your original node.

> **Running nodes on different platforms**
>
> OpenShift can run on any x86_64 server that can run CentOS 7 or Red Hat Enterprise Linux 7. In theory, your OpenShift cluster can stretch across multiple platforms like these:
>
> - Bare-metal servers
> - Virtual machines like VMWare, Ovirt, and Hyper-V
> - Public cloud providers like Amazon Web Services and Microsoft Azure

> **(continued)**
> Communication between OpenShift nodes requires a quality connection with relatively low latency. You'll get the best performance if you locate your cluster on a single platform. For building out larger clusters across multiple types of server infrastructure, you should consult a company like Red Hat (or at least its documentation) for best practices and example architectures.

For our new node, we're using an additional VM with similar resources, hostname, and IP address (see table A.5). Any additional server that can run CentOS 7 will work if it has network connectivity to your existing cluster.

Table A.5   New application node specs

Resource	Value
VCPU	2
RAM	8192 MB
OS disk	10 GB
Data disk	20 GB
Hostname	ocp3.192.168.122.102.nip.io
IP address	192.168.122.102

Configure your new node using the same steps as the original application node covered in this appendix. These steps are summarized in table A.6.

Table A.6   Summary of steps in configuring an application node

Command	Description
`yum -y install origin origin-clients vim-enhanced atomic-openshift-utils NetworkManager python-rhsm-certificates`	Installs base OpenShift packages
`systemctl enable NetworkManager --now`	Enables and starts NetworkManager
`setsebool -P virt_use_nfs 1` `setsebool -P virt_sandbox_use_nfs 1`	Sets SELinux to allow NFS persistent storage
`yum -y install docker libcgroup-tools`	Installs docker and cgroup management tools
`cat <<EOF > /etc/sysconfig/docker-storage-setup` `DEVS=/dev/<CONTAINER_STORAGE_DISK> VG=docker-vgEOF`	Creates the docker-storage-setup configuration file
`docker-storage-setup`	Runs the docker-storage-setup utility

After your new application node is provisioned and configured, reboot it to make sure all changes take effect. The server is now ready to be added to your cluster. The workflow to add your node is executed on your master server, like deploying your original cluster. Let's discuss that next.

A.9 Configuring the master node

The first step in configuring your master node is to add the root user's SSH to your new application node. Doing this allows the Ansible playbook that adds your node to access your new application node. To do this, run the following `ssh-copy-id` command. If you used a different IP address for your new node, be sure to use it when running the command:

```
ssh-copy-id root@192.168.122.103
```

You're prompted for the root user's password that you set during the CentOS installation process. This command sets up the SSH key from your master to provide access to the root user on your new node. With this complete, make sure the installer packages are up to date for your master server.

A.9.1 Updating OpenShift playbooks

To make sure you have the most up-to-date version of the OpenShift installer, run the following `yum` command on the master node:

```
yum update atomic-openshift-utils
```

If there are updated playbooks for your version of OpenShift, this command will install them on your master, notifying you when complete. Next, add your new node to the OpenShift installer's inventory.

A.9.2 Updating your OpenShift inventory

When you deployed OpenShift, you created an Ansible inventory file at /root/hosts on the master node. To add the new node to OpenShift, you need to edit this inventory before running the Ansible playbook that scales your cluster.

> **NOTE** Red Hat supports OpenShift clusters as large as 2,000 application nodes. For clusters that large, services on the master, like etcd, are separated onto their own servers to provide better performance and scalability.

To add your new node, create a group that contains the information for your node by editing your inventory file directly, as shown in listing A.5. Be sure to name this group new_nodes. Also include any labels it needs (none in this case), and tell the installer to make this node schedule-able for workloads.

Listing A.5   new_nodes group to contain your new node's information

```
[new_nodes]
192.168.122.102 openshift_node_labels="{}" openshift_schedulable=True
```

Next, you need to tell the OpenShift playbook that the new_nodes group is part of your OpenShift cluster. To do this, add the new_nodes group to the [OSEv3:children] group, as shown in the following listing.

Listing A.6   new_nodes group added to the OSEv3:children group

```
[OSEv3:children]
nodes
nfs
masters
etcd
new_nodes
```

The final step of editing your inventory is to define the variables your new_nodes group needs to function properly. You need to create this group so you can define the variables to disable a few of the resource checks that the installer performs by default because of the limited resources on the nodes. You can copy the [nodes:vars] group and change the name to [new_nodes:vars], shown in the following listing.

Listing A.7   Creating the new_nodes:vars group

```
[new_nodes:vars]
openshift_disable_check=disk_availability,memory_availability,docker_storage
openshift_deployment_type=origin
```

**Copy the content from nodes:vars and use it to
create a new group called new_nodes:vars.**

After creating the new_nodes and new_nodes:vars groups, and adding new_nodes to the OSEv3:children group, you're ready to scale your OpenShift cluster.

A.10   Adding the node

There's an Ansible playbook on your master node that will add your new node to your existing OpenShift cluster. You run it using the ansible-playbook command, specifying your newly edited inventory with the -i parameter. To start this process, run the following command on your master server:

```
ansible-playbook -i /root/hosts  /usr/share/ansible/openshift-
➥ ansible/playbooks/byo/openshift-node/scaleup.yml
```

Once scaleup.yml completes successfully, your new node has been added to your OpenShift cluster. You can confirm this by running oc get nodes while being logged in as the admin user:

```
# oc get nodes
NAME                              STATUS                      AGE
➡ VERSION
ocp1.192.168.122.100.nip.io       Ready,SchedulingDisabled    3d
➡ v1.6.1+5115d708d7
ocp2.192.168.122.101.nip.io       Ready                       3d
➡ v1.6.1+5115d708d7
ocp3.192.168.122.102.nip.io       Ready                       2d
➡ v1.6.1+5115d708d7          ◁
```

The new ocp3 node is visible to OpenShift and ready to handle workloads.

This process is repeatable as your OpenShift cluster grows over time, to make sure your OpenShift cluster always has resources to handle your workloads.

appendix B
Setting up a
persistent storage source

The purpose of this appendix is to configure NFS and export a volume to use as the backend for persistent volumes in your OpenShift cluster. In the examples, you'll set up the OpenShift master as the NFS server. If you want to use a different server, the setup is similar. The main thing you need to be sure of is that your NFS server has connectivity to your OpenShift cluster. In the following sections, you'll install and configure your OpenShift master as an NFS server.

B.1 Installing the NFS server software

The NFS server software is provided by the nfs-utils package. The first step is to confirm whether this package is installed on the master. The command to do that uses the yum package manager. The output indicates whether nfs-utils is installed. If the package isn't installed, there's no output. In a terminal window, run the following command at the prompt to see if the nfs-utils package is installed on your master server:

```
# rpm -q nfs-utils
nfs-utils-1.3.0-0.33.el7_3.x86_64
```

If you need to install nfs-utils, running the following yum command in the same terminal will install all the services required to act as an NFS server:

```
yum -y install nfs-utils
```

When you have nfs-utils installed on your master server, you need to configure the filesystem that NFS will use for storage. This is detailed in the next section.

B.2 Configuring storage for NFS

In appendix A, you created your master node with two disks. In the example in appendix A, which used VMs on a Linux laptop, the second disk device's name is /dev/vdb. If you created your VMs using a different platform, or if you're using physical machines for your cluster, the device name of this disk may be different. If you don't know the device name for your second disk, you can use the lsblk command on your master server to see all the block devices on your server:

```
# lsblk
NAME                  MAJ:MIN RM  SIZE RO TYPE MOUNTPOINT
sr0                    11:0    1 1024M  0 rom
vda                   252:0    0   10G  0 disk
├─vda1                252:1    0    1G  0 part /boot
└─vda2                252:2    0    9G  0 part
  ├─cl-root           253:0    0    8G  0 lvm  /
  └─cl-swap           253:1    0    1G  0 lvm  [SWAP]
vdb                   252:16   0   20G  0 disk
```

B.2.1 Creating a filesystem on your storage disk

In appendix A, when you selected your disk configuration options, you unchecked the second disk on the system. That instructed the installer to ignore that disk when it installed the OS. Now you need to create a filesystem on the second disk. For your needs, an ext4 filesystem will do everything you need. (The ext4 filesystem is a standard filesystem format for Linux servers.) To create a filesystem, you can use the mkfs.ext4 command:

```
# mkfs.ext4 /dev/vdb
mke2fs 1.42.9 (28-Dec-2013)
Filesystem label=
OS type: Linux
Block size=4096 (log=2)
Fragment size=4096 (log=2)
Stride=0 blocks, Stripe width=0 blocks
1310720 inodes, 5242880 blocks
262144 blocks (5.00%) reserved for the super user
First data block=0
Maximum filesystem blocks=2153775104
160 block groups
32768 blocks per group, 32768 fragments per group
8192 inodes per group
Superblock backups stored on blocks:
    32768, 98304, 163840, 229376, 294912, 819200, 884736, 1605632, 2654208,
    4096000

Allocating group tables: done
Writing inode tables: done
Creating journal (32768 blocks): done
Writing superblocks and filesystem accounting information: done
```

NOTE If you'd like more information about the ext4 filesystem and what makes it work, check out the article "An Introduction to Linux's EXT4 Filesystem" (David Both, *opensource.com,* https://opensource.com/article/17/5/introduction-ext4-filesystem).

The next step is to configure your master server so that it's properly mounted when the server starts up.

B.3   Mounting your storage disk at startup

The NFS shared volume you're creating needs to be available all the time. That means you need to configure your NFS server to mount your newly created filesystem when the host boots up.

B.3.1   Creating a mountpoint directory

In Linux, every mounted filesystem needs a directory to act as a mountpoint. For your NFS server, you need to create that directory in /var to mount your filesystem in. The following command creates the /var/nfs-data directory to serve as the mountpoint for the NFS filesystem:

```
# mkdir /var/nfs-data/
```

After the directory is created, you need to gather some information about the filesystem you created to hold your NFS volumes. This information will be used to edit the Linux server to make it mount this filesystem correctly when it boots up.

B.3.2   Getting your storage drive's block ID

Each block device has a *unique identifier* (UUID) in Linux. You can view these UUIDs using the blkid command-line tool. Here's an example of the output:

```
# blkid
/dev/vda1: UUID="bdda3896-5dbc-4822-b008-78bba4898341" TYPE="xfs"
/dev/vda2: UUID="KsWi8Z-PNi0-Hdgt-akAP-RWfF-9Myp-oL0eKr" TYPE="LVM2_member"
/dev/vdb: UUID="607b9d47-9280-433d-a233-0f40f060ec51" TYPE="ext4"
/dev/mapper/cl-root: UUID="88a37ff5-eaba-4358-80a7-119edf6d30a7" TYPE="xfs"
/dev/mapper/cl-swap: UUID="4a2d0c5c-33f9-46d3-b8e7-4e8c53d562ce" TYPE="swap"
/dev/loop0: UUID="e7a6c25e-d482-4082-bc7d-a845fd2aef17" TYPE="xfs"
/dev/mapper/docker-253:0-12995325-pool: UUID="e7a6c25e-d482-4082-bc7d-
➥ a845fd2aef17" TYPE="xfs"
```

In this example, we used the /dev/vdb block device to create the NFS storage filesystem. You can see in the output that our UUID is "607b9d47-9280-433d-a233-0f40f060ec51". Make a note of the UUID for your device; you'll need it in the next section.

The next step is to configure your server to automatically mount the volume correctly when it boots up.

B.3.3 Editing /etc/fstab to include your volume

On a Linux server, /etc/fstab is the configuration file that contains all the filesystems and partitions that should be mounted automatically when the server boots up, along with their mount options. The following listing shows an example /etc/fstab file; the same file should be similar on your system.

Listing B.1   An example /etc/fstab configuration file

```
#
# /etc/fstab
# Created by anaconda on Fri May 12 19:39:58 2017
#
# Accessible filesystems, by reference, are maintained under '/dev/disk'
# See man pages fstab(5), findfs(8), mount(8) and/or blkid(8) for more info
#
/dev/mapper/cl-root          /                       xfs     defaults       0 0
UUID=bdda3896-5dbc-4822-b008-78bba4898341 /boot                     xfs
➥ defaults        0 0
/dev/mapper/cl-swap     swap                    swap    defaults       0 0
```

Each mountpoint in /etc/fstab has several parameters. They're as follows, from left to right:

- *Device to be mounted*—In this case, you'll use the UUID that you noted earlier.
- *Mount point for the block device*—This is the /var/nfs-data directory that you created earlier.
- *Type of filesystem*—This is ext4 for your new line in /etc/fstab.

The rest of the options are beyond the scope of this appendix. You can use `defaults 0 0`. In this example, the following line was added to the end of /etc/fstab:

```
UUID=607b9d47-9280-433d-a233-0f40f060ec51 /var/nfs-data    ext4    defaults 0 0
```

B.3.4 Activating your new mount point

After adding your new line to /etc/fstab, you can use the `mount -a` command to have the server re-read /etc/fstab and mount anything that isn't already mounted. After it completes, you can make sure it's mounted properly by running the `mount` command with no additional parameters. Following are examples of these commands and their output:

```
# mount -a
# mount
...
/dev/mapper/cl-root on /
      type xfs (rw,relatime,seclabel,attr2,inode64,noquota)
selinuxfs on /sys/fs/selinux type selinuxfs (rw,relatime)
systemd-1 on /proc/sys/fs/binfmt_misc type autofs
➥ (rw,relatime,fd=31,pgrp=1,timeout=300,minproto=5,maxproto=5,direct)
```

```
hugetlbfs on /dev/hugepages type hugetlbfs (rw,relatime,seclabel)
debugfs on /sys/kernel/debug type debugfs (rw,relatime)
mqueue on /dev/mqueue type mqueue (rw,relatime,seclabel)
nfsd on /proc/fs/nfsd type nfsd (rw,relatime)
/dev/vda1 on /boot type xfs (rw,relatime,seclabel,attr2,inode64,noquota)
sunrpc on /var/lib/nfs/rpc_pipefs type rpc_pipefs (rw,relatime)
tmpfs on /run/user/0 type tmpfs
➥ (rw,nosuid,nodev,relatime,seclabel,size=388192k,mode=700)
/dev/vdb on /var/nfs-data type ext4
➥ (rw,relatime,seclabel,data=ordered)         ◁──┐  /dev/vdb is mounted at /var/nfs-data,
                                                   │  just like we want.
```

At this point, the filesystem is ready to go. The next step is to configure NFS to share /var/nfs-data over the network.

B.4   *Configuring NFS*

Because several examples in this book require NFS storage, you'll need to export five different NFS volumes. In NFS, an exported volume is a unique directory specified in the /etc/exports configuration file. You need to create these directories in /var/nfs-data. You can create them all with a single command, as follows:

```
# mkdir -p /var/nfs-data/{pv01,pv02,pv03,pv04,pv05}
```

After creating your export directories, the next step is to add them to your NFS server's configuration.

By default, the /etc/exports configuration file is empty. You'll edit this file to add all the volumes you want to export, along with their permissions, as shown in the following listing.

Listing B.2   Configuration to add to /etc/exports for your cluster

```
/var/nfs-data/pv01 *(rw,root_squash)
/var/nfs-data/pv02 *(rw,root_squash)
/var/nfs-data/pv03 *(rw,root_squash)
/var/nfs-data/pv04 *(rw,root_squash)
/var/nfs-data/pv05 *(rw,root_squash)
```

Looking at each line in this file from left to right, let's break down what the configuration means for each export:

- *Directory to be exported by NFS*—One entry for each of the directories you just created.
- *Servers allowed to connect to this NFS share*—The asterisk allows any server to access these shares.
- *Mount permissions*—These options are in parentheses. For these exports, you'll allow read-write (rw) access and not allow the root user to mount the volume (root_squash).

Because you aren't allowing the root user to mount any of these NFS volumes, you need to make sure the permissions on the directories are correct.

B.4.1 Setting ownership of the mountpoint

OpenShift will connect to the NFS shares using the nfsnobody user: a special user used by NFS servers that's used when root user access isn't allowed. You can use the chown and chmod commands to properly set the ownership of /var/nfs-data and allow access to the directory only for the nfsnobody user. After setting the proper ownership and permissions, you can confirm them:

Confirms that the ownership and permissions for /var/nfs-data are correct

Sets ownership to nfsnobody, using the -R option to act on the directory recursively

Sets the mode so that only the nfsnobody user and group can access the directory, using the -R option again to act recursively

```
# chown -R nfsnobody.nfsnobody /var/nfs-data/
# chmod -R 0770 /var/nfs-data/
# ls -al /var/nfs-data/
total 24
drwxrwx---.  7 nfsnobody nfsnobody 4096 Jun 17 21:27 .
drwxr-xr-x. 20 root      root       283 Jun 17 01:13 ..
drwxrwx---.  2 nfsnobody nfsnobody 4096 Jun 17 21:16 pv01
drwxrwx---.  2 nfsnobody nfsnobody 4096 Jun 17 21:16 pv02
drwxrwx---.  2 nfsnobody nfsnobody 4096 Jun 17 21:27 pv03
drwxrwx---.  2 nfsnobody nfsnobody 4096 Jun 17 21:27 pv04
drwxrwx---.  2 nfsnobody nfsnobody 4096 Jun 17 21:27 pv05
```

Because NFS is a filesystem served over a network, you need to make sure the network firewall on your master server will allow the NFS traffic through. This is covered in the next section.

B.5 Setting firewall rules to allow NFS traffic

You'll be using NFS version 4 (NFSv4) to connect to these exported volumes. This version of the NFS protocol requires TCP port 2049 to be open. You can check that status using the following command:

```
# iptables -L -v -n | grep 2049
    0     0 ACCEPT     tcp  --  *       *           0.0.0.0/0
  ➥ 0.0.0.0/0           state NEW tcp dpt:2049
```

If you don't get any output from this command, you can add a rule to your firewall using the following iptables command:

```
# iptables -I INPUT -p tcp --dport 2049 -j ACCEPT
```

After running this command, you can rerun the previous iptables command, and you should see a result. If you do, then you've configured your firewall correctly.

The last thing you need to do for your network configuration is to save your new settings. You do so using the following service command in Linux:

```
# service iptables save
```

NOTE   The default firewall utility for CentOS and RHEL 7 is firewalld. Open-Shift is still working to integrate completely with this tool. Currently, the OpenShift installer disables firewalld. For our example, because we're using the OpenShift master as our NFS server, we're using the older `iptables` commands and the `service` command to save our firewall rules. If you're using a different server, you can set up NFS using firewalld.

With this completed, the last things to do is to enable and start the NFS services.

B.6   *Enabling and starting NFS*

What we call NFS is actually a collection of four services that you need to enable and start:

- `rpcbind`—NFS uses the RPC protocol to transfer data.
- `nfs-server`—The NFS server service.
- `nfs-lock`—Handles file locking for NFS volumes.
- `nfs-idmap`—Handles user and group mapping for NFS volumes.

B.6.1   *Starting NFS services*

If you're using the OpenShift master as your NFS server, these services are already enabled and turned on. In that case, you need to restart the services, using the following command that loops through all the services that make NFS work properly:

```
for i in rpcbind nfs-server nfs-lock nfs-idmap;do systemctl restart $i;done
```

If you're using another server to host your NFS server, enable these services and start them using the following command:

```
for i in rpcbind nfs-server nfs-lock nfs-idmap;do systemctl enable
➥ $i;systemctl start $i;done
```

Now you can check your system to make sure your new volume is exported.

B.6.2   *Confirming that your NFS volume is exported and ready to use*

To see all the volumes exported by NFS in Linux, you can use the `exportfs` command-line tool. On the OpenShift master, you'll see several exported volumes, similar to the following example. On an independent server, you'll see only the volumes you exported in the /var/nfs-data directory:

```
# exportfs
/var/nfs-data/pv01
        <world>
/var/nfs-data/pv02
        <world>
/var/nfs-data/pv03
        <world>
/var/nfs-data/pv04
        <world>
/var/nfs-data/pv05
```

Indicates that the volume is exported and ready for use as an NFS volume. The <world> notation means any host can access the volume, just as you configured in /etc/exports.

```
        <world>
/exports/registry
        <world>
/exports/metrics
        <world>
/exports/logging-es
        <world>
/exports/logging-es-ops
        <world>
```

And that's it! You now have an NFS volume that's ready to be used by OpenShift to provide persistent storage to your containerized applications.

appendix C
Working
directly with Docker

Docker has its own command-line tool, aptly named `docker`. To get the information you need to dig deeper into how containers isolate applications in OpenShift, the `docker` command is your starting point.

> **NOTE** To interact directly with docker, you need to SSH into your application node and run the commands in this chapter as the root user.

The first thing we'll walk through is how to get a list of all currently running containers on an application node.

C.1 Getting running containers

After you log in to your application node, run `docker ps` at the command prompt. This command returns a list of all containers currently running on the application node. Each line in the output from `docker ps` represents a running container. The first value in each line is a shortened version of the container ID for that container. You can use this short ID—for example, `fae8e211e7a7`—to specify a container when you need to interact with it using the `docker` command. You can confirm whether the container is for app-cli or app-gui by the name of the image used to create the container.

The `docker ps` output will be longer on your application node, including information about containers that house both your image registry and your HAProxy load balancer. The following has been trimmed to show only the output for the app-cli and app-gui containers you'll deploy in chapter 2. These two applications are what you'll use for examples through chapter 4. You'll deploy app-cli using the OpenShift command-line tool and then deploy app-gui using the Open-Shift web interface.

This appendix uses those applications as the example:

OK status code
from a header

```
# docker ps
CONTAINER ID
  ⇥ IMAGE
  ⇥ COMMAND                     CREATED          STATUS          PORTS
  ⇥ NAMES
⌞→ fae8e211e7a7
     docker-registry.default.svc:5000/image-uploader/
  ⇥ app-cli@SHA256:
```

Docker-registry.default.svc is
the internal IP for the registry.

```
     cef79b2eaf6bb7bf495fb16e9f720d5728299673dfec1d8f16472f1871633ebc
     "container-entrypoint"   32 hours ago        Up 32 hours
  ⇥ k8s_app-cli_app-cli-4-18k2s_image-uploader_45e4431b-9f1d-11e7-
  ⇥ 8afe-001cc4000001_1efbbe3967e47
  ⇥ docker-registry.default.svc:5000/image-uploader/app-gui@SHA256:
  ⇥ 2f98cd2ce28aa32faf60bbd7dab14320c95e5af744c50b2d5bc202fa437aa3e2
  ⇥ "container-entrypoint"   32 hours ago        Up 32 hours
  ⇥ k8s_app-gui_app-gui-2-165d9_image-uploader_42965321-9f1d-11e7-
  ⇥ 8afe-001cc4000001_1
```

The registry listens on
port 5000 by default.

The unique SHA256 ID beginning
with cef279 ensures the correct
container image for this app-cli
deployment is always pulled.

How OpenShift pulls container images

The URL that points to the container image in the OpenShift registry may seem a little strange if you've downloaded an image from any container registry before. A standard registry-request URL contains a container name and a corresponding tag, like docker.io/jeduncan/php-demo-app:latest. This registry URL can be broken down into four components:

- *docker.io*—URL for the registry. In this case, Docker Hub.
- *jeduncan*—User account for the registry. In this case, jeduncan, the account for Jamie Duncan.
- *php-demo-app*—Name of the container image to download.
- *latest*—Tag, or specific version, of the container image.

The value `latest` is the image tag you want to download. *Image tags* are arbitrary values that specify a version of the image to be downloaded. Instead of using tags to specify a version of an image, OpenShift uses the unique SHA256 hash value for each version of a container image.

Downloading a container image by its SHA256 hash is a security benefit for OpenShift. Tags are mutable, meaning multiple tags can point to different image versions at different times. SHA256 hashes are immutable and always point to a single container image, regardless of any tags associated with it. If a container image changes for any reason, its SHA256 hash changes, even if its tags don't.

In the previous output, the container with a short ID `fae8e211e7a7` is the app-cli container. You can be sure of this because it was created from the app-cli custom container image in the OpenShift registry.

C.2   *Using docker inspect*

The `docker inspect` command displays all the low-level runtime information about a container. If you don't specify any parameters, `docker inspect` returns a long list of information about the container in JSON format.

Using the `-f` parameter, you can specify the part of the JSON output that you want to view using JSON's dot-notation *property accessor*. Using the container short ID for app-cli you obtained using `docker ps`, you can get the PID for the app-cli container using `docker inspect`, as the following example and its resulting output demonstrates:

```
# docker inspect -f '{{ .State.Pid }}' fae8e211e7a7
4470
```

> **TIP**   The JSON data format dot-notation property accessor is a way to describe and access a specific piece of data in a JSON dataset. (You can learn more at http://mng.bz/26Nm.) You can run `docker inspect <container short id>` on your application node to see all the data available from docker about a running container. Using this output, you can use JSON dot notation to specify only the data you want from all the available information.

If you delete the app-cli pod or stop the container using docker directly, OpenShift will create a new container using the same image and configuration, but it will have a different PID. The PID will also change if you reboot your application node or redeploy your applications. In a similar fashion, the container's short ID will change under the same circumstances. These aren't permanent values on your application node. In chapters 3, 5, and 9, you'll interact with docker to pull low-level information about your containers as you investigate how containers function on a Linux server.

Another task you'll need to do is to start an interactive shell in a running container.

C.3   *Interactive shells in a container*

To start an interactive shell session in a running container, edit the following command to reference your container's short ID:

```
docker exec -it f3cce9147cd1 bash
```

The `-i` option provides an interactive user session, `-t` creates a TTY session in the container, and `bash` launches the bash shell terminal program on the TTY you created in the container. You've effectively entered your running container. Instead of just providing the output of the command, the interactive parameter provides you with an active bash shell.

appendix D
Configuring
identity providers

Many different user databases are available to IT professionals for managing access and authentication. To interoperate with as many of these as possible, OpenShift provides 11 identity providers that interface with various user databases, including the Allow All provider that you've been using in your cluster up to this point. These providers are as follows:

- *Allow All*—Allows any username and non-empty password to log in
- *Deny All*—Doesn't allow any usernames and passwords to log in
- *htpasswd*—Authenticates with Apache htpasswd database files
- *Keystone*—Uses OpenStack Keystone as the authentication source
- *LDAP*—Authenticates against an LDAP provider like openLDAP
- *Basic*—Uses Apache Basic authentication on a remote server to authenticate users
- *Request Header*—Uses custom HTTP headers for user authentication
- *GitHub*—Authenticates with GitHub using OAuth
- *GitLab*—Authenticates with GitLab using OAuth
- *Google*—Uses Google OpenID Connect for authentication
- *OpenID Connect*—Uses OpenID Connect with a source other than Google

Different authentication providers have different options that are specific to each provider's unique format. For example, the options available for the htpasswd provider are different than those required for the GitHub provider, because these providers access such different user databases.

In the next section, you'll change your OpenShift cluster's configuration to stop using the Allow All provider and start using htpasswd provider. To use this provider, you'll need to create an htpasswd database file on the master server.

Why is htpasswd spelled this way?

The htpasswd utility is an old one. It goes all the way back to the first versions of the Apache web server in the later 1990s. Back then, computers had so much less memory that the name of an application could affect system performance.

Application names were typically limited to eight characters. To fit this tight requirement, characters were often removed wherever possible—and thus htpasswd was born.

D.1   Introduction to htpasswd

The htpasswd provider uses Apache-style htpasswd files for authentication. These are simple databases that contain a list of usernames and their corresponding passwords in an encrypted format. Each line in the file represents a user. The user and password sections are separated with a colon (:). The password section includes the algorithm that was used to encrypt the password, encapsulated by $ characters, and the encrypted password itself. Here's an example htpasswd file with two users, admin and developer:

```
admin:$apr1$vUqfPZ/D$sTL5RCy1m5kS73bC8GA3F1
developer:$apr1$oKuOUw1t$CEJSFcVXDH5Jcq7VDF5pU/
```
← admin user with a password encrypted using the default apr1 algorithm

You create htpasswd files using the `htpasswd` command-line tool. In appendix A, you installed this tool on your master server. By default, the `htpasswd` tool uses a custom encryption algorithm based on MD5 hashing.

> **NOTE** Full documentation on the Apache `htpasswd` application and file format is available at http://mng.bz/ZqaG. Full documentation on possible encryption formats is available at http://mng.bz/3CVh.

D.2   Creating the htpasswd database

To create an htpasswd database file, you need to SSH to your master server. On the master server, the configuration files for the OpenShift master processes are in /etc/origin/master. There, you'll create an htpasswd file called openshift.htpasswd with three users—developer, project-admin, and admin—to act as the database for the htpasswd provider to interact with.

> **TIP** The location of the htpasswd file is important. Be sure to take note, because you'll need it in the next section.

You need to run the `htpasswd` command to add each user. The first time you run the command, be sure to include the `-c` option to create the new htpasswd file.

> **TIP** Be sure to only use the `-c` option the first time, or it will overwrite your file each time. The `-i` option takes the password information from the command's standard input. Without this option, the tool will prompt you twice for the password through an interactive prompt.

Use the following commands to create the htpasswd file with three users:

```
# echo developer | htpasswd -i -c
➥ /etc/origin/master/openshift.htpasswd developer    ◁─┐  Creates the file and adds
Adding password for user developer                      │  the developer user
```

```
# echo project-admin | htpasswd -i                                Adds the project-
  ➥ /etc/origin/master/openshift.htpasswd project-admin  ◁─┘     admin user
Adding password for user project-admin
```

```
# echo admin | htpasswd -i /etc/origin/master/openshift.htpasswd
➥ admin                        ◁──────┐
Adding password for user admin         │ Adds the admin user
```

With your htpasswd database created and populated with users, you're ready to use it for authentication in OpenShift. To configure your new identity provider, you need to edit the configuration for your OpenShift master server. That's what you'll do in the next section.

D.3   *Changing authentication providers*

The configuration file for your OpenShift master is /etc/origin/master/master-config .yaml, and it's more than 150 lines long. When you configured OpenShift, this section enabled the default Allow All provider that we discussed earlier. The following options are common to all providers:

- challenge—Defaults to true. Ensures that web clients receive challenge HTTP headers. These headers instruct non-web clients like the oc command-line tool to be sure users are logged in before access is granted.
- login—Defaults to true. Redirects unauthenticated sessions to the login page for the provider.
- mappingMethod—Defines how users interact with the user database. The default value, claim, provisions a new user with the preferred login if the name isn't available.

We'll concentrate on the identityProviders stanza. This section controls which authentication providers are implemented in OpenShift. Here's a default identity-Providers section from master-config.yaml:

```
identityProviders:
  - challenge: true
    login: true
    mappingMethod: claim
    name: allow_all              ◁── Name for the provider
    provider:
      apiVersion: v1
      kind: AllowAllPasswordIdentityProvider       ◁── Provider to use
```

> **NOTE** You can find full information about configurations for all the identity providers at http://mng.bz/bjMJ.

The options for the htpasswd identity provider are similar to those of the Allow All provider. It requires one additional option: a file parameter that references the location of your htpasswd database file. The other big difference is the kind value, which is the name of the provider you want to use. In this case, you need to make sure the value for kind is HTPasswdPasswordIdentityProvider.

To configure the htpasswd provider, edit the identityProviders section in your master-config.yaml file as shown next.

> **Listing D.1 master-config.yaml configured to access your htpasswd database**

```
identityProviders:
- name: my_htpasswd_provider          ◁──┐ Name for your
  challenge: true                          │ new provider
  login: true
  mappingMethod: claim
  provider:
    apiVersion: v1
    kind: HTPasswdPasswordIdentityProvider    ◁── kind value
┌─▷ file: /etc/origin/master/openshift.htpasswd
```
**Location of the htpasswd
database file**

After you make the changes and save your new configuration, restart the OpenShift master services with the following command:

```
systemctl restart origin-master
```

Once the origin-master service is restored, the new configuration is in effect. You can verify this by attempting to log in as the dev user you've been using in your cluster. Access should be denied at this point. Access for your newly created users—developer, project-admin, and admin—should work, with their configured passwords.

index

283